D1137439

V A R I O U S

A T W O O D S

BATH SPA UNIVERSITY
LIBRARY

DISCARD

B.S.U.C. - LIBRARY

00324676

VARIOUS

Essays on the Later Poems, Short Fiction, and Novels

ATWOODS

LORRAINE M. YORK, EDITOR

Anansi

Copyright © 1995 by House of Anansi Press

All rights reserved. No part of this publication may be reproduced or
transmitted in any form or by any means, electronic or mechanical,
including photocopying, recording, or any information storage and
retrieval system, without permission in writing from the publisher.

Published in 1995 by
House of Anansi Press Limited
1800 Steeles Avenue West
Concord, Ontario
L4K 2P3
Tel. (416)445-3333
Fax (416)445-5967

Canadian Cataloguing in Publication Data

Main entry under title:

Various Atwoods: essays on the later poems, short fiction, and novels

Companion vol. to: The art of Margaret Atwood.
ISBN 0-88784-548-7

1. Atwood, Margaret, 1939–   Criticism and interpretation.
I. York, Lorraine M. (Lorraine Mary), 1958–

PS8501.A78Z96 1995   C813'.54   C95-930060-8
PR9199.3.A78Z96 1995

Cover design: Brant Cowie / ArtPlus
Typesetting: Tony Gordon

Printed and bound in Canada

House of Anansi Press gratefully acknowledges the support of the Canada
Council, the Ontario Ministry of Culture, Tourism, and Recreation, Ontario Arts
Council, and Ontario Publishing Centre in the development of writing and
publishing in Canada.

BATH SPA UNIVERSITY
NEWTON PARK LIBRARY

Class No. 813.54 ATw 4	
AMAZON 2014/07	

Contents

Acknowledgements

TO SAY THAT THIS COLLECTION belongs more to Arnold E. Davidson than to me is no cliché — as all of the contributors to this volume will heartily acknowledge. I thank him for his ever-present professional, critical, and personal generosity.

It has been a very great pleasure to work with Martha Sharpe, our editor at Anansi, who has devoted many hours to this project. I am grateful for her professional expertise and for her unshakeable optimism.

Lorraine M. York

Introduction

WHEN ARNOLD AND CATHY DAVIDSON intro-
duced their Anansi volume, *The Art of Margaret Atwood: Essays in
Criticism*, in 1981, they perhaps unwittingly sowed the seeds of
the present volume. "Margaret Atwood," they reflected, ". . . is
at least four authors in one," "a writer of many facets" whose
"diversity" demanded the "multiplicity of approaches" represented in the collection's thirteen essays (9-10). Fourteen years
later, the facets are steadily increasing; just as Margaret Atwood's
inventiveness continues to surprise and to impress her readers,
so have the critical and theoretical discussions of her texts
exceeded the boundaries of one set of hard covers. *Various
Atwoods*, then, is a necessary supplement to an energetic and
heterogeneous critical discourse — a supplement, that is, in
philosopher Jacques Derrida's sense: an addition that simply
signals the never-completedness of the prior text, and that itself,
of course, is never-to-be-complete.

Various Atwoods. The title, borrowed from Robert Fulford's
1977 reference to "the various Atwoods of our imagination,"
glances in a couple of directions: there is the protean, endlessly
inventive Atwood, and there are the "various Atwoods" that
readers and critics continue to construct. As a supplement, this
volume also necessarily glances backward and forward in time.
Included here are three contributors who appeared in *The Art of
Margaret Atwood* fourteen years ago: Sandra Djwa, Sherrill E.
Grace, and Linda Wagner-Martin. Each of these essays, implicitly

or explicitly, grounds itself upon / against the prior essay. As such, then, the present volume has much to say about acts of critical re-vision. At the same time, represented here are critics who have emerged during this fourteen-year period — another generation of Atwood scholars, such as Shannon Hengen and Nathalie Cooke. Judging from the continued vigour of critical engagements with Atwood's texts, I'll look forward to reading *their* retrospective essays in the year 2009, in a volume most likely entitled: *Multiplicitous Atwoods*! But any easy categorization of the critical discourses engaged here according to generation is bound to lead to oversimplification, for those critics returning to Atwood in this volume discover her anew, and those who are at the beginning of their investigations touch base, consciously or unconsciously, with the considerable body of thought on Atwood's writing already on record. I think that's why I prefer to call this volume a "supplement" rather than a "retrospective," though the latter term will creep into this introduction from time to time; like Elaine Risley in *Cat's Eye*, I fear that the word "retrospective" has too much of the clanging of the coffin lid about it: "first the retrospective, then the morgue" (16).

That said, I must indulge in some retrospection for a moment, before I offer some comments about how the essays in this volume work together and singly. How *are* the various Atwoods of 1995 distinct from the ones investigated and celebrated in *The Art of Margaret Atwood*? To begin with, the Atwood of fourteen years ago was remarkably comfortable in a number of genres; as Arnold and Cathy Davidson enumerated, she was "poet, short story writer, novelist, and critic" (9). Over the intervening years, though, Atwood has taken her multigeneric career to a further, exciting stage: the writing of intergeneric texts like *Murder in the Dark* (1983) and *Good Bones* (1992). Indeed, as Patricia Merivale argues in the present volume, these genre-challenging texts tended to replace Atwood's lyrics; in our fourteen-year period, only two "poetry collections" as such appeared, and early on at that (*True Stories* 1981; *Interlunar* 1984). As for fictional modes, with *The Handmaid's Tale* (1985) Atwood added the dystopic to her repertoire. *Cat's Eye* (1988) explored fictional territory eerily reminiscent of the stories of Alice Munro, while *The Robber Bride* (1993) reminded readers that Atwood had by no means relinquished the satirical and the sardonic. It is as though Atwood has playfully corrected her readers' predictions for her fiction, as she did when, bemused by reviewers' claims that, in *Two-Headed Poems*, her satirical, power-political edge was somehow "softened" by motherhood, she struck back with the torture poems of *True Stories*.

But if Atwood's textual practices seem, in T. S. Eliot's words, to multiply "variety in a wilderness of mirrors," no less is true of the burgeoning critical industry fueled by her works. When *The Art of Margaret Atwood* appeared, Sherrill E. Grace's pioneering volume, *Violent Duality*, was but a year off the presses, but the intervening years have seen a number of critical volumes devoted to her work, both collectively authored (essays edited by Sherrill E. Grace and Lorraine Weir [1983], Kathryn Van Spanckeren and Jan Garden Castro [1988], Judith McCombs [1988]) and singly Frank Davey's *Margaret Atwood: A Feminist Poetics* [1984], Jerome H. Rosenberg's "Twaynification" — to use Atwood's own term — of Atwood in 1984, and, more recently, J. Brooks Bouson's *Brutal Choreographies: Oppositional Strategies and Narrative Design in the Novels of Margaret Atwood* and Shannon Hengen's *Margaret Atwood's Power* [both 1993]). The driving force behind most of the monographs has been, not surprisingly, the similarly burgeoning field of feminist theory. And since feminist theory continues its permutations, its fruitful and challenging interfaces with postcolonial, autobiographical, postmodern, queer, and other theory, it will no doubt continue to be a dominant force in Atwood criticism.

AS THE ESSAYS in this volume demonstrate, however, no one set of theoretical assumptions, however "dominant," will have the

Atwoodian field to itself. Indeed, rereading the essays, I am struck by how the growing awareness of theoretical assumptions that has characterized the North American literary academy in the 1980s and 1990s has enriched and diversified studies of Atwood's work. In the present volume, Atwood meets parodic intertextuality, postmodernity, postcolonialism, deconstruction, semiotics, Foucauldian theory, dialogism, confessional theory, cultural criticism, and theories of canon formation.

Sandra Djwa opened *The Art of Margaret Atwood*, and she opens *Various Atwoods* too, not merely for reasons of pleasing symmetry, but because her present essay, "Back to the Primal: The Apprenticeship of Margaret Atwood" is an absorbingly self-conscious act of critical revision. As Djwa explains, "I have come to the conclusion that her apprentice verse should first be related to T. S. Eliot and fertility myth, and only then to Frye and a Canadian poetic tradition" (the latter two influences being those amply explored in Djwa's first essay, "The Where of Here: Margaret Atwood and a Canadian Tradition"). Here, Djwa traces the process of Atwood's adoption and rejection of an Eliotic cosmology in her apprenticeship poetry, much of it not readily accessible in print. Revising Eliot's modernism, as Djwa says, "from a woman's point of view," Atwood embraces the "primal" as her own special area of concern — right up to some of her most recent work, such as *The Robber Bride*.

Djwa's sense that Atwood has, in the years since her first essay, become "an international woman of letters" is given ample support by the very presence of the next contributor, Coral Ann Howells, self-described as a "transatlantic reader." Howells's essay, "It all depends on where you stand in relation to the forest: Atwood and the Wilderness from *Surfacing* to *Wilderness Tips*," is, like Djwa's, retrospective in nature, though what she traces is Atwood's own revisionary reading of her earlier renderings of "wilderness." In the light of the "late modern" and "postmodern" worlds, argues Howells, Atwood "has moved from representing wilderness to Canadians as their culturally distinctive national space to a much bleaker contemporary revisionary reading, where simple binary nationalist oppositions disappear." The Atwood of *Wilderness Tips* is, says Howells, more aware of an international audience, and she uses that widening readership to address issues of global concern on a planet where wilderness has "reced[ed] into myth." So too has nationality; unlike the early Atwood of *Surfacing*, the Atwood of *Wilderness Tips*, of postmodernity, is very much aware of the constructedness of national demarcations in a global village whose Chernobyls know no boundaries.

Linda Wagner-Martin, another original contributor, turns her retrospective glance to the poetry that Atwood has published since Wagner-Martin's 1981 article, "The Making of *Selected Poems*, the Process of Surfacing." She charts the course of the genre questioning of the 1980s, and concludes that "Atwood's choice of poems for the second *Selected* collection shows something of her confusion about how to define 'poem.'" As in her essay for *The Art of Margaret Atwood*, there is the sense of the Atwood collection — including the *Selected* volumes — as a thing shaped rather than a victim of arbitrary marketing needs; for instance, Wagner-Martin makes the striking claim that "Whether Atwood felt that the didacticism of some of the more outspoken of these [her *True Stories* poems] was inappropriate, or whether she faulted them as poems, she made choices that left *Selected Poems II* gutted of much of her most interesting work." Moving right up to *Good Bones*, Wagner-Martin draws a portrait of "Atwood's poetry during the past fifteen years," and concludes that "she has finally convinced herself of the efficacy of play." For Wagner-Martin, Atwood the trickster, the playful creator of "provocative texts that avoid being what her readers expect," truly deserves the plural designation, *Various Atwoods*.

Diana Brydon's essay on *Bodily Harm* is retrospective criticism of yet another variety. In "Atwood's Postcolonial Imagination:

Rereading *Bodily Harm*," Brydon opens up a whole new field of Atwood study: "I believe," writes Brydon, "it will be impossible to fully appreciate Atwood's artistic achievement and its limitations without accounting for the postcolonial contexts of her vision." What better place to start the postcolonial retrospect, one might think, than Atwood's 1981 novel set in the Caribbean, *Bodily Harm*? As Brydon shows, however, postcolonial critics have not been slow to take note of Atwood's often neglected novel, but their notice has been, for the most part, deprecatingly critical. What Brydon does is to refocus the postcolonial debate on *Bodily Harm*, opting to acknowledge both the imperialist blindnesses and the postcolonial insights of the novel. The result is an engrossing ideological complexity; *Bodily Harm* is both a weakened "counterdiscourse to imperialism" and "an important document of Canada's ambivalent positioning within the 'home ground/foreign territory' of imperialist Eurocentrism."

Hilda Hollis's essay brings another major theoretical outgrowth of the 1980s to bear on Atwood's work: deconstruction. And, like Diana Brydon, she glances back to the beginning of that decade, to reread another 1981 Atwood text anew: the poetry collection *True Stories*. But in "Between the Scylla of Essentialism and the Charybdis of Deconstruction," Hollis does not merely use deconstruction to critique Atwood; the process is a resolutely two-way one. Although Atwood, like deconstructionist thinkers, explodes the myth of the "true story," it is the female body, and violence to that body, that for Hollis put the brakes on deconstruction's "ever-spiraling irony," its reluctance to acknowledge any truths in any stories. But this feminist stand places Hollis — and, she argues, Atwood — between the Scylla of essentializing corporeality and the Charybdis of "proliferating indeterminacy." For Hollis, Atwood's corporeal materialism makes her invocation of the body a nonessentialist one: "In acknowledging the *aporia* of language, she attempts to draw us beyond language to a recognition of pain."

Sherrill E. Grace's paper takes up this issue of true stories in bringing together Atwood's story of the Franklin voyage in *Wilderness Tips*, "The Age of Lead," and other tellings of that story, particularly the CBC documentary, which serves as an intertext in Atwood's version. As Grace points out, Atwood's "The Age of Lead" "includes but goes beyond a deconstruction of the film. Although it also affirms that the past is accessible through the present . . . and that present and past are linked to confirm, validate, and establish, . . . Atwood questions notions of truth and belief in the accurate reading of signs." Building on her early study of Atwood's "violent duality," as it appears both in her 1980 book of that name and in her essay for *The Art of Margaret Atwood*, Grace explores "how" and "why" "The Age of Lead," in her words, "recapitulates her persistent concern with the aesthetics of doubling and the semiotics of the 'space between.'" For Grace, the key to Atwood's fascination with the Franklin myth lies "in our continuing, insistent demand for answers, our rapacious need to uncover and possess, our transgressive, objectifying gaze, our continued search for the Northwest Passage to origins and truth." Here, Grace touches base with Coral Ann Howells's study of the postmodernizing of "wilderness" in the same short story collection; in the face of global apocalypse, the need for a "space between" egotistical certainties has never been stronger.

Grace's analysis of the contrapuntal texts-within-texts in Atwood's "The Age of Lead" (the Franklin documentary that Jane watches on TV and the cross-cut narrative of her lover's death), presages Glenn Willmott's study of the dialogism of film and fiction in *The Handmaid's Tale*(s) — novel and film. In "O Say, Can You See: *The Handmaid's Tale* in Novel and Film," Willmott works from the assumption that the two "media are different forms of power" as well as "different forms of language," and "in a story about power, such as *The Handmaid's Tale*, one is concerned about how power will be communicated in both the medium and its message." One way in which, for Willmott,

Atwood's novel meditates on power is through temporal multi-ple imaging: the layering of a number of historical states or states of desire within one visual space. Of course, this happens time and time again in *The Handmaid's Tale*, as Offred relentlessly details for us what certain visual signs would have signified in pre-Gilead society, signs that are both sent and negated in Gileadan space. But Willmott is then moved to the inevitable question: how can a visual medium like film subvert a Gileadan tyranny of the one, supreme visual signifier that wishes to negate other historicized states of desire? "Intermittently" seems to be the answer — in, for instance, Volker Schlondorff's use of the double representation of filmed TV footage in the film.

Willmott takes up philosopher Richard Rorty's term for this visual tyranny — "ocular knowledge" — but this concern is also at the heart of the next essay in the collection, Molly Hite's "An Eye for an I: The Disciplinary Society in *Cat's Eye*." Moving to Atwood's next novel after *The Handmaid's Tale*, Hite demonstrates that the ocular knowledge which so governs Gilead is not that foreign to the mid-twentieth-century Ontario of *Cat's Eye*. Invok-ing Michel Foucault's example of the Panopticon as the model of the "modern disciplinary society," Hite reveals that Elaine Risley's choice of profession, painting, like the Panopticon, in-vests power in the "one-way gaze." Atwood, building on her reading of John Berger's observations about women as objects, not subjects, of sight, notes that the one-way gaze of painting is, not surprisingly, "usually reserved . . . for men." This ocular tyranny, which segregates seeing from being seen and, therefore, judging from being judged, is deeply implicated, for Hite, in *Cat's Eye*'s painful study of the psychology of blame. Like Willmott, Hite asks, in effect, is there any (representable) way out of this subjection of the sighted? Mothering and mercy alone, in *Cat's Eye*, Hite suggests, have the power to integrate rather than to sever.

Nathalie Cooke's essay, "The Politics of Ventriloquism: Mar-garet Atwood's Fictive Confessions," fittingly opens with an act of seeing through the eyes of a (fictional) other: a reader's temptation to sympathize with the confessions of a fictional character. Like Willmott with the film medium, however, Cooke is quick to point out that such an exchange is one of power as well as language. In her theorizing of "fictive confessions," Cooke dramatically revises the literary tradition of seeing confession as generic, and sees it, instead, as "a rhetorical and ethical *strategy*" driven by power exchange. Touching base with Hollis and Grace, Cooke suggests "that the confessional tradition provides a model for analysing something that is central to Atwood's oeuvre: not truth itself (Atwood would strongly deny such an essentialist assumption), but rather the dynamics of truth-telling" — that is, the power relations involved in the telling of true stories rather than the enshrining of "the true story."

Just as there are, for Atwood, true *stories* but no true story, there are arguably "various Atwoods" but no Atwood. In my own essay, "'Over All I Place a Glass Bell': The Meta-Iconography of Margaret Atwood," I explore Atwood as a constellation of cultural signs — an icon, in short. What's more, this literary icon has herself critiqued "iconization, that powerful aesthetic and emotional desire to reify." In the paper, I chart the course of this meta-iconographical process, "from fairly straightforward iconoclasm, based on dualities, to the complex realization of the inherent instability of icons," to "a renewed, reformulated desire for the iconic" in her "most explicitly iconographical novel," *Cat's Eye.*

Patricia Merivale brings together two texts that stand at opposite ends of the period in Atwood's career that this volume studies: her two prose poem collections, *Murder in the Dark* (1983) and *Good Bones* (1992). Paying close attention to the constructedness of the prose poem cycles, she charts Atwood's movement from lyric to Baudelairean prose poet, in her "subversion of prose genres through compact parody and canny intertextuality." Rather than conflating the two collections, though, Merivale argues that they grow out of different generic areas of

Atwood's career: *Good Bones*, with its more "narrative" "kind of metatextuality" growing out of Atwood's prose, and *Murder in the Dark* moving "towards prose poem from the direction of Atwood's poetry." Merivale gives us, then, an Atwood who, in Canada, is almost singly occupying "the Baudelairean mode" of prose poem (as contrasted with the "lyrically surreal and melodious prose poems" of Phyllis Webb or the "abstractedly meditative and philosophical" ones of John Ashbery). Even so, Merivale shows, Atwood occupies the mode playfully, to work witty gender inversions and meta-elegies.

In the closing paragraph of Shannon Hengen's essay, "Zenia's Foreignness," and hence of *Various Atwoods*, the words "gender, nationalism, and ethnicity" are invoked. They are not offered, however, as a summarizing trinity of prioritized critical agendas, but as examples of the issues that Hengen believes may be cross-discussed when critics open themselves to a pluralism that, instead of erasing methodological and ideological differences, productively acknowledges and explores them. Postcolonialism's interventions into the fields of postmodernist and feminist theory, to re-member therein the critical roles of agency and history, is an example that lies at the heart of this paper. Accordingly, Hengen touches base with some of the most significant current debates in Canadian literary circles — postmodern irony's relationship to agency and the construction of Canadian canons — not to settle upon "winners" and "losers," but to perceive a crucial critical dialogism. Fittingly, her analysis of *The Robber Bride* enacts, on another level, this preference for dialogism over debate; refusing the "good (Canadian) girl"/"bad (foreign) girl" opposition with which Atwood tempts her readers, Hengen explores what she calls a "postimperial . . . third subject position." Zenia is the difference that challenges the distinctions and assumptions of Charis, Roz, and Tony — not because she is "other" and "exotic," but because she continually frustrates the others' desires to "other" her. The parallels with a postcolonial retheorization of difference are plain and forceful: postcolonial reading strategies prompt us to ask not why and how are works "Canadian" — especially when the works in question are produced by communities that have been consistently "othered" or exoticized in Canadian life — but, instead, how do these works deconstruct and revise our notion of "Canadianness"? In this light, what Hengen calls "that dangerous term," "postfeminism," is in her hands not a Real Women rallying cry, but a feminism critically revised by the interventions of women of colour and/or working class women and/or lesbians — the feminism of Adrienne Rich in *Blood, Bread and Poetry.*

And so, this closing essay *opens*, to my eyes, another way in which this collection constructs various Atwoods: not only by presenting various critics, each duly armed with a critical approach, but by suggesting that we might each perceive a variety of critical paths, those "third [and fourth, and fifth . . .] eye(s)" potentially available to a reader at any one time. As usual, though, Atwood has gotten there long before me:

> There is no
> either/or

Sandra Djwa

Back to the Primal: The Apprenticeship of Margaret Atwood

Sir James Frazer regards her as "either Demeter or her double, Persephone."

ROBERT GRAVES, THE WHITE GODDESS

I'm Isis of Saïs,
If you'd know what my way is,
Come riddle my riddle-me-ree

JAY MACPHERSON, THE BOATMAN

[Isis] the Egyptian Queen of Heaven and Earth was . . .
gathering up the pieces of the . . . body of her lover Osiris . . .
She was creating the universe by an act of love.

MARGARET ATWOOD, WILDERNESS TIPS

TO GO BACK TO THE POETRY and prose of Margaret Atwood after a decade's absence is to feel like a female Rip Van Winkle rubbing one's eyes in a new landscape. Ten years ago I wrote about Atwood's generation and Canadian nationalism, the influence of Northrop Frye, and the new feminism anticipated by her use of the Persephone myth. I also suggested that Atwood had created "her own version of a primal fertility myth," and related this to an evolutionary tradition in Canadian poetry (Djwa 24). My assumptions were that Atwood was primarily a poet, that her significant context was Canadian, and that she occupied a transitional position between the inherited 1950s concept of woman and the new feminism of the late 1960s and 1970s.

I now see her work somewhat differently. During these past ten years Atwood has changed from a Canadian poet to an international woman of letters. And despite some *sotto voce* anti-American volleys (or pro-Canadian, it is easy to confuse the two), her context, if we are to judge from the bulk of recent criticism, is most often international.[1] She has published three books of poetry — *True Stories* (1981), *Interlunar* (1984), and *Selected Poems II* (1986) — but five novels: *Life Before Man* (1979), *Bodily Harm* (1981), *The Handmaid's Tale* (1985), *Cat's Eye* (1988), and *The Robber Bride* (1993); several books of short stories including *Bluebeard's Egg* (1985), *Wilderness Tips* (1991), and *Good Bones* (1992); a number of essays, and a collection of early criticism, *Second Words* (1982).

At its best Atwood's fiction combines intelligent, witty, and sometimes profound social satire with high seriousness. Like Washington Irving or Nathaniel Hawthorne (or their lineal descendant, T. S. Eliot) she writes the moral fable *de nos jours* that is structured, like poetry, through a series of dominant metaphors and which, unlike realistic fiction, works on the deeper level of myth and allegory. *The Edible Woman* (1969), *Surfacing* (1972), *Life Before Man*, and *The Handmaid's Tale* are all metafictions that critique the society they depict through central metaphors. *Surfacing*, for example, is structured by a complex of metaphors (lost father, drowning brother, dead frog, aborted fetus), all of which associate in a young woman's mind following a climactic descent into water. This primal myth of descent and return, central to Atwood's work, first appears in the poetry. And after reading the early verse, much of which was published in journals in the late 1950s and early 1960s and not collected, I have come to the conclusion that her apprentice verse should first be related to T. S. Eliot and fertility myth, and only then to Frye and a Canadian poetic tradition.

Atwood has now become a symbol of the feminist movement, albeit somewhat reluctantly. Like many women artists of the 1950s, she inherited the traditional notion of a woman's role, a view expressed by one of the speakers in "The Triple Goddess: A Poem for Voices" (1960):

> Haven't I done all the things I should?
> Basted the roast and folded the bedding,
> Dusted the tops of the books and ledges,
> Loved my husband, and clipped the hedges,
> And gone to my brother's daughter's wedding . . . (11)

These were notions that she promptly began to revise. As the allusion to "the triple goddess" shows, Atwood's challenge to the traditional views of the feminine was based on new anthropological theories, especially those advanced by Robert Graves in *The White Goddess* (1947), celebrating the power of the Great Mother Goddess in her triple aspects of Persephone-Demeter-Hecate. For Atwood's Matron, Woman and Girl, latter-day versions of Graves's trio, the pressing question is "What to do?" Should one, like Atwood's Matron, accept the prevailing norms to marry and have children, or should one, like Atwood's Girl, attempt to escape generation and its discontents, much like Blake's Thel? As I suggested in my 1981 article, very early in her career Atwood appears to have been exploring myths of a woman's role with a view to reshaping patriarchal versions[2] partly in rejection of conventional social roles, partly in response to contemporary women writers, and possibly, as I will argue, in rejection of the dominant male voice of the period.

Women in the 1950s tended to turn to classical literature, especially to myths of the feminine, when probing their own identity. The primary myth of the female principle, as depicted from the Homeric Hymns to D. H. Lawrence's *The Lost Girl* (1920), was that of Demeter-Persephone-Hecate. Described by early moderns like Sir James Frazer in *The Golden Bough* (1890; abridged 1922), the myth of the Great Goddess was reinterpreted by Graves, by Eric Neumann in *The Origin and History of Consciousness* (1954), and by women poets like Edith Sitwell, Kathleen Raine, and Jay Macpherson. Graves celebrated the concept of female sexual power, but Lawrence and Neumann were fearful. The lament of Eliot's woefully timid Prufrock — "Do I dare to eat a peach?" (17) — interpreted through Freud, that 1950s authority, expresses a similar anxiety regarding female sexuality.

For women the myth of the mother goddess is emotionally charged, expressing as it does the primal aspects of female experience: sexual initiation (the descent), followed by gestation and new birth. Not surprisingly many women writers were empowered by it, especially by the possibilities that the myth offered for changing the traditional name of woman as passive victim (Persephone) to woman as all-powerful goddess (Demeter or Hecate). Nonetheless, early women modernists tended to focus on Persephone, the least threatening figure, and to soft-pedal their concerns, as did Sitwell, with jaunty parody:

WHEN
Sir
Beelzebub called for his syllabub in the hotel in Hell
     Where Proserpine first fell,
Blue as the gendarmerie were the waves of the sea (61)

Closer at hand, at the University of Toronto, Atwood was taught by Macpherson in 1958–59, whose first book, *The Boatman*

(1957), also parodies traditional myth, especially in "Isis," "Mary in Egypt," and "The Rymer":

> Hear the voice of the Bard!
> Want to know where I've been?
> Under the frost-hard
> Ground with Hell's Queen, . . .
> Not everybody's dame,
> But a sharp baby
> All the same. (23)

Here, Macpherson depicts the crone aspect of the triple goddess, "Hell's Queen," but elsewhere, especially when writing on the myth of Narcissus and in poems like "Eve in Reflection," she presents the more affective aspects of the daughter goddess.

Views of the feminine in the context of classical myth, largely negative, were also available to the 1950s reader in Eliot's *The Waste Land* (1922). Atwood recalls that she read the poem in 1957, just before her first year at the University of Toronto where Eliot's work figured largely in the undergraduate study of English.[3] I do not mean to imply that Atwood was, as she says, a "lump of featureless dough":[4] poets respond to those elements in other poets that resonate to their own concerns and experience. Yet, as a product of the myth-centred 1950s, Atwood began to publish when Eliot was the most highly respected modern poet in North America and when the exploration of his allusive, mythic technique was a staple of the New Criticism taught at universities. Finally, as a young poet in the late 1950s at the University of Toronto, Atwood would have been subject to the prevailing concept of poetry as an aesthetic construct (*The Well Wrought Urn* 1947), a view expressed not only in Eliot's criticism but also in the myth-oriented theories of Frye and the poetic techniques of Macpherson. It was an exciting time to be an undergraduate at Victoria College; a fellow student recalls animated discussions with Atwood about Eliot's *The Waste Land*, Macpherson's *The Boatman*, and Frye's theories of symbolism.[5]

Atwood has remarked that when she first read *The Waste Land* she did not understand it and that she came to modern poetry through Canadian poetry.[6] She meant this remark half jokingly to refer to her graduate years at Harvard, beginning in 1961, when, being female, she had access to the Widener library, which held Canadian poetry, but not the Lamont library, which held the main modern poetry collection. More important, however, were Atwood's undergraduate years. When she first came to the University of Toronto in 1956–57, Victoria College was acknowledged as a centre for Canadian poetry. Several members of the faculty — including E. J. Pratt who had just retired, Frye, and Macpherson — were identified with the discipline. Victoria also had the best library of Canadiana on the campus. In her third and fourth years at university Atwood was taught by Macpherson, and in 1959–60 when house-sitting for her, she recalls that she read Macpherson's collection of Canadian poetry, including A. J. M. Smith's anthology, *The Oxford Book of Canadian Verse* (1960). At that time Atwood would also have had access to books gathered by Macpherson in preparation for a text on Greek myths: these included Graves's *Greek Myths* (1955), the one-volume edition of Frazer's *The Golden Bough*, together with *Adonis, Attis, Osiris*. Atwood also knew Margaret Murray's *Greek Myths* and already owned a copy of *The White Goddess*, which was, as a contemporary recalls, practically "a source book for poetry" for the younger poets like Atwood who read their verse aloud at the Bohemian Embassy.[7]

While at Toronto, Atwood was also taught by Frye who had published his first study of Blake's archetypal myth, *Fearful Symmetry* (1947), and his theory of modes, *Anatomy of Criticism: Four Essays* (1957). Throughout the 1950s Frye wrote the annual surveys of Canadian poetry for the *University of Toronto Quarterly*, columns Atwood read avidly. There he reviewed the four best books of the decade: Leonard Cohen's *Let Us Compare Mythologies* (1956), Macpherson's *The Boatman*, James Reaney's *A Suit of Nettles* (1958), and Margaret Avison's *Winter Sun* (1960) — all characterized by what Eliot, in an early review of Joyce's *Ulysses*, had called the "mythical method," that is, literature structured by developing a continuous parallel between classical myth and contemporary reality, a method Eliot also employed in *The Waste Land*. The advantage of this technique, praised by Frye and characterized by Eliot in an early review of Joyce, is that it provides a way of "controlling . . . of giving a shape and a significance to the immense panorama . . . of contemporary history" (177).

Reading through Atwood's early and uncollected verse is to see that Eliot's influence is more pervasive than has been recognized,[8] and that it was reinforced both by Frye's criticism and Canadian poetry, especially Macpherson's. The apprentice Atwood appears to have responded both to Eliot's ideas and to his allusive technique. Not only did the mythic technique of *The Waste Land* help shape the structural myth and allusion of her early poetic, but following an early period of parody Atwood rejected Eliot's thesis to develop her own version of a primal myth that drew both on classical fertility myth and on the evolutionary myths and metaphors of Canadian poetry. Aspects of her interest in myth have been identified by earlier critics including myself.[9] I would like to explore, here, the way in which a parodic technique and what Atwood describes in a review of Avison's poetry as "chips of myth" ("Some Sun" 19) entered her poetic, shaping the sensibility of the early poems and reappearing in later novels and short stories. Because much of the early verse is not easily accessible, I will quote extensively to document her development.

Like Pratt and Frye, her predecessors in the Victoria College magazine, *Acta Victoriana*, Atwood's early publication in *Acta* began with parody and collage. From the late 1950s to 1961 her references to Eliot range from parody to pastiche, and she reworks concepts drawn from several of Eliot's major poems, including "The Love Song of J. Alfred Prufrock." The parodied piece, written with Dennis Lee under the *nom de plume* Shakesbeat Latweed, consists of a short verse "Spratire" on the subject of Jack Spratt, for whom "Canada Packers is the cruellest brand" (22). A further essay, written by Lee alone under their joint pseudonym, "In Dispraise of James J. Eliot" (1960), conflates Joyce with Eliot and condemns Eliot's attitude to religion. However, the metaphors of Atwood's early poetry suggest that it is Eliot's use of fertility myth to express contemporary sexuality that intrigues her. Particularly relevant is "The Burial of the Dead" section from *The Waste Land*:

> That corpse you planted last year in your garden,
> Has it begun to sprout? Will it bloom this year? (65)

Also relevant is the section of "The Fire Sermon" in which Eliot parodies the classical theme of the departure of the nymphs. But where Eliot dramatizes spiritual and sexual impotence — the burial of the dead is not followed by a resurrection — Atwood inverts the myth. After a brief flirtation with the hollow men in the wasted land she moves on to a revisionist interpretation that, building upon Graves's version of the white goddess, presents what we might describe as the female generative principle: a series of poems in which sexuality and/or the burial of the dead is followed by spring resurrection or fruition.

The first poem Atwood had published in the college paper (November 1958) was a parody of Eliot, entitled "The Conversation," and signed, Eliot-like, *M. E. Atwood*. A pastiche of images and themes from Eliot's poetry juxtapose a Prufrockian speaker against images of a potentially threatening landscape. There is an insistence on surfaces and neurasthenia that suggests Eliot's

"Portrait of a Lady," and a "do I dare" motif suggestive of "Prufrock." The implied "he," the narrator, refuses to acknowledge the necessity of descent into the psychological or sexual self.

> But
> Shall I peer
> Over the edge?
> Shall I see you squirm
> Exposed, in the dark abyss,
> In the tangled jungle, rank,
> Reeking of rotted vines,
> That is your mind? (11)

Atwood's diction, especially the "jungle, rank, / Reeking," suggests the sexuality of "rank" Grishkin from Eliot's "Whispers of Immortality," an association reinforced by the sexual innuendo of the following lines that also carry evolutionary overtones: "Will you slip your hand . . . / Down slippery stems / To roots sunk in the ooze and slime of years?" (11). The poem ends with the narrator's denial of human connection and a witty parody of Eliot's conversational tone:

> and
> "What were you saying about Roberta?
> Yes, she's sometimes rather low;
> good taste, I think, is *so* essential;
> Yes. And anyway . . .
>   shall we go?" (11)

Eliot's invitation in "The Love Song of J. Alfred Prufrock," "Let us go then, you and I" (13), leads to the recognition of a hollow man who has divorced dream from reality, head from body, and, by implication, art from life. Above all, Prufrock fears and rejects the "overwhelming question" (13) that initiates sexual relations. Yet the penalty for stasis is psychological death by engulfment:

> We have lingered in the chambers of the sea
> By sea-girls wreathed with seaweed red and brown
> Till human voices wake us, and we drown. (17)

That Atwood chooses to treat this aspect of the poem ironically suggests that she was in the process of rejecting the negative aspects of *The Waste Land*. In later poems her version of metamorphosis and "Death by Water" is primarily life-giving.

A year later in 1959 she published "Knell and Nativity" in *Acta Victoriana*, again signed *M. E. Atwood*. This is an early example of the fertility myth poem that draws upon the same elements described by Eliot in "The Burial of the Dead," but reaches opposite conclusions:

> I
>
> Bury the harvest, spade the dead down deep;
> The furrow fertilize with passive sleep.
>
> II
>
> Again the earth turns, and a cycle slow
> Returns the rain.
> A newer birth burns, and the seed below
> Swells in its pain.
> Now the moist moments burst the husk, and flow;
> The resurrected shoots take root and grow. (19)

In general, the poems and reviews that Atwood wrote and published between 1958 and 1962 in *Acta Victoriana*, the *Canadian Forum*, and *Alphabet* suggest that she was experimenting with forms and concepts borrowed from Eliot and Graves while learning from her contemporaries, especially Macpherson.

"Pastoral Elegy" (1961), for example, shows Atwood experimenting with Eliot's characteristically ironic tone and form. Atwood's version of the departure of the nymphs begins with a familiar landscape, presumably in April, which subverts the usual associations of "roots" and "spring":

> My landscape is becoming disarranged.
>   The gardener is digging up the willows
>   because their roots have grown into the sewers; this spring
>   has been warmer than most, but the early burgeoning
>   is not my arrangement: I find
>   too many flowers get in the way.
>   The only nymphs I could obtain
>   this year, were less satisfactory than usual: they
>   refused to unloose their crimped hair,
>   simpered, demanded extra pay,
>   and strewed used tissues on the lawn.
>
> Something has changed.
>
> Yesterday, I tried
>   Hiring another musician to provide
>   the right atmosphere, but he insisted on
>   set hours, union rates, and the saxophone, which was
>   really not what I had in mind.
>   Once, I seem to recall, someone died,
>   I think. I can find no evidence of it here;
>   this clean sky denies all sense of rain;
>   eddies of swallows swirl again
>   into the hollow branches, and
>   the gardener is digging up the willows. (4)

The tone of the speaker, again an implied male, is dry and matter-of-fact, which suggests that Atwood's characteristic tone, and certainly her ironic use of form, owes much to Eliot. But here *The Waste Land* is brought up-to-date with sardonic allusions to "used tissues" and "union rates." God is divorced from myth, and the speaker, unlike Eliot, finds religion and its mythic manifestations (the desired rain of the wasted land) irrelevant: "I can find no evidence of it here; / this clean sky denies all sense of rain." However, this assertion of the difference between the arid present and the implied spiritual past is presented in a form that echoes the emblem verse of George Herbert's "Easter Wings." Ironically, Eliot's divorce of spirit from flesh is subverted through Atwood's butterfly image: her tone parodies Eliot's high seriousness while her iconic form, an emblem of metamorphosis, denies his negative conclusions.

Atwood's parodic treatment of Eliot's themes in "The Conversation" and "Pastoral Elegy" prefigure her later development because, having drawn Prufrock within Eliot's cosmology, she moves on in subsequent poems of the early 1960s to reject both the figure and the cosmology in favour of a number of poems with a female narrator (sometimes embodying the myth of Persephone), in which sexual initiation, descent through water, and winter death are followed by spring rebirth. Around the mid-1960s Atwood begins to fuse fertility myth with an evolutionary (and sometimes threatening) landscape, drawn from Canadian poetry perhaps, as "The Descent of Dissection" (1964) suggests, through Pratt.

"The Triple Goddess" suggests that by 1960 Atwood saw Graves's triad through Macpherson's poetry. I say this because the female archetypes are placed in a context that echoes Macpherson's poem "Poor Child." Macpherson's poor child is archetypal — from "Achilles" to "Prufrock, and you and you . . ." (5). For Macpherson "the child is mortal; but Poor Child / Creeps through centuries of bone" (5). This construct and language reappears in Atwood's poem "The Triple Goddess," where the protagonist asks, "Are these my mother's, sister's, or my own / Pattern in my inevitable bone?" (11). Also common to both poems is the Blakean concept of genesis: speakers in each poem express the desire to "return / To the once-green place" (11), the Eden that exists before generation.

Although Frye associates Eden with the innocence of the pastoral, the poems of both Macpherson and Atwood suggest Blakean experience. Eden is a central locale in patriarchal fiction because the myth of the Fall is an important justification for the subordination of women: *The White Goddess*, however, offered alternative woman-centred Eden myths. Graves's cosmology is apparent in "The Harvesters," one of Atwood's most striking Eden poems from this period:

> Just-fallen woman and new-risen man
> Walk lightly under trees that once they were
> He on the ground, she on the topmost bough
> Once writhed a root and spired a furled flower;
> They cannot tell in this first sentient hour
> Vegetable man, mammalian tree
> Where tendril stops or tender limbs begin
> Or which the crimson leaf, which the bloodgreen skin.
>
> Moved by a hunger that was never theirs
> While earth and air flowed in their other veins
> They crop the fruit that curves the fingered branch
> Or heavy drops to rot the foot of bark;
> They cannot hear the wail or see the dark
> Pain on the trunk as with stained hands they tear
> Children from a green womb once their own:
> Eating their kindred flesh, breaking their former bone. (60)

In Atwood's Eden poem the archetypal "he" and "she" become separated from the great "green womb" of being. This version of the Fall is not the Genesis Fall into a consciousness of sexual sin, but rather, a Fall from vegetable to animal life accompanied by human consciousness. Wittily, the difference between the two sexes — her Fall and his Rise — is given an organic basis. But as we learn from Graves, man's rise is at woman's expense. In *The White Goddess* Graves speaks of iconotrophic distortion in the Genesis story of Adam and Eve; he argues that in the original fertility myth, from which the Biblical myth derives, there was no Jehovah but only the Great Mother Goddess who expelled man from her "fertile riverine dominions" because he attempted to usurp her function (276). In effect, Atwood is reworking the Genesis story of fertility myth as expounded by Graves. Her version ignores Biblical Genesis and "sin" to concentrate on the issue of power (her fall and his rise). This also appears to be the earliest poem in which she sets out a mythic rationale for metaphors expressing the movement from vegetable to animal to man, a characteristic movement in what is to become her own version of a primal creation myth.

Atwood the critic was conscious of the strategies employed by Atwood the poet. In February 1961 she reviewed the newly founded journal *Alphabet*, a magazine organized around mythic themes, which had announced itself in its subtitle as "*A Semiannual Devoted to the Iconography of the Imagination.*" The title echoes one of Graves's preoccupations, the old poetic "alphabet," associated with the worship of the Mother Goddess. Atwood characterizes *Alphabet* as "not just another 'little' magazine [but] . . . a 'way of looking at things,'" which she describes in Frygian terms as "indicative of a growing tendency to regard the individual piece of writing . . . as a work whose real context is provided by literature as a whole." However, she does observe that the general structure of the little magazine "is designed both to relate the various works to each other and to a central figure — Narcissus this issue — and to place them along an axis whose poles are Art and Life. Just about everything fits, from the poetry . . . to Jay Macpherson's pertinent article" ("Narcissus" 15).

In the same article in *Acta Victoriana*, when reviewing Marie-Claire Blais's novel *Mad Shadows*, which draws upon the Narcissus myth, Atwood acknowledges the power of such mythic literature: "The world of Miss Blais . . . is a world of the imagination, of myth. . . . It possesses almost ritual undertones and is able to create strangely evocative images out of strangely intense relationships. It gets down to the primal . . ." (16). Atwood's use of "primal" seems to imply both "early in time" and "primitive": the powerful drives towards sexuality and death associated with basic instincts. Getting "down to the primal," Atwood recognizes, means that "naturalism" and "subtlety" might be sacrificed in fiction but "the sacrifice is justified in a work so rewardingly original." This is an important discovery because it acknowledges the power of myth as structure and privileges the exploration of human sexuality. It is this primal male-female territory that Atwood will subsequently make her own (Djwa 26).

In this movement Macpherson may have offered Atwood some direction. Her essay, "Narcissus: Some Uncertain Reflections," alluded to in Atwood's review, contained the following passage:

> The narcissus in general is associated with the underworld powers and used in the rites of the mysteries and the burial of the dead. It is sinister from its first appearance in literature, the story of its origin given in the "Homeric Hymn to Demeter." Zeus secretly agreed to give his daughter Persephone to his brother Hades. When she was gathering flowers one spring morning, Earth in accordance with the will of Zeus put forth "as a trick" a wonder never seen before by the gods or mortal men, the narcissus, irresistibly beautiful. As Persephone reached out to pick it, the earth opened and Hades sprang out in a black-horsed chariot and grabbed her. (45–46)

Atwood certainly knew of the Persephone myth as early as high school, but I would speculate that Macpherson's retelling of the story helped to make the myth numinous, prompting Atwood to recognize that Persephone was the antithesis of the Prufrock figure she had been exploring in the earlier, Eliot-influenced verse.

Shortly after, in the spring of 1961, Atwood published the first in a series of Persephone poems. The goddess initially appears as Proserpine, perhaps because the Latinate form of the name was a favourite of the English poets, especially Milton, Shelley, and Swinburne, who adopted it from Ovid's *Metamorphosis*. When describing Eden in *Paradise Lost*, for example, Milton speaks of "*Proserpina* gath'ring flow'rs/ Herself a fairer Flow'r by gloomy *Dis* / Was gather'd" (284). Similarly, Shelley's "Song of Proserpine" associates Proserpine the "Sacred Goddess, Mother Earth" with the new life of "Gods, and men, and beasts . . . / Leaf and blade, and bud and blossom" (606).

The link between Persephone, death, and regeneration is part of the tradition of English poetry, and Atwood's versions of the myth also emphasize rebirth. Her first version of the story appears to be "The Field of Souls" (March 1961):

> The same unopened trees and flowers
> Float in the green light
> That tinged Proserpina walking this plain
> Before the dark earth parted, and she sank from sight; (2)

In "Proserpine," which appeared in the spring 1961 issue of *Jargon*, Atwood, like Macpherson, emphasizes the moment of sexual descent but centres this within the rebirth cycle:

> And though this May she raises
>   The roots bones living from the dead
> All green all flesh is gathered up at last
>   And sunk within her head

But the dark watcher from the hills
   Looking far down, only sees
A young girl bent among the daffodils,
   And gores his foaming steeds. (4)

This poem, especially in the penultimate and last stanzas, leads into Atwood's first chapbook, *Double Persephone* (1961).

Double Persephone represents Atwood's first sustained use of Eliot's "mythical method" as technique; however, her myths of the feminine appear to owe the most to Graves, while her style suggests the wit and intelligence of Macpherson. In the late 1950s, when Atwood was a student at Victoria, Macpherson was a guru to a group of younger poets who read, admired, and talked about her difficult, Blakean poetry,[10] which combines snippets of Greek, Roman, and Biblical myth, fairy tale, and ballad in a style that moves from the formal to the colloquial voice. If one reads *Double Persephone* from the perspective of Graves on the White Goddess (as mediated by Macpherson's style) certain aspects of a puzzling poetic cycle are clarified. Graves tells us that Frazer regards the White Goddess as "either Demeter or her double, Persephone" (58), which suggests a source for Atwood's title, *Double Persephone*. The reference to "double" suggests the opposing cycles of innocence and experience, the goddess as creator and destroyer, and it is from this context that Atwood writes.

The last and title poem "Double Persephone" is the most difficult of the sequence:

The field of hieroglyphics lies
   Open under graven skies
      But kneeling in the shadowed wood
      No flower of air can do her good
Where letters grown from branch and stem
   Have no green leaves enclosing them (np)

However, when read in relation to Graves, some of the more puzzling references become transparent. The references to "hieroglyphics," "lies," and "graven skies," providing a textual and physical setting for Persephone, can also be read as puns. Graves argues that the ancient hieroglyphics of the old Minoan poetic alphabet honouring the White Goddess were revised, first by invaders from central Asia and then by the Greek philosophers, notably Plato, with the intention of shifting power from the old matriarchal line of the White Goddess to a new patriarchal Apollonian order, a change also recorded by Frazer in *The Golden Bough*. In this revision the myths (expressed in hieroglyphs) regarding a female creator goddess were twisted in meaning to accommodate myths of patriarchal power. Thus they became "lies." However, under "graven skies" the field now "lies / Open" because under Graves's tutelage we have learned to read the original hieroglyphics of the "tree alphabet" that attest to the primacy of the Mother or White Goddess. The second and last stanzas of the poem can be read in a similar manner with explicit references to Graves.

To see further examples of this allusive technique in action we might turn to "Iconic Landscape," the third poem of *Double Persephone*, which alludes to a number of images or icons suggestive of the White Goddess.

> The twisted paths are hidden; the lost mother
> Listens for a sound she cannot hear,
> A deadened child's-cry; sister and brother
> Cover their lips with wild-strawberry leaves; (np)

The first allusion to "the lost mother" refers at one level to Demeter and her search for Persephone, but at a secondary level it is the White Goddess herself who is lost to contemporary memory. The "sister and brother" (note the word order) remind us that the matriarchal principle of the female fertility goddess was lost and superceded by male authority. In this process the female fertility goddess and her consort were changed by successive mythographers into sisters and brothers: this pair suggests Artemis and Apollo, described by Graves as children of the White Goddess. In the shift from matriarchy to patriarchy Apollo took over the goddess's role as the patron of poetry.

The final stanza of the poem combines a number of puzzling references: there is the "idiot girl," paradoxically described as sustaining the landscape and associated with an "owl," a cold "sun," and a "nest among the billows." The owl is traditionally associated with Minerva, the sun with Diana, and a nest in the rocking billows suggests Venus as Aphrodite. Graves provides a more explicit family tree with a quotation from Apuleius which tells us that "terrible Proserpine" is also the "Cecropian Minerva" (owl), the "Dictynnian Diana" (cold sun), Ceres (Demeter), and the Paphian Venus (63–64). We can therefore speculate that Persephone sustains the landscape as fertility goddess — all new life flows from her. Why then does Atwood add to Graves's catalogue a description of Persephone as "an idiot girl"? Perhaps because she was a silly girl to go wandering off alone, inviting trouble; perhaps Atwood is punning: *idiot* is derived from the Greek *idios*, a private citizen, one who does not engage in public debate.[11] Atwood may be using the word here because it was the Greeks, and especially Plato, who revised the old myths to disparage, and thus disenfranchise, women.

This sustained use of concepts gleaned from *The White Goddess* suggests not only that Atwood has applied Eliot's "mythical method" to *Double Persephone* but that Graves's *The White Goddess* has the same one-to-one relationship to her chapbook as Jessie L. Weston's *From Ritual to Romance* (1920) has to *The Waste Land*. Considerations of comparative value aside, Atwood's poetic cycle cannot be fully understood without reference to her source text.

Atwood's exploration of the archetype of the White Goddess took an academic form at Harvard in the early 1960s when she read Rider Haggard, summarizing some of her findings in an essay published in *Alphabet* as "Superwoman Drawn and Quartered: The Early Forms of *She*," which schematize Haggard's allegorical forms of the female principle. The basic distinctions, however, can be encompassed within the "ice woman" versus "earth-mother" categories, which Atwood claims in *Survival: A Thematic Guide to Canadian Literature* (1972) characterize presentations of the female in Canadian writing, categories she frankly admits derive from *The White Goddess* (*Survival* 199).

Much of the biting social comedy of Atwood's first novel, *The Edible Woman* (1967), builds upon the fertility goddess concepts treated in the early verse. The Prufrockian Leonard Slank is terrified of "Birth. Fecundity. Gestation. It's obscene . . ." (159) but is nonetheless "led flower garlanded to his doom" (86) as consort to Ainsley, would-be Great Mother and her "goddamn fertility-worship" (214). The ever-pregnant Clara, "spen[ds] most of her time being absorbed in, or absorbed by, her tuberous abdomen" (130), and so risk[s] allowing "her core to get taken over by the husband. And when the kids come, she wakes up one morning and discovers she doesn't have anything left inside, she's hollow . . ." (236). Significantly, Atwood's protagonist, the archetypal Mary (Marian McAlpin), is, as another character from the novel says in a somewhat different context, "trying to find her role as a Woman" as "one sexual role after another is presented to her . . ." (194).[12] Marian cannot be either a powerful fertility goddess or a compliant, modern-day Persephone. Trapped and anguished, she weeps, runs away, and hides. Ultimately, she finds that her body rejects the dictates of her head, instinctively escaping from a feminine role that destroys her integrity by compromising her intelligence: "my mind was at first as empty as though someone had scooped out the inside of my skull like a cantaloupe and left me only the rind to think with" (83). To be a hollow man may be fashionable in the poetry of T. S. Eliot, but to be a hollow woman in real life in the 1960s, Atwood argues, is intolerable.

After *Double Persephone* Atwood moves away from the explicit correlations of classical myth to develop her own version of a primal myth within a distinctively Canadian landscape. What is new in Atwood's early and mid-1960s poetry is a landscape derived from Canadian poetry (particularly the poetry of E. J. Pratt, F. R. Scott, and A. M. Klein, and often expressed as the descent into water) and what might be described as a Canadianized version of Ovidian metamorphosis: that is, the tendency to see the human in terms of landscape and the penchant for evolutionary metaphors that regularly turn the human into landscape or the landscape into the human.

Aside from Eliot's "Death by Water" and Poe's "The City in the Sea," Atwood's emphasis on water, evolution, and metamorphosis may represent a fusion of a number of influences from Canadian poetry. It is clear that Macpherson's Eve-Persephone (the "lost girl gone under the sea") contributes as does her sequence "The Island" from *The Boatman*:

> No man alone an island: we
> Stand circled with a lapping sea.
> I break the ring and let you go:
> Above my head the waters flow. (53)

An early Atwood poem, "We and Our Lost Selves" (March 1961), echoes the sea, crystal/glass, and island imagery of this sequence from Macpherson. Moreover, the concept of an island in association with human relationships and a circle suggests some of the imagery in *The Circle Game*, where the female narrator speaks of breaking the circle in order to break out of a disastrous relationship. Klein's poem about underwater meta-morphosis, "Portrait of the Poet as Landscape" (and Milton Wilson's explication, "Klein's Drowned Poet: Canadian Varia-tions on an Old Theme"), also contributes as do Scott's poems, especially "Lakeshore" and "Laurentian Shield." Finally, Atwood appears to draw upon a number of poems by Pratt, including "The Cachelot" and *Towards the Last Spike* (1952). All three poets present variations on the man-into-landscape or landscape-into-man metaphor, often in an evolutionary context. Atwood has remarked that Klein's poem with its drowned poet ("At the bottom of the sea" [335]) has influenced her and in my first essay I traced the influence of Pratt and Scott on one of her more striking underwater poems from this period "A Descent Through the Carpet" (Djwa 1966, 26). I would now like to add to this discussion the way in which her early preoccupation with Eliot and fertility myth diffused into a specifically Canadian poetic landscape.

Atwood's emphasis on landscape can be seen as a continuation of the early verse; the focus on a *Canadian* landscape may repre-sent a response to the literary nationalism of the 1960s leading up to the centenary of Canada's Confederation in 1967. Frye, in his "Conclusion" to the *Literary History of Canada* in 1964, for example, had consolidated much of his earlier criticism by em-phasizing the centrality of landscape to the Canadian poetic tradition and identifying Pratt as the major poet. To judge from the verbal echoes of three poems written between April and September in 1963, Atwood was also responding to Pratt's poetry in Smith's *Oxford Book of Canadian Verse*. Smith reprinted Pratt's "The Cachelot" together with two selections from *Towards the Last Spike*, where man becomes landscape: "Foreheads grew into cliffs, jaws into juts. / The meal, so changed, engaged the follicles: / Eyebrows came out as gorse, the beards as thistles," (347). These excerpts are echoed in Atwood's poem "Poor Tom," published in *Alphabet*, June 1963.

> . . . the earth grows
> out through him, immanent
> in sandy bramble-hair, the chilblained
> bedrock of his jawbone, rough redpine
> of spine (52)

Atwood had merged man / woman with landscape in the earlier poem "The Harvesters," but the difference is that here, as in Pratt's *Towards the Last Spike*, man takes on the physical aspects of the landscape from which he developed. Moreover, this is no longer a literary Eden, but rather, a distinctly Canadian northern shield. Finally, Atwood is describing the body as landscape as do Pratt and Klein.

In the poem "The Descent as Dissection," (*Canadian Forum*, March 1964), Atwood continues a Prattian strain in a description of a journey into the body, which also becomes a descent into the evolutionary past. Typographically the poem appears on the page as two long skinny poems with a space between; thus, one may read the whole poem from left to right or each half from top to bottom as in a descent.

> I was cutting off small   pieces, intricate grafts
> with my fingernail   scalpel, making cross
>   sections
> when all at once   (though I was being
>   careful)
> it all   fell away; those over
> coats and under   shirts I found
> under the skin, the layer   of fur, the lizard scales
> pceled off and then
>
>   I was inside
> a long cavern, a room   of ribs, it seemcd
> of some gigantic fish,   a bedrock fossil
> stranded in this granite land

I had been so far inland   for so long
I had forgotten   that the sea
was once   here, also

but around me grew   stone ferns
old forests   creatures from the first
thick tepid floors,   greening with warmth
             again

When I have waded
       through   these swampy fens
and reached the beaches   of the heart —
lands, great lakes   where earth and water
             verge

each other, I will know   how it could all
have been contained   within this one dead
man. (280)

The initial description of the cadaver's ribs as like some gigantic fish suggests the description of the interior of the giant rib cage of the whale in Pratt's "The Cachelot," and here, as in several Pratt poems, notably "Silences" and "Come Away, Death," there is a descent into the evolutionary past. At first a descent into the human body, Atwood's poem becomes a descent into the animal past, with fur and lizard scales, then a descent into a gigantic fish, rather like Pratt's Cachelot (or Frye's whale that serves as a metaphor for the Canadian landscape [*LHC* 284]). Then the narrator is further back in time, inside ribs and bedrock fossils, where the sea once had been; there we find old forests, stone, firs, ferns, creatures from the first thick tepid floors, "greening with warmth." This dissection of the human body, ultimately passing through swamp, will finally end at the heartlands where earth and water merge. This is man's evolutionary journey "away back, down deep" into water described by Pratt in "Silences" (77–78).

In April 1964 Atwood published "The Willowpattern Plate,"

her first description of a descent into the water with a "You" and "I," apparently lovers. In the next version of the water poem "After the Flood, We," published in September 1964, Atwood combines the Genesis version of the flood with an earlier version from Ovid's *Metamorphosis*, the story of Deukalion and Pyrrha, who ride out the flood in an ark and then throw the bones of the mother (i.e., the rocks of mother earth) behind them to repopulate the world. In Atwood's poem there are again "you" and "I," apparently he and she. She gathers the bones of the "drowned mothers" while he walks ahead, speaking of the beauty of the morning, not even noticing there has been a flood, tossing pebbles behind, not hearing, not seeing, "the almost-human / brutal faces forming / (slowly) / out of stone" (131). This poem, depicting man's savage beginnings, associates the flood with a new Genesis of metamorphosis from inanimate to animate life.

It is on the basis of these poems that Atwood develops her own primal myth, one that organizes her first major collection, *The Circle Game*. The book is framed — begins and ends — with images of watery metamorphosis. The first poem, "This Is a Photograph of Me," evokes a drowned narrator:

> (The photograph was taken
> the day after I drowned.
> I am in the lake, in the center
> of the picture, just under the surface. . . .) (11)

This poem is recalled in Milton Wilson's article, "Klein's Drowned Poet: Canadian Variations on an Old Theme," where he describes the poet-photographer of Klein's "Portrait of the Poet as Landscape," who has "resurrected his own drowned body" (14): "the last picture to be developed under water is that 'single-camera view'" (Wilson 15). The relevance of Wilson's comment to "This Is a Photograph of Me" is simply that this poem also describes a drowned "me" in an underwater photograph.

This primal myth of descent and metamorphosis also reappears in the second poem, "After the Flood, We," and in a later
poem, "A Descent Through the Carpet":

> . . . in the green halflight
> I drift down past the
> marginal orchards branched
> colourful
>
> > feathered. . . .
>
> into the long iceage
>
> > > the pressures
>
> of winter
>
> > the snowfall endless in the sea. (21)

The narrator, after a descent into an underwater world suggestive of both Pratt and Scott (Djwa 26–29), is brought back by
the sound of a gun, "breaking the membrane of water . . . / fossil
bones and fangs . . . / I was born . . . / the night these wars
began" (23). What Atwood has added to the Canadian underwater poem is the concept of uterine waters, a concept that reappears in *Surfacing*.

In "Pre-Amphibian" the return is again to the primal past:

> . . . this warm rotting
> of vegetable flesh
> this quiet spawning of roots. . . .
>
> but here I blur
> into you   our breathing sinking
> to green millenniums
> and   sluggish   in our blood
> all ancestors
> are warm fish moving (63)

In the last two poems of the book, "The Explorers" and "The Settlers," the myth of descent is given a Canadian context. One speaker, apparently the voice of a skeleton, suggests that the coming explorers (presumably the discoverers of Canada) won't be able to tell which of the two skeletons was the survivor (78). In the last poem, "The Settlers," the humans metamorphose into trees and grass as a part of an organic cycle:

> They dug us down
> into the solid granite
> where our bones grew flesh again,
> came up trees and
> grass. (79)

These are preliminaries for the evolutionary, sexual, and psychic journeys taken by the narrators in *The Journals of Susanna Moodie* and *Surfacing*. In *Surfacing*, published three years later, in 1972, Atwood combines fertility myth with social satire (on the phenomena of Americanization). The central scene at the core of the novel is again the journey "away back, down deep" into water, which is a return not just to the Indian and evolutionary past but also to the primitive unconscious and the uterine waters. In the Persephone myth the pattern is that of descent through water followed by impregnation by Pluto and spring rebirth. In *Surfacing* the pattern alters somewhat in that the protagonist descends into water questing for knowledge but she "surfaces" with a new understanding of herself. Thus she becomes the agent of her own redemption. She then seeks impregnation, as both Annis Pratt and Sherrill E. Grace[13] have noted, like the female figure of fertility cults.

> The baby will slip out easily as an egg, . . . I'll lick it off and bite
> the cord, the blood returning to the ground where it belongs;

> the moon will be full, pulling, in the morning I will be able to
> see it: it will be covered with shining fur, a god . . . (162)

Characteristically, as is common to the Canadian poetic tradition, the narrator becomes part of the landscape:

> I lean against a tree, I am a tree leaning. . . .
> I am not an animal or a tree, I am the thing in which the
> trees and animals move and grow, I am a place. (195)

Here again, as in the early poetry, Atwood is metamorphosing
body into landscape. To be sure, the novel offers the possibility
of an hallucinogenic mushroom, but the underlying logic of this
metaphor is also Frye's belief in the contiguity of Canadian
identity and Canadian landscape.

Atwood's development shows the essentially hybrid nature of
Canadian literary modernism. In her case the influence of international modernism by way of Eliot was reenforced by Frye's and
Macpherson's emphasis on myth, but it was given a particular-
ized Canadian application, partly through Atwood's adaptation
of the man-into-landscape metaphors of Pratt, Scott, and Klein,
and partly because of her response to the Canadian literary
nationalism in the 1960s. Tracing the development of her early
verse up to the first collection, *The Circle Game*, reveals that her
poetic technique has developed from what might be considered
the major mode of the twentieth century, the parodic mode. As
Linda Hutcheon remarks in *A Theory of Parody* (1985), the parodic
form distances and changes (32–33); Atwood, in reworking
Eliot's conventions in "The Conversation" and "Pastoral Elegy"
was, in fact, distancing and changing from a woman's point of
view. In *Double Persephone* Atwood is no longer simply parodying
content, but is implementing Eliot's technique while rejecting
many of his concepts. In her later poetry the structure of specific

myths are sometimes left behind while "chips of myth" are used within primal myths and metaphors of Atwood's own devising.

In her development as an artist Atwood has moved from a one-to-one parody of Eliot to a mastering of the parodic use of myth and allusion. In this progression she is very much a part of the mainstream of twentieth-century writing. As Hutcheon has observed, ". . . parody in this century is one of the major modes of formal and thematic construction of texts. And, beyond even this, it has a hermeneutic function with both cultural and even ideological implications. Parody is one of the major forms of modern self-reflexivity" (2). For Atwood, we may conclude, the hermeneutic function is closely associated with self-definition as a woman and an artist.

If, as we found, Atwood's early poems are suggestive of the spring solstice with new birth following winter death, the later prose — especially *Cat's Eye*, *Wilderness Tips* (1991), and *The Robber Bride* (1993) — suggest the summer solstice with stories of aging, betrayal, the loss of fertility and the fact of death. Zenia, Atwood's female version of Grimm's "The Robber Bridegroom," is clearly woman as Hecate, "an ancient statuette dug up from a Minoan palace: there are the large breasts, the tiny waist, the dark eyes, the snaky hair" (546). In *Wilderness Tips* there are also allusions to fertility goddesses and buried bodies; however, the ethos of the book suggests "The Age of Lead," the title of one finely crafted story, when compared to earlier (and younger) ages of silver and gold. Particularly self-reflexive is the story "Isis in Darkness," about an aging male academic and his relationship with a young woman, a Gwendolyn MacEwen-like poet. He is provided with a past that sounds remarkably like Atwood's:

> He'd been good with words then. He'd had several of his poems
> published in the university literary magazine, and in two little
> magazines, one of them not mimeographed. Seeing these poems

in print, with his name underneath — he used initials like T. S. Eliot, to make himself sound older — had given him more satisfaction than he'd ever got out of anything before. (62)

Years before, in a coffee house (suggestive of the Bohemian Embassy), the young woman read (as had Margaret Atwood) a series of lyrics, "Isis in Darkness," which described the search of the Egyptian Queen of Heaven and Earth for the dismembered body of her lover Osiris (65). The myths of Isis and Osiris are Egyptian allegories of resurrection, versions of the Persephone-Pluto myth; however at the surface level in Atwood's story the myth is invoked ironically. The narrator, too, had once wanted to be a poet, but his career and his relationship with the young woman have been unsuccessful. At a deeper level, however, the myths of Isis and Osiris become resonant when the male figure takes on aspects of the nurturing Isis. After the young woman's death, he settles on the role of archaeologist, sifting through their joint past in an attempt to re-create it (just as Isis searched for Osiris) by discerning the mythic patterns that give life meaning:

> He will only be the archaeologist. . . . In the ruined sanctu-
> ary. . . . groping for the shape of the past. He is the one who will
> say it has meaning. . . . summoning up whatever is left of his
> knowledge and skill, kneeling beside her in the darkness, fitting
> her broken pieces back together. (82–83)

In one sense the narrator's search is for the woman-poet as Isis, the creator, one of the many forms of the White Goddess; in the largest sense his search is the writer's quest for meaning.

I see this story as self-reflexive because in later novels, such as *Life Before Man* and *Cat's Eye*, Atwood, as poet-turned-novelist, has become an archaeologist of contemporary society, sifting through the primal, putting the pieces together, showing their mythic numinousness, and so attempting to discern meaning.

This task, first undertaken in the early poetry, is now transferred to prose, perhaps because what she wants to say requires an extended medium, perhaps because (as suggested by three titles in *Selected Poems II*, which include the formula "Aging female poet . . . ") poetry is a young woman's, as well as a young man's, game. In any event, it is Atwood's search for articulated meaning and her belief that even the so-called meaninglessness of contemporary life can be intelligently and wittily explored that I find most impressive. Her unflinching reports on (so far) the two ages of women are increasingly valid for most generations, particularly now as women continue their search for self-definition in personal terms. Atwood's wry vision speaks to the complexity of this quest: the disappointments sometimes tainted by anger, the humorous aspects sometimes tainted by bitterness, the small, often qualified, successes. It is because of this that she continues to be read and appreciated.

NOTES

1. Of the twenty-seven entries in the 1990 MLA listing (excluding DAI), five articles appeared in Canadian journals, and the balance were predominantly in American publications. Two important critical collections were published in 1988 by American publishers: Judith McCombs, ed. *Critical Essays on Margaret Atwood* (Boston: G. K. Hall & Co., 1988), and Kathryn Van Spanckeren and Jan Garden Castro, eds., *Margaret Atwood: Vision and Forms* (Carbondale: Southern Illinois UP, 1988). The first collection is equally balanced between Canadian and non-Canadian contributions; the second consists largely of American critics.

2. I suggest briefly in my 1981 article that Atwood is rewriting patriarchal myth. Gail Greene explores the question of feminist metafiction in *Changing the Story: Feminist Fiction and the Tradition* (Bloomington: Indiana UP, 1991).

3. Margaret Atwood to Sandra Djwa, interview, March 13, 1975.

4. Margaret Atwood to Sandra Djwa, letter, June 26, 1992.

5. David Donaldson to Sandra Djwa, interview, September 7, 1993.

6. Margaret Atwood to Sandra Djwa, interview, March 13, 1975. This comment and the following details are from this interview.

7. David Donaldson to Sandra Djwa, interview, September 7, 1993.

8. A number of critics have identified echoes of Eliot in Atwood's prose and poetry; Walter Swayze has linked the tone of Atwood's criticism in *Survival* with that of the early and dogmatic Eliot; Gail Greene has explored the ways that many of the central concerns of *Life Before Man* can be traced back to "The Love Song of J. Alfred Prufrock" and "The Hollow Men" and Jerome Rosenberg has noted that Atwood's metaphors in *The Circle Game* echo a phrase from Prufrock.

9. See note 1. See also Sherrill E. Grace, "In Search of Demeter: The Lost, Silent Mother in *Surfacing*," in *Margaret Atwood: Vision and Forms*, 35–47; Gillian Ladousse, "Some Aspects of Theme and Metamorphosis in Margaret Atwood's Poetry," *Études Canadiennes* 2 (1976) 71–77.

10. David Donaldson to Sandra Djwa, interview, September 7, 1993.

11. In a late nineteenth-century Canadian poem by Archibald Lampman, "The City at the End of Things," there is a reference to an "idiot" that draws upon its Greek meaning.

12. Alan Dawe, in his 1973 introduction to *The Edible Woman*, makes the point that Marian's experience parallels that of Fischer's exposition of sexual roles in *Alice in Wonderland*.

13. Sherrill E. Grace, "In Search of Demeter: The Lost, Silent Mother in *Surfacing*," in *Margaret Atwood: Vision and Forms*, 35–47; and Annis Pratt, "*Surfacing* and the Rebirth Journey," *The Art of Margaret Atwood*, eds. Cathy N. and Arnold E. Davidson (Toronto: Anansi, 1981) 139–57.

WORKS CITED

Atwood, Margaret. "After the Flood, We." *The Canadian Forum* (September 1964): 131.

———. "The Conversation." *Acta Victoriana* (November 1958): 11.

———. *The Circle Game*. Toronto: Contact Press, 1966.

———. "The Descent as Dissection." *Canadian Forum* (March 1964): 280.

———. *Double Persephone*. Toronto: Hawkshead Press, 1961. np.

———. *The Edible Woman*. Toronto: McClelland & Stewart, 1969.

——. "The Field of Souls." *Acta Victoriana* (March 1961): 2.

——. *The Handmaid's Tale*. Toronto: McClelland & Stewart, 1985.

——. "The Harvesters." *Canadian Forum* (June 1960): 60.

——. [Shakesbeat Latweed, pseud.]. "In Dispraise of James J. Eliot." *Acta Victoriana* (November 1960): 11–12.

——. "Knell and Nativity." *Acta Victoriana* (February 1959): 19.

——. "Narcissus: Double Entendre." *Acta Victoriana* (February 1961): 15–16.

——. "Pastoral Elegy." *The Sheet* 3 [n.d.]: 4.

——. "Poor Tom." *Alphabet* 6 (June 1963): 52.

——. "Proserpine." *Jargon* (Spring 1961): 4.

——. *The Robber Bride*. Toronto: McClelland & Stewart, 1993.

——. "Some Sun for This Winter." *Acta Victoriana* (January 1961): 18–19.

——. [Shakesbeat Latweed, pseud.]. "Spratire." *Acta Victoriana* (December 1958): 22.

——. "Superwoman Drawn and Quartered: The Early Forms of *She*." *Second Words: Selected Critical Prose*. Boston: Beacon Press, 1982/1984. 35–54.

——. *Surfacing*. Toronto: General (1972) 1983.

——. *Survival: A Thematic Guide to Canadian Literature*. Toronto: Anansi, 1972.

——. "The Triple Goddess: A Poem for Voices." *Acta Victoriana* (April 1960): 8–13.

——. "We and Our Lost Selves." *Acta Victoriana* (March 1961): 2.

——. *Wilderness Tips*. Toronto: McClelland & Stewart, 1991.

——. "The Willowpattern Plate." *Canadian Forum* (April 1964): 23.

Djwa, Sandra. "The Where of Here: Margaret Atwood and a Canadian Tradition." *The Art of Margaret Atwood*. Eds. Cathy N. and Arnold E. Davidson. Toronto: Anansi, 1981. 15–34.

Eliot, T. S. "The Love Song of J. Alfred Prufrock," "The Waste Land." *Collected Poems 1909–1962*. London: Faber & Faber, 1963. 13–22, 61–79.

——. "*Ulysses*, Order, and Myth." *Selected Prose of T. S. Eliot*. London: Faber & Faber, 1975. 175–78.

Frye, Northrop. Conclusion, *Literary History of Canada: Canadian Literature in English*. Ed. Carl F. Klinck. Toronto: U of Toronto P, 1966. 821–49.

Graves, Robert. *The White Goddess*. New York: Vintage, 1960.

Hutcheon, Linda. *A Theory of Parody: The Teaching of Twentieth-Century Art Forms*. New York/London: Methuen, 1985.

Klein, A. M. *The Collected Poems of A. M. Klein*. Toronto: McGraw-Hill Ryerson, 1974. 330–35.

Macpherson, Jay. *The Boatman*. Toronto: Oxford UP, 1957.

———. "Narcissus: Some Uncertain Reflections." *Alphabet* 1 (September 1960): 41–57.

Milton, John. "Paradise Lost." *John Milton: Complete Poems and Major Prose*. Ed. Merritt Y. Hughes. New York: Odyssey, 1957. 208–469.

Pratt, E. J. *The Collected Poems of E. J. Pratt*. Toronto: Macmillan, 1958. 345–88.

Shelley, Percy Bysshe. "Song of Proserpine." *The Complete Poetical Works of Percy Bysshe Shelley*. Ed. Thomas Hutchinson. London: Oxford UP/Humphrey Milford, 1927. 606.

Sitwell, Edith. *The Canticle of the Rose: Selected Poems 1920–1947*. London: Macmillan, 1950.

Wilson, Milton. "Klein's Drowned Poet: Canadian Variations on an Old Theme." *Canadian Literature* 6 (Autumn 1960): 5–17.

Coral Ann Howells

"It all depends on where you stand in relation to the forest" : Atwood and the Wilderness from *Surfacing* to *Wilderness Tips*

If you stand very close, you can see the molecules inside the tree. Move back, you see a green thing in the distance. Where are we standing here? Are we right close to the individual author? In which case, it's the author's voice, not the Canadian voice. Do we stand back a little bit, and see a region? Do we say, there's a Quebec voice? an Ontario voice? . . . Standing quite far back, you can say, "Yes, there is a Canadian voice."

CONVERSATIONS 199–200

ATWOOD'S DISCUSSION OF CANADIAN VOICE and how it is perceived by readers at varying distances might serve as emblem for this essay, which is concerned with perception and perspective. How does a transatlantic reader perceive Atwood's changing perceptions of Canadian wilderness over a period of twenty years? It is worth looking a little more closely at the language of the above passage with its landscape markers, its curious elision of "hearing" into "seeing," its emphasis on location. This use of spatial metaphors would seem to indicate a crucial feature of Atwood's construction of Canadian identity, though perhaps a more distinctive formulation is the one in *Surfacing*: "Now I am on my home ground, foreign territory" (11). Such a paradoxical configuration seems to work for Atwood as the sign of Canadianness, "constructing a spatial metaphor which codes in a distinctively Canadian positioning in relation to culture and ideology, to history, to place, to identity, suggesting continuity between a New World mythology of wilderness and a contemporary postmodern awareness." [1] Atwood's fiction is so well known internationally that in all likelihood her voice is now heard across the Atlantic as "the" Canadian voice. Though there are disadvantages to this single (white, anglophone) representation of a bilingual, multicultural society, I would argue that these are not as great as they might be, given her active engagement with cultural politics, not only in Canada but on the international scene, where Canada may be the "First Postmodern State" in a world that British sociologist Anthony Giddens describes as belonging to the "post-traditional order of late modernity." [2] Atwood's fiction is a response both to her experiential context ("Every piece of writing exists in its surround," [3]) and to the wider ecological threats that late modern globalization projects impose with their "socialisation of nature" and their "colonisation of the future." [4] It is this double response that has caused a shift of emphasis over the past twenty years in Atwood's writing; she has moved from representing wilderness to Canadians as their culturally distinctive national space to a much bleaker contemporary revisionary reading, where simple binary nationalist oppositions disappear. In *Wilderness Tips* an identifiably Canadian voice addresses an international audience, arguing for our shared recognition of complicity in her strong warnings against global pollution as wilderness recedes into myth.

Arguably "wilderness" was already a Canadian cultural myth when Atwood inherited it as a child in the 1940s. For her, wilderness is a concept based on experiential knowledge and cultural conditioning, and she has written frequently about her bush childhood in northern Ontario and Quebec as the daughter of an entomologist, about her summers at Ontario camps in the 1940s and 1950s with their Europeanized versions of the wild, and about her early Canadian reading where "Seton's stick-and-stone artefacts and live-off-the-land recipes in *Wilder-nessWisdom* were readily available, and we could make them quite easily, which we did." [5] As a result of her own upbringing, Atwood has constructed her literary figurations of the wilder-ness as unexplored natural environment, a territory without monuments or landmarks, emptied of signs of human presence. (Signs of aboriginal presence were indecipherable and, there-fore, invisible.) For her first complete figuring of wilderness we should turn to *The Journals of Susanna Moodie* (1970), though there are earlier versions in her unfinished novel *The Nature Hut* (c. 1966), and her unpublished story "Transfigured Landscape," described by Atwood as "the first, very first bit of *Surfacing* to emerge. Winter 64–5?"[6] *Susanna Moodie* is the paradigmatic representation of a female European immigrant's response to the Canadian wilderness as undifferentiated bush landscape, the site of immense and threatening (because unknown) otherness. Through her Moodie persona, Atwood articulates her complex construction of the Canadian psyche, which is spelled out in the famous Afterword:

> We are all immigrants to this place, even if we were born here. The country is too big for anyone to inhabit completely, and in the parts unknown to us we move in fear, exiles and invaders. (62)

In this poetic sequence, wilderness is projected as New World chaos, the binary opposite of Old World civil order; but as Jacqui

Smyth suggests, there is a blurring of boundaries between the two as the "I"/Susanna Moodie figure breaks down or, more significantly, is "broken into by branches, roots, tendrils." [7] "Crept in upon by green," Susanna Moodie experiences the dawning of new perceptions of the wilderness as living natural order. Metaphors change over the three Journals, imaging the process of shifting subjective perceptions, and the English-born pioneer woman is resurrected as a witness to the presence of the past in late 1960s Toronto:

> There is no city;
> This is the centre of a forest
> your place is empty. (61)

So Atwood establishes her conception of wilderness as Canadian cultural myth: it may be buried, but it does not vanish.

Atwood uses this wilderness as the sign of a distinctive heritage when she addresses Canadian readers in *Surfacing* and *Survival*. Both are products of 1970s Canadian cultural nationalism, the historical specifics of which are clearly set out in Peter Dale Scott's useful essay, which focuses on the "Emergent Nation Syndrome" and its attendant problems of national identity;[8] Atwood's two texts may be read as symptomatic of this period. Though *Surfacing* was written before *Survival*, there is a symbiotic relationship here, for writing her novel made Atwood realize certain common themes that her fiction shared with other Canadian writings, and *Survival* in its turn shows Atwood creating the context in which to read her fiction. Setting out to answer the question, "What is distinctive about Canadian literature?" Atwood's project is clearly related to raising cultural self-consciousness as she describes key patterns in selected texts which are "like field markings in bird-books: they will help you to distinguish this species from all others, Canadian literature from the other literatures [English and American] with which it is often compared or confused" (13). Operating within an already nascent Canadian consciousness of a literary tradition (Djwa 15–34) that she acknowledges when she defines her project as an answer to Northrop Frye's question, "Where is here?" Atwood's definition of Canadianness hinges on the subject's position in relation to wilderness:

> Literature is also a map, a geography of the mind . . . We need such a map desperately, we need to know about here, because here is where we live. For members of a country or a culture, shared knowledge of their place, their here, is not a luxury but a necessity. Without that knowledge we will not survive. (18–19)

Atwood then proceeds to construct a bleak (dominantly anglophone) Canadian literary tradition from the early nineteenth century to the 1970s, which has been criticized for its obsession with victims and with nature as monster. It is time we dropped that myopic reading to emphasize the resonance of the title, *Survival*, with its specific historical and cultural implications; for what Atwood does (and I shall argue, she does again in *Wilderness Tips*) is to diagnose a contemporary malaise. *Survival* presents several arguments for revisionary readings of a "Canadian signature" (237) in order to move beyond the encoded colonial predicaments: rewriting quests as searches for spiritual reintegration; advocating that victims take responsibility and assume power, thereby ceasing to be victims; restructuring perceptions of wilderness so that Canada ceases to feel like "foreign territory" and becomes "home ground." *Survival* also moves outside the genre of literary history to address questions of national and cultural survival, as Atwood urges her fellow Canadians to

> control our own space, physical as well as cultural. But that space must be controlled with love, or it will be the control typical of

> tyranny; there will not be that much difference between Cana-
> dian ownership and the absentee landlord draining the land we
> already live under. If choices destructive of the land are made,
> it doesn't much matter finally who makes them. (244)

Several of Atwood's most consistent preoccupations surface
here: her ecological interests, her belief that art has a social
function, and her concern with Canada–United States relations.
It is also evident that her faith in the power of language to
transform perception is strongly written in at the end, when she
talks about "a 'jail-break,' an escape from our old habits of looking
at things, and a 're-creation,' a new way of seeing, experiencing
and *imaging* — or imagining — which we ourselves have helped
to shape" (my emphasis, 246). This is a visionary ending that
resonates with the language of empowerment in *Surfacing*.

SURFACING BEGINS AND ENDS with the forest, for just as wilderness
is significant in Atwood's version of a Canadian nationalist literary history, so it is in the story of one woman's quest to find an
appropriate language to write about her changing perceptions of
her own identity as Canadian and female. The *Toronto Star* review
(September 12, 1972) described *Surfacing* as "a Canadian fable in
which the current obsessions of Canadians become symbols in a
drama of personal survival: nationalism, feminism, death, culture, art, nature, pollution," all of which signals early recognition
of the emblematic status of this novel, though the reviewer
underplays gendered perceptions of wilderness in a text that now
may also be read as eco-feminist. A great deal of critical attention
has been paid to *Surfacing*, so in my reading I propose to highlight
only the dual emphases on the regenerative powers of wilderness
and language.

As George Woodcock has written, "The environment is the
great theme in *Surfacing*," [9] and one of the great strengths of this

novel is its sense of specific location as the unnamed female narrator (whom I shall call the surfacer, following W. J. Keith) leaves the city to travel back to her home in the bush on the Ontario-Quebec border. The area has been identified as the Canadian Shield, northwest of North Bay, near Lake Kipawa.[10] However, if this is wilderness in the early 1970s, it is not far away from the effects of civilization, for the white birches are dying from acid rain, the land is being vandalized by weekend hunters and fishermen, and the area is being invaded by new tourist roads. As the highway signs show their "mélange of demands and languages" (English-English, American-English, and French), the district already has a local history of colonization that goes back to the narrator's childhood memories of a paper mill and a dam built sixty years ago to "control" the lake. The socialization of nature is already in progress in the marks of human habitation and exploitation, the disappearance of the Native population ("The government had put them somewhere else, corralled them" [85]), and the small community on the lake which represents a hybrid colonial culture. Yet the forest landscape is still capable of regenerating itself and of offering a protective cover: "The peninsula is where I left it, pushing out from the island shore with the house not even showing through the trees" (32).

Coming home is to enter not only another place but another time dimension, as the narrator tracks back to an almost forgotten past that belongs both to her own private history and to the Amerindian prehistory of the region:

> In the cool green among the trees, new trees and stumps, the stumps with charcoal crusts on them, scabby and crippled, survivors of an old disaster. Sight flowing ahead of me over the ground, eyes filtering the shapes, the names of things fading but their forms and uses remaining, the animals learned what to eat without nouns. . . . Beneath it the invisible part, threadlike underground network . . . (149–50)

The living forest with its cycle of life and death still bears traces of the past in the present, functioning like a text in another language. This, as the narrator comes to understand, is a language of changing natural forms, for the forest is the place of dynamic transformation:

> Out of the leaf nests the flowers rise, pure white, flesh of gnats and midges, petals now, metamorphosis. . . . energy of decay turning to growth, green fire. I remember the heron; by now it will be insects, frogs, fish, other herons. My body also changes, the creature in me, plant-animal, sends out filaments in me. (167–68)

The imagery encodes not only analogy but also harmony between the forest and the pregnant woman, establishing connections between human and non-human at the basic level of life processes. Where Susanna Moodie left the wilderness knowing there was something she had not learned, the surfacer construes "new meanings," immersing herself in "the other language" of the forest and the "multilingual water" of the lake.

Indeed, *Surfacing* might be read as the record of a gendered search for a new language which is more responsive to an organic conceptualization of reality, and perhaps some of the most interesting questions the novel raises are linguistic. These are the same questions that Atwood raised in an interview in 1986:

> How do we know "reality" ? How do you encounter the piece of granite? How do you know it directly? Is there such a thing as knowing it directly without language?[11]

Initially the surfacer has a deep distrust of words, seeing them as instruments of deception and domination rather than of communication: As a woman she feels "trapped in a language that wasn't mine," placed in the position of victim in male power games of love and war (106); as an anglophone in Quebec she has to confront problems of translation "when people could say words that would go into my ears meaning nothing" (11); as a Canadian she feels compromised by American cultural influences:

> If you look like them and talk like them and think like them then you are them, I was saying, you speak their language, a language is everything you do. (129)

So her quest for self-rehabilitation is also a quest to find her own "dialect" amidst all the languages available to her, "It was there in me, the evidence, only needing to be deciphered" (76).

This journey of resistance and recovery proceeds through a series of clearly marked stages, encounters with wilderness that teach her not only how to "see" but how to "act." It is a visionary education where psycho-spiritual experience and the physical sensation of sight are presented as parallel modes of perception. The process begins with the blurred image of discovery when she dives into the lake (142). No passage in Atwood has been so exhaustively reread, so I shall merely make the point that the redemption of a personal past is presented here as sacralized response to the wilderness:

> These gods, here on the shore or in the water, unacknowledged or forgotten, were the only ones who had ever given me anything I needed; and freely, (145)

Left alone on the island, her vision of the primeval forest looms with the clarity of hallucination after she has eaten the magic mushrooms ("Something has happened to my eyes" [181]):

> The forest leaps upward, enormous, the way it was before they cut it, columns of sunlight frozen; the boulders float, melt, everything is made of water, even the rocks. In one of the

languages there are no nouns, only verbs held for a longer
moment.

The animals have no need for speech, why talk when you are
a word

I lean against a tree, I am a tree leaning (181)

In this world of dynamic process, reality consists of a continuous,
uninterrupted flow of energy in perpetual metamorphosis rendered as kaleidoscopic vision. However, to be "crept in upon by
green" would mean the deconstruction of individual identity, a
submergence in undifferentiated process. In order to survive as
human, there is a need to "break surface" and to "stand" separate
again, marking one's discontinuity from the earth. The need for
separation is confirmed in the surfacer's vision of her father's
ghost as wilderness monster, standing as terrible warning against
the abolition of borders: "he wants the forest to flow back into
the places his mind cleared" (186). Immediately after this comes
the crucial moment of recovery, where sight and insight fuse in
the brief episode of a fish jumping.

From the lake a fish jumps
An idea of a fish jumps
A fish jumps, carved wooden fish with dots painted on the
sides, no, antlered fish thing drawn in red on cliffstone, protect-
ing spirit. It hangs in the air suspended, flesh turned to icon, he
has changed again, returned to the water. How many shapes can
he take.

I watch it for an hour or so; then it drops and softens, the
circles widen, it becomes an ordinary fish again. (187)

This is an exceptionally detailed record of how perceptions of an
object alter it, so that a real fish becomes first a visual image, then
a word and an idea which may undergo multiple transformations
in the mind of the perceiving subject, changing into the wooden

trophy seen earlier in the village bar, then into the antlered fish in the copy of the Indian rock paintings, then into the shadow of a dead father's body, till it finally becomes a fish again, dropping into the water. These transformations are effected through subjective vision and registered in language that is closer to poetry than to prose.

The surfacer is at last able to tell her life story and to offer another model for remembering when she realizes that her story, too, is always multiple and open to revision. Having heard the other language of the wilderness, she has also realized that words are a human necessity, for to be alienated from words is to be alienated from other human beings. The last chapter is a curious blend of definition and indeterminacy. It begins with an assertion: "This above all, to refuse to be a victim. . . . The word games, the winning and losing games are finished" (191). However, a new language still has to be invented, and as the surfacer contemplates returning to her lover, Joe, she faces the double possibility of love and trust and also of compromise and failure "through the intercession of words." Her story ends tentatively, as she stands hidden among the trees watching Joe who is calling her name, poised to step forward but not yet moving. I prefer to read the ending as optimistic, for as the surfacer realizes, "withdrawing is no longer possible and the alternative is death." She no longer hears the voice of the wilderness which has become indifferent to her: "The lake is quiet, the trees surround me, asking and giving nothing" (192). Joe, on the other hand, is offering her *something*.

The narrator has surfaced through patriarchal language with its definitions of "woman" and "victim," and she has found an appropriate form within a quest narrative that mixes realism and fantasy. Yet this is a quest that is markedly incomplete. At this point it is worth turning back to the signal in the title, coded into the part of speech employed. *Surfacing* is a gerund (a noun made out of a verb), indicating process or activity (like the fish jumping), not fixity or completeness. Perhaps the best explanatory gloss on the role of language in conceptualizing reality is provided by Atwood herself:

> Well, let me put it this way. There are a number of Indian languages which are very interesting: in one of them there are no nouns. What we would call a noun is a variation of a verb. So that you don't say, "A deer is running across a field." You say something like "fielding" or "something which is being a field is manifesting something which is being a deer." That is, the whole language is composed of verbs. The mode of linguistic expression militates against seeing objects as distinct from their backgrounds . . . the whole area of your perception is behaving in a certain way.[12]

Similarly, *Surfacing* argues for a change in subjective perceptions of reality and for a restructuring of language ("the language is wrong" [76]) in a shift beyond traditional binary oppositions towards a holistic vision. Atwood commented on her project in an interview in 1972:

> You can define yourself as innocent and get killed, or you can define yourself as a killer and kill others. I think there has to be a third thing again; the ideal would be somebody who would neither be a killer or a victim, who could achieve some kind of harmony with the world, which is a productive or creative harmony, rather than a destructive relationship towards the world. Now in neither book [*Surfacing* or *Survival*] is that actualized, but in both it's seen as a possibility finally, whereas initially it is not.[13]

SURVIVAL ENDS WITH two questions addressed to Canadian readers: Have we survived? If so, what happens after survival? Twenty years later, *Wilderness Tips* offers the same challenge, not only to

Canadians, but to Atwood's international readership. Now, however, there is a marked shift to an emphasis on loss and disempowerment, and a bleaker vision of survival on a globalized scale. Binary oppositions are indeed eroded in these fragmented narratives that insistently double back on themselves, but the effect is not one of "productive or creative harmony," but rather of contamination and complicity in a late modern world, "which we ourselves have helped to shape." These stories show us a world on the verge of breakdown as they signal the contemporary collapse of the grand narratives of history and of national myth, registering a disintegration of traditional systems of order associated with the postmodern/late-modern condition. While they retain their distinctive "field markings" with their references to Canadian wilderness, history, and geography, national identity is exposed as cultural construction and possibly cultural myth. Atwood's writing in the feminine challenges traditional assumptions while at the same time it recognizes and seeks to evade the "male textual spaces within which we traditionally operate." [14] The three stories I propose to discuss ("Age of Lead," "Death by Landscape," and "Wilderness Tips") all betray high anxiety levels which are both personal and cultural: anxieties about history and how it might be interpreted from a late twentieth-century female perspective; anxieties about geography and the blurring of boundaries between home ground and foreign territory; anxieties about culture where wilderness as distinctive Canadian signature is under threat of erasure; and anxieties about pollution where the question assumes a globalized dimension of risk and danger.

"AGE OF LEAD" is Atwood's story about Canada's most famous Arctic exploration, and it is about disaster. A woman in Toronto sits watching a television program in the late 1980s showing the exhumation and de-icing of the frozen bodies of three sailors who died on Sir John Franklin's ill-fated expedition in 1845 to discover the Northwest Passage. The expedition spectacularly disappeared, and all that was found were some bones, an abandoned lifeboat, a pile of tins, and three graves. Though many search parties were sent out nobody knew what had happened, until over a hundred years later, in 1984, permission was obtained to exhume the three bodies, and forensic tests showed that the men had probably died of lead poisoning from their tinned food. As Atwood comments in her historical account, "The Franklin expedition, through its reliance on 'state-of-the-art' technology, had unwittingly poisoned itself." [15] The men died wandering aimlessly across the arctic wilderness, carrying piles of useless gear.

Retelling history in a doubled narrative, Atwood draws a parallel between lead poisoning in the Arctic a hundred years ago and conditions in the contemporary polluted urban wasteland, where people are contracting mysterious diseases, and like Franklin's young sailors, are dying earlier than they should. Atwood opens with the historical narrative that lurches out of the past into the present via the picture on the television screen, where the youngish woman Jane watches a bizarrely Gothic resurrection as she confronts the corpse's ferocious stare, "an indecipherable gaze like a werewolf meditating . . . caught in the split second of his tumultuous change" (159). Running parallel to this is Jane's private narrative of her friend Vincent, who died less than a year ago of a mysterious viral disease, and who had to lie packed in ice in the hospital to ease the pain. The two stories comment on each other, establishing correspondences between the two young men, both victims of the malign effects of science and technology, dying one hundred years apart, and "suffering the consequences to things you didn't even know you'd done" (174). As Jane watches, the figures start to superimpose, and the two stories blur in her mind: the two bodies packed in ice, and the reference to John Torrington's lead poisoning from tinned food, which parallels Vincent's joke as he lies dying, "It must have been something I ate" (173). Suddenly Jane has a vision of total dereliction, where the littered Toronto pavement looks to her like a city under bombardment from which the populace is fleeing and, in the process, discarding "the objects that were once thought essential but are now too heavy to carry" (175). The story ends with a sense of threat and risk as it shifts from a localized cause of death like lead poisoning to the globalized threat of pollution.

This is not a story about national or gender identity, despite its historical subject and Jane's memories of her mother's warnings about the "consequences" for girls of sexual activity; such particularity is subsumed in the context of high consequence risk. In this survival narrative gone wrong, Atwood writes a new version of the classical myth of the Age of Gold, challenging readers to reinterpret history. While Jane mourns her dead friend, she is also anxious about late twentieth-century pollution where the poison, "like a colourless gas, scentless and invisible" is seeping into everything (172). Past and present alike are contaminated in this representation of a world where everybody is a victim, and where national boundaries no longer mark off "home ground" as safer than anywhere else.

"DEATH BY LANDSCAPE" and "Wilderness Tips" are in some ways more traditional stories, being situated within the Canadian cultural mythology of wilderness; though both question that referential framework and by doing so position themselves as postmodern fictions which expose the fabrication of the very traditions to which they allude. One story reads wilderness through the most famous nationalist school of landscape painting; the other looks at the literary construction of the wilderness tradition and speculates on its prospects for survival in post-traditional Canadian society.

Set in present-day Toronto, "Death by Landscape" relates

specifically to the wilderness paintings of the Group of Seven, signaled on the second page by a catalogue of the best known names and a description of the paintings:

> They are pictures of convoluted tree trunks on an island of pink wave-smoothed stone, with more islands behind; of a lake with rough, bright, sparsely wooded cliffs; of a vivid river shore with a tangle of bush and two beached canoes, one red, one grey; of a yellow autumn woods with the ice-blue gleam of a pond half-seen through the interlaced branches. (110)

Displayed here are those "landscapes voiced of human presence," which Jonathan Bordo argues construct "a distinctive wilderness aesthetic of the Laurentian Shield," [16] a male narrative of silent wilderness, centred on a significant subject, frequently symbolized by a "single foregrounded tree." Bordo has written a fascinating essay on the semiotics of the Group of Seven paintings, but Atwood's story views these works from a different perspective, for what you see "depends on where you stand in relation to the forest." Told retrospectively by an elderly woman, Lois, who collects these landscapes in memory of a traumatic summer camp experience in the 1940s, this story ironizes the Group's representation of wilderness, its pieties of place, and its exclusion of Native inhabitants. By multiplying trees and rocks and shifting time frames, Lois's narrative exposes the "woodsiness" of summer camp culture as phoney and Eurocentred, while reasserting the strong spiritual forces of wilderness landscape with its inhuman strangeness.

The story title indicates another frame of reference, too, for it harks back to *Survival* with its "Death by Nature" motif:

> In Death by Nature something in the natural environment murders the individual, though the author . . . often disguises the foul deed to make it look like an accident. (54–55)

In this case the "foul deed" looks like a teenaged girl's suicide by drowning when she jumps from a cliff into a lake, but (and here I follow Atwood's own procedure in *Survival* for reading Earl Birney's long poem *David* [56–58]), the survivor's reconstruction "casts a different light on the story." Any facts are speculative because nobody saw what happened, though Lois who was nearest (and later made the scapegoat for her friend Lucy's mysterious disappearance) thought she heard a shout at what could have been the crucial moment: "Not a scream. More like a cry of surprise, cut off too soon. Short, like a dog's bark" (123). Incidentally, this comparison raises a further speculative element: Has Lucy turned into something else in the wilderness? Again, we never know. Structured as Lois's indirect narrative, switching back and forth between present and past, and fixated on the riddle of Lucy's vanishing, this increasingly unstable text finds its focus in Lois's collection of the Group of Seven paintings. By doing so, it offers a revisionist reading of that wilderness discourse with its male proprietory ethic, for while both the paintings and the story represent what Bordo calls "experiential records of the subject's response to wilderness," [17] the subject of this story is different. Here a Canadian woman haunted by loss is seeking insistently in the paintings not for traces of herself but for traces of the hidden other, her lost friend Lucy. Erased from the landscape of real life, Lucy does not vanish, but continues to exist as "another shadowy life" on the margin of Lois's own. From Lois's perspective the Group of Seven aesthetic of absence becomes more than a convention, for these pictures come to represent the site of her loss:

> She looks at the paintings, she looks into them. Every one of them is a picture of Lucy. You can't see her exactly, but she's there, in behind the pink stone island, or the one behind that . . . but if you walked into the picture and found the tree, it would be the wrong one, because the right one would be further on. (129)

This catalogue at the end, which is an exact repetition of the catalogue at the beginning, has one crucial addition: Lucy's ghost, for this is a reading of wilderness landscape as haunted maze, figuring a decentred female subject incessantly searching for her absent other. By returning to the paintings, Atwood offers another contemporary perspective on wilderness, where landscape is transformed into art object. These paintings hang on the wall of a condominium in downtown Toronto; they are "good investments." However, the story retains its contradictory movement to the last with Lois's perception: "She is here. She is entirely alive," as a reminder of the slippages within this utterly unstable text.

◖◖◗ ◗◗

"WILDERNESS TIPS" codes slippage into its title, for "tips" is an unstable part of speech ("He was not immediately sure whether this word was a verb or a noun" [207]), and this story (which also gives its name to the whole collection) about tradition and inheritance ends with a woman's vision of a drowning landscape as the forest slides gradually down into the lake. The story opens in the present tense in the summer of 1990, with a group of middle-aged Canadians (three sisters, one brother, and one husband) at their summer cottage by a lake. To all appearances, the cultural myth of wilderness is in place. However, right from the start, what looks like a shared framework of reality shows its cracks in the first conversation between Prue (one of the daughters of the house) and her sister's husband George, a Hungarian immigrant of the 1950s:

> "It's the forties look," she says to George . . . "Rosie the Riveter. From the war. Remember her?"
>
> George, whose name is not really George, does not remember. (197)

George is the outsider who has learned in adult life to be a Canadian, and it is mainly through his ambiguous vision that the tradition of wilderness is interrogated. There are a number of complementary preoccupations here, to do with the construction of cultural traditions, with problems of authenticity and origins, with questions of inheritance and survival. The narrative ponders these matters, so that the question of inheritance becomes a questioning of inheritance, played out in this summer cottage scenario where familiar domestic rhythms barely contain the transgressive forces that threaten to overwhelm its fragile order.

No wonder the cottage is called Wacousta Lodge, after Major John Richardson's nineteenth-century historical romance, a wilderness tale of revenge and betrayal, split selves, and multiple identities that Michael Hurley describes as "problematising the whole notion of a stable coherent national or personal identity."[18] *Wacousta* provides a pattern of thematic motifs and structural perspectives which Atwood acknowledges as her own literary inheritance in this story, just as Wacousta, the hero with a double name, who is a Scottish aristocrat disguised as an Indian, stalks like a totemic ancestor behind the two male figures, Roland and George. The two would appear to be opposites, with Roland the Canadian-born traditionalist and George the immigrant existentialist who has "married" Wacousta Lodge by marrying Portia, one of Roland's sisters. They despise each other's principles, George believing that Roland must have "the inner life of a tree, or possibly of a stump" (200), and Roland convinced that if George could get Wacousta Lodge he would convert it into a "retirement home for the rich Japanese" in order to make a huge profit from Nature (212). Yet the Wacousta figure establishes a shadowy correspondence between the two. This particular tract of domesticated wilderness is "sacred ground" for them both: it is Roland's inheritance by birth and upbringing; it is George's inheritance by adoption, for he has reinvented the wilderness tradition for himself through assiduous reading just as he has reinvented himself as an English-speaking Canadian.

The story celebrates and subverts anglo-Canadian wilderness literary traditions, thematized in Wacousta Lodge and elaborated in the catalogue of books in the great grandfather's collection at the cottage presented through George's eyes (only he has read all of them). The titles trace the genealogy of this indigenous tradition whose documentary sources are revealed to be the work of white male imperialists fascinated by the otherness of the wild, with its forests and animals and Indian lore. However it is *Wilderness Tips* that highlights the ambiguities of tradition, for that most authentic-looking text, described in documentary detail from cover to contents to page references, is Atwood's own invention. So, what is authenticity when the wilderness tradition finds its most complete expression in an imaginary text? The model is clearly Ernest Thompson Seton, from whose *Book of Woodcraft and Indian Lore* I quote:

> The ideal Indian stands for the highest type of primitive life. He was a master of woodcraft and unsordid, clean, manly, heroic, self-controlled, reverent, truthful, and picturesque always. (8)

There is no mention in this book, however, of the Indian and white footprints that so fascinated Roland, but only drawings of animal spoors. Could it be that Atwood is referring to that other manual by Seton, *Wilderness Wisdom*, which she named in *Survival*? Roland, the avid boyhood reader of *Wilderness Tips*, had needed those Indians to be there, and he remains a true witness to a vanished past that perhaps had never existed:

> How can you lose something that was never yours in the first place? (But you can, because *Wilderness Tips* was his once, and he's lost it. He opened the book today, before lunch, after forty years . . . It was dust.) (214)

Through Roland's anxieties about being dispossessed, the story articulates its anxious concerns about the survival of the wilderness tradition, which is shown here to be a cherished anglophone cultural myth in need of revision in a postmodern, post-traditional, multicultural Canada. Yet in the face of imminent change, the story urges the case for tradition:

> She wants everything on this peninsula to stay exactly the way it always has been. And it does, though with a gradual decline into shabbiness. George doesn't mind the shabbiness, however. Wacousta Lodge is a little slice of the past, an alien past. He feels privileged. (203)

But love of tradition cannot prevent anything. George commits adultery with Portia's other sister Pamela in the boathouse, an act overheard by Portia (though not by Roland who is obliviously stacking wood), who runs away from this revelation into the lake. The story ends with her two moments of vision as she lies there floating: one is a vision of wilderness "tipping," "as if there'd been a slippage in the bedrock" (221), and the second is a vision of imminent destruction where Portia races naked through the ballroom of the Titanic screaming, "Don't you see? It's coming apart, you're sinking. You're finished, you're over, you're dead!" (221). Portia's revelation goes unheeded; apocalypse is denied and then reconstructed as mere repetition: "And nothing has happened really, that hasn't happened before."

Slippage has occurred, however: taboos have been broken at Wacousta Lodge, and trust has been violated. As Portia and Roland take the position of silent victims like the Indians before them, who will inherit and what will remain in this contemporary drama of survival of the fittest? Tradition and evolution become complementary themes held in a precarious balance. The sense of crisis and irresolution in this story pervades the time-haunted narratives of this short story collection, documenting a white anglophone Canadian female writer's response to a late modern, post-traditional world. (The very list of qualifiers here suggests a contemporary crisis of ontological security!) Atwood's conception of futures already being shaped by the present and foreshadowed by the past makes for dire warnings, yet she continues to write, diagnosing the symptoms of a general malaise as they appear in her specifically Canadian context. The wilderness may be in danger of receding into myth, yet it is perhaps through the very power of myth to transform perceptions that hopes for regeneration and survival may lie. To end with the words of Giddens, whose social theory has helped to situate this reading of Atwood's changing perspectives on wilderness:

> The dramatising of the risks humanity now faces is a necessary enterprise, and some of the social pressures and movements it has helped to stimulate represent our best hope for the future. (173)

NOTES

1. Coral Ann Howells 319.
2. Anthony Giddens 5. "Canada: The First Postmodern State?" was the title of the 1993 Annual Conference of the British Association of Canadian Studies at Cambridge, where Margaret Atwood was the keynote speaker; Anthony Giddens, professor of sociology at the University of Cambridge, gave the plenary address.
3. Quoted in Earl Ingersoll 210.
4. Giddens 166.
5. Margaret Atwood, *Survival*, 29–30.
6. *The Nature Hut*, unpublished novel (Margaret Atwood Papers, Box 17, Folders 6–7); "Transfigured Landscape," unpublished story (Margaret Atwood Papers, Box 79, Folder 26).
7. Jacqui Smyth 151.
8. Peter Dale Scott 10–14.
9. George Woodcock 53.

10. *North Bay Nugget*, Oct. 3, 1976.

11. Quoted in Ingersoll 209.

12. Ibid 92. See Ronald Lowe, *Basic Sight Inuvialuit Eskimo Grammar* (Inuvik, Northwest Territories: Committee for Aboriginal People's Entitlement, 1985) for a clear description of the way syntax works in one Native language that is similar to what Atwood describes. The language uses word bases and suffixes from which words are made by expanding the base and so giving it a grammatical form: "Such word bases are not parts of speech, but momentary arrangements of word-forming elements put together in discourse" (15–16).

13. Quoted in Graeme Gibson 27.

14. Linda Hutcheon 110.

15. Owen Beattie and John Geiger 21.

16. Jonathan Bordo 102.

17. Ibid 117.

18. Michael Hurley 4.

WORKS CITED

Atwood, Margaret. "Concerning Franklin and His Gallant Crew." *Books in Canada* 20 (May 1991): 20–26.

———. *The Journals of Susanna Moodie*. Toronto: Oxford UP, 1970.

———. *Surfacing*. London: Virago, 1979.

———. *Survival*. Toronto: Anansi, 1972.

———. *Wilderness Tips*. London: Virago, 1992.

———. Boxes 17 and 79, Ms Collection 200, Margaret Atwood Papers, Thomas Fisher Rare Book Room, Robarts Library, University of Toronto.

Beattie, Owen, and John Geiger. *Frozen in Time: Unlocking the Secrets of the Franklin Expedition*. Saskatoon: Western Producers Prairie Books, 1987.

Bordo, Jonathan. "Jack Pine — Wilderness Sublime or the Erasure of the Aboriginal Presence from the Landscape." *Journal of Canadian Studies/Revue d'études canadiennes* 27.4 (1992–93): 98–128.

Djwa, Sandra. "The Where of Here: Margaret Atwood and a Canadian Tradition." *The Art of Margaret Atwood: Essays in Criticism*. Eds. Arnold E. Davidson and Cathy N. Davidson. Toronto: Anansi, 1981: 15–34.

Gibson, Graeme. *Eleven Canadian Novelists*. Toronto: Anansi, 1973.

Giddens, Anthony. *Modernity and Self-Identity: Self and Society in the Late Modern Age*. Cambridge: Polity, 1991.

Howells, Coral Ann. "No Transcendental Image: Canadianness in Contemporary Women's Fiction in English." *Canada on the Threshold of the 21st Century*. Eds. C. H. W. Remie and J. M. Lacroix. Amsterdam/Philadelphia: John Benjamins B.V., 1991.

Hurley, Michael. *The Borders of Nightmare: The Fiction of John Richardson*. Toronto: U of Toronto P, 1992.

Hutcheon, Linda. *The Canadian Postmodern: A Study of Contemporary English-Canadian Fiction*. Toronto: Oxford UP, 1988.

Ingersoll, Earl, ed. *Margaret Atwood: Conversations*. London: Virago, 1992.

Keith, W. J. *A Sense of Style: Studies in the Art of Fiction in English-Speaking Canada*. Toronto: ECW Press, 1989.

Scott, Peter Dale. "The Difference Perspective Makes: Literary Studies in Canada and the United States." *Essays on Canadian Writing* 44 (1991): 1–60.

Seton, Ernest Thompson. *The Book of Woodcraft and Indian Lore*. New York: Doubleday, 1927.

Smyth, Jacqui. "Divided Down the Middle: A Cure for the Journals of Susanna Moodie." *Essays on Canadian Writing* 47 (1992): 149–62.

Linda Wagner-Martin

"Giving Way to Bedrock": Atwood's Later Poems

DURING THE LATE 1970s and 1980s, Margaret Atwood, established poet and novelist, took on three apparently new roles. One was that of disrupting the conventional genre divisions she had formerly respected. From her earliest publications, Atwood had written poems that were both wryly lyric and blunt, savage in their ability to defy readers' expectations. Simultaneously, she had written stories and novels complete with interesting characters, plot lines, and resolution. Like Erica Jong and Marge Piercy, who also wrote authoritatively in both genres, Atwood excelled in poetry as well as prose. By 1976, when her *Selected Poems* appeared, she was one of the most important women writing in North America. The work that was to come in the late 1970s and 1980s, however, showed dramatic changes in form, and implied that she was questioning the validity of genre distinctions.

Another change in Atwood during the mid-1970s was the result of her becoming a mother. She wrote with her acerbic wit about what readers expected once her daughter was born — that she would become "instantly warm and maternal."[1] The un-flinching, and often macabre, humour of Atwood's earlier work did seem to go underground for a time, while she wrote poems that explored family dynamics and cultural assumptions about mothers and daughters. But nothing could erase the root of her frustration, which was the inherent conflict between the roles of woman as a socially conditioned and passive being, and woman as writer, whose function was the aggressive telling of the truth. As she wrote in "On Being a 'Woman Writer': Paradoxes and Dilemmas,"

> a woman's place was in the home and nowhere else . . . anyone who took time off for an individual selfish activity like writing was either neurotic or wicked or both, derelict in her duties to a man, child, aged relatives or whoever else was supposed to justify her existence on earth.[2]

To live as a working writer meant defying the opinions of most of the men, and women, around her — and becoming a mother had only intensified that conflict.

A third shift was Atwood's move from being a feminist voice, a woman angered by inequities based on sex and gender, to becoming a spokesperson for human rights. As specific gender concerns fell away from her writing, readers found what seemed to be a new sensibility, a poet of witness whose caring voice now spoke about social wrongs. Atwood described her new involvement with human rights issues as "not separate from writing. When you begin to write, you deal with your immediate surroundings; as you grow, your immediate surroundings become larger. There's no contradiction. . . . I began as a profoundly apolitical writer, but then I began to do what all novelists and some poets do: I began to describe the world around me."[3]

These changes were, of course, linked. As she saw more and felt more, and became increasingly impatient with the social ills that blotted her landscape (especially as she felt herself less powerful than a male writer would be in helping to resolve such issues), Atwood began breaking out of literary traditions she found confining. In nearly every case, when she left a traditional poetic form, it was to give a woman speaker's voice more prominence and more control.

Two-Headed Poems **and** True Stories

ATWOOD'S DIFFICULT 1978 collection shows her working through all three of these conflicts. The title, *Two-Headed Poems*, comes in part from a metaphor for the woman writer that she used in a review of Erica Jong's *Half-Lives*: "the woman who is a writer who is also a woman, with the Siamese twins pulling uneasily against each other, the writer feeling suffocated by the woman, the woman rendered sterile by the writer." Here, Atwood first voiced what she saw as an irrefutable dichotomy;[4] so long as women continue to be judged by their beauty, or lack of it, for them the defamation of the grotesque — that is, being half of a Siamese twin — ruins lives. Ugliness is more than cosmetic. Rather than the separate faces of the connected twins, Atwood prefers a paperbag head, one literally empty, because through it she can speak "a repertoire / of untold stories, / a fresh beginning."[5] Such freshness and optimism contrasts with the sad remnants of the worn and betraying language of the title poem, stale mouths giving out only "wrinkled" words, "swollen with other words":

> Your language hangs around your neck,
> a noose, a heavy necklace;
> each word is empire,
> each word is vampire and mother. (67)

Rather than seeing in the poet's trusting language a means of salvation, here, Atwood shows the falsity of privileged word choice. "Two-Headed Poems" is also a clearly political poem, the devastation of nuclear war providing its central metaphor. Salvation — Atwood as poet says — occurs only through new language, and the ability to create that language. As for history, that revered record of the past, she notes, "For so much time, our history / was written in bones only." Her later pervasive imagery of death begins here.

While "Two-Headed Poems" is successful in only some of its eleven segments, Atwood emphasizes the dangers of speaking without listening. Her sombre closing image is of the two heads, so closely joined, singing a duet; but because both singers are deaf, discord is predictable.[6]

The powerfully grim tone recurs in "Four Small Elegies," a sequence about women and children left to die in conflicts that occur throughout history. Atwood brings the lament into the present by insisting,

> This year we are making
> nothing but elegies.
> Do what you are good at,
> our parents always told us,
> make what you know.
>
> This is what we are making,
> these songs for the dying . . . (55)

The poet's frustration wins out in these poems, too, because her accomplishment of creating poems, like flowers, is so minor: "We gather them, keep them in vases, / water them while our houses wither" (55).[7]

True to what is to become her pattern, Atwood voices her most positive sentiments in *Two-Headed Poems* in the single prose poem, "Marrying the Hangman." Here, the woman protagonist, "condemned to death by hanging," uses wit (becomes a female trickster figure) to coerce the hangman into marrying her (by law, the hangman may not kill his wife). Saved from the system, she explains her wisdom: she is a creator who wills her life-saving strategy out of imaginative force.

> In order to avoid her death, her particular death, with wrung neck and swollen tongue, she must marry the hangman. But there is no hangman, first she must create him, she must persuade this man at the end of the voice, this voice she has never seen and which has never seen her, this darkness, she must persuade him to renounce his face, exchange it for the impersonal mask of death. . . . She must transform his hands so they will be willing to twist the rope around throats that have been singled out as hers was, throats other than hers. (48)

And the successful woman is also a listener: "My friends, who are both women, tell me their stories, / which cannot be believed and which are true. They / are horror stories and they have not happened to me, / they have not yet happened to me, they have / happened to me but we are detached, we watch our / unbelief with horror." Complicit in the telling of stories is providing witness, so the poet must both absorb and relate the horrors of her friends' narratives, and, as she writes near the close of the poem, "The fact is there are no stories I can tell my friends / that will make them feel better. History cannot be / erased, although we can soothe ourselves by / speculating about it." Atwood's 1981 poem collection, *True Stories*, charts that absorption as well as the poet's continuing frustration with her mission in life, to bring readers to understand.[8]

Atwood's title signals her impatience with genre, and tests that nebulous line between poem and story. "True Stories" should be fictions — though the coupling of "true" with "story" returns to the old dichotomy that "fiction" is fantasy, anything but fact, denigrated because it is made of the imaginary rather than the true. Atwood insists here that stories are "true," and that the most incredible narratives may well be factual. Accounts of torture, rape, incest, abuse, assassinations, and simple unkindness blot her canvas — and her personal horror at the academic, intellectual resistance to believing such accounts gives her work its bitter undertone. In *True Stories* Atwood approaches the "landscape / reduced to the basics" she described in "Daybooks I,"[9] continuing the description of horrors she had attempted in "Footnote to the Amnesty Report on Torture."

True Stories pounds relentlessly at the reader's sensibilities. Negating in every respect as she declares "The true story is vicious / and multiple and untrue," Atwood's collection assails the reader during its first half and then creates a firestorm in the second, "Notes Towards a Poem That Can Never Be Written," which includes the poems "Torture," "The Arrest of the Stockbroker," "French Colonial," "A Women's Issue," "Christmas Carols," "Vultures," "Last Poem," and others. In the title poem of that section — dedicated to American poet Carolyn Forché, whose poems about El Salvador in *The Country Between Us* were an early expression of the terror of torture — Atwood gives bleak voice to the desperation of the writer, unable to create the horror she feels, unable to do her work, which is to affect her readers and thereby change unbearable situations. Part five of "Notes Towards a Poem That Can Never Be Written" is a controlled, frustrated lament:

> The facts of this world seen clearly
> are seen through tears;
> why tell me then
> there is something wrong with my eyes?
>
> To see clearly and without flinching,
> without turning away,
> this is agony, the eyes taped open
> two inches from the sun.

Blending images of torture with the poet's inadequacy, Atwood questions whether what she sees is hallucination, mirage, or fact, and then she concludes,

> The razor across the eyeball
> is a detail from an old film.
> It is also a truth.
> Witness is what you must bear. (69)

For all its convincing moral outrage, however, Atwood's *True Stories* is a groping collection, with many of its most anguished poems expressed so flatly that the reader feels disappointment. Just as she had feared, her language does not reach the reader; writing "That's your hand sticking out of the rubble" does not necessarily re-create nuclear chaos. Atwood seemed driven to use a dulled, prose-like language in the urgent poems of this time, as if only the most objective words could present the emotion she desired. The effect of that purposeful flatness, however, was sometimes ineffectual.

There are a number of nature and love poems in the *True Stories* collection. These poems seem numb at the centre with a sense of loss, but still employ the language of romance. They do introduce a more positive undercurrent to the tone of the whole, but their complacency is jarred by the most successful part of the book: the five prose poems titled collectively — and ironically — "True Romances." In three separate narratives, Atwood deflates all pretensions about love, and her invective in each of the wry tales colours the other, less cynical poems. Placed at the end of the first half of the book, and closing with the poet's admission that once again she is frustrated in her quest to imagine stories perfectly, this five-part prose work helps draw the separate poems into unity. The structure of *True Stories* as a collection shows that Atwood is broadening her understanding of the essential values of "timing in narrative. . . . Writing on the page is after all just a notation, and all literature, like all music, is oral by nature."[10]

In her struggle to find effective voices to express her growing horror with the facts of twentieth-century reality. Atwood worked towards a mélange of poetry and prose. In fact, some of her most effective writing is in the prose poem form.

Murder in the Dark

THE PROSE POEMS and short fictions that comprise this 1983 collection both culminate Atwood's previous poetic themes and foreshadow the angst of her 1985 novel, *The Handmaid's Tale*. In her search for effective ways of presenting the meaning of her immediate culture, Atwood finally breaks through her neat division of poetry and prose. In 1980 she had written, "I believe that poetry is the heart of the language, the activity through which language is renewed and kept alive. I believe that fiction writing is the guardian of the moral and ethical sense of the community."[11] By 1983, however, she saw that no poetry could avoid expressing a moral and ethical purpose. After several books that tried to keep poetry in a separate sphere, even while it was infused with her outrage at human behaviour, Atwood produced these successful, witty, bitter, and bleak prolegomena. *Murder in the Dark* is Atwood's dark night of the soul, appropriately couched in flip and often cantankerous language, and based on the trope of life — and death — as game.[12]

The title piece describes the game itself, a search for the player designated as "murderer." The rules dictate that the murderer must lie, and lying effectively is the way to win. Atwood images the setting for the game in actual life and appoints herself the liar, creating a conundrum for the truth-telling poet. Poised to act as murderer, she then plays with the confusion of roles through self-reflection: "by the rules of the game, I must always lie. / Now: do you believe me?"[13] The reader is led on a quirky and amusingly sinister romp through the poet's observations on love and romance, civilization, destruction (in the fine "Simmering"), literary conventions ("Women's Novels"), and the writer's own life (foreshadowing her later novel, *Cat's Eye*).

These thirty seemingly disparate selections are like surreal tapestries, woven out of imaginative play, and yet they interrelate. From the rich interplay of ideas in "Women's Novels," with its comic distortion of language and meaning, Atwood moves to the parodic "Happy Endings," which contains various narratives about John and Mary (choose the ending you like best). In this spoof of literary convention, Atwood grounds her fantasy endings with the hard-hitting closing couplet:

> The only authentic ending is the one provided here:
> *John and Mary die. John and Mary die. John and Mary die.* (40)

She then meditates upon the act of writing, and leads her reader to the purely fantastic "Bread," three of its six segments opening with the imperative, "Imagine — a loaf of bread, a famine, a prison." As Atwood spins her narratives from these exercises, her powers of invention dazzle the reader. The progression continues into the next selection, "The Page," a moving meditation on the writer and the location for her language. Yet different as these subjects might appear, all Atwood's meanings cohere and relate, in one way or another, to a central, ironic paragraph in "Women's Novels":

> I no longer want to read anything sad. Anything violent, anything disturbing, anything like that. No funerals at the end, though there can be some in the middle. If there must be deaths, let there be resurrections, or at least a Heaven so we know where we are. Depression and squalor are for those under twenty-five, they can take it, they even like it, they still have enough time left. But real life is bad for you, hold it in your hand long enough and

you'll get pimples and become feeble-minded. You'll go blind. (35)

Angry at the self-indulgence of the insistently moral writer, which she herself is at times, Atwood uses the raw sexual image of masturbation to shock the polite reader, who is one of the sources of the complaint about the violence and unpleasantness of contemporary literature. The question remains, what *is* the role of literature? — with its corollary issue, what *is* the role of the writer?

Bereft of the "true stories" she believed her readers wanted, Atwood spun these webs of imagination that she thought might — if they were successful — force open minds long closed to new ideas. *Murder in the Dark* is an attempt to win acceptance through humour, to employ the macabre in the service of farther-reaching truths.

In "Iconography" Atwood returns to her familiar theme of women as objects, bluntly stating the inequities of power in her opening: "He wants her arranged just so. He wants her, arranged. He arranges to want her. / This is the arrangement they have made . . ." (52). Linking this piece with three others — "Liking Men" ("It's time to like men again. Where shall we begin?"), "She," and "Him" — Atwood once more meditates on women's powerlessness. But she counters that helplessness with the description of women's real powers, both sexual and clairvoyant, in her ending selections, "Hand" and "Instructions for the Third Eye." In the latter prose poem, she insists that every reader can be made to see, even though vision is painful: "the third eye can be merciless, especially when wounded." The poet's effort, like the writer's conscience, is directed towards bringing first vision and then voice to the reader. In *Murder in the Dark*, Atwood concentrates on making the reader understand vision; she insists, "someone has to see these things. They exist. . . . this truth is not the only truth." And she also promises, "After that there are no more instructions because there is no more choice. You see. You see" (62).

Interlunar and *Selected Poems II*

IF ATWOOD'S writing during the early 1980s can be seen as a prelude to *The Handmaid's Tale*, her bitter parable about the meaninglessness of both language and women's lives, then her 1984 poetry collection *Interlunar* deserves investigation. Its stark testimony to disaster — with the poet and all humankind described as "some doomed caravan" — is voiced through a series of mythic personae, anthropomorphized in animal speakers (a series of snake poems), and generally different from the usual Atwoodian persona. Atwood's attempt to approach the mythic heart of experience may not have succeeded, but as she said in an interview at the time, she wanted poetry to move beyond the personal and toward the "unconscious mythologies" that motivate most human beings.[14]

"The Words Continue Their Journey" expresses that continual effort to translate the personal into the mythic, narrated in the voice of the traveler who sees where the "pilgrimage" took a wrong turn. Life now consists of death and dryness, and of human camaraderie "perishing . . . vanishing out of sight, / vanishing out of the sight of each other, / vanishing even out of our sight".[15] "No Name" continues the horror, as a wounded man, "blood leaking out," becomes "man in the act of vanishing," remote from the poet's attempts to help. The poet's emphasis on returning to a primitive form — the snake — might be one kind of answer, but the "Snake Poems" sequence seems inconclusive. Complete with suggestive sexual imagery, the presence of the snake both terrifies and reassures — but its power is severely limited. The poet, like the reader, wonders how long any inscribing voice can continue to relate terror, as Atwood questions in "Orpheus," "Whether he will go on singing / or not, knowing what he knows / of the horror of this world" (2). The keystone of the collection sounds in the bleakness of "Precognition" (Living backwards means only / I must suffer everything twice"), and from this book it is only a step to the harrowing dystopia of *The Handmaid's Tale*.

Atwood's interest in parable, in narrative with wide implications for moral instruction, drives the 1985 novel, which is itself a kind of prose poem. Specific description glossed to stylized paradigm, it seems as though this novel intended to leave most questions unanswered. Impugning only patriarchal and religious authority, leaving shades of difference for the chiaroscuro of realism, Atwood wrote her harshest commentary about contemporary society, with gender relations at the heart of her anguish. The framing tale of academic discovery, with its account of the bungled tapes of the Handmaid's story, creates a mockery of truth-telling that echoes the ironic narratives of the earlier *True Stories*. Of what value is even the truest of stories if no one listens seriously? And by moving to an oral tale, complete with its diminishing sexual innuendoes, Atwood positions women's narratives as the most endangered of today's languages.

The section "New Poems, 1985–1986" in *Selected Poems II* expresses many of the motifs contained in *The Handmaid's Tale*. One of Atwood's personae is named "aging female poet," and she occupies herself variously, and without potency: sitting on a balcony, reading little magazines, doing " a lot of washing" as she tries to get things clean, get things right. She is paired with various female types — a mother, a snake, a weary porcupine, a schoolgirl tempted by nightshade, a woman experiencing yet more pain. In this late poem, "The Rest," Atwood identifies with a group of watchers whose role is to observe the anguished woman:

> The rest of us watch from beyond the fence
> as the woman moves with her jagged stride
> into her pain as if into a slow race.
> We see her body in motion
> but hear no sounds, or we hear
> sounds but no language; or we know

> it is not a language we know
> yet. We can see her clearly
> but for her it is running in black smoke. . . .

The absence of language ("We would like to call something / out to her. Some form of cheering") does not relieve her arduous task, and the poem closes, "There is pain but no arrival at anything" (139). Again, to depict senseless and unidentified pain leads to nothing — no alleviation, no resolution. But Atwood the poet at least sees the existence of pain, and her expression of its existence gives it reality.

The group of poems works as a unit. This one is followed by "Another Elegy," reminding the reader of the continuation of sorrow from the earlier "Four Small Elegies," and it is preceded by a long-lined tarantella of grief, "Machine. Gun. Nest." Although this poem is divided into couplets, it reads like a prose poem and that restless synergy may account for some of its force. It begins,

> The blood goes through your neck veins with a noise they call
> singing.
> Time shatters like bad glass; you are this pinpoint of it.
>
> Your feet rotting inside your boots, the skin of your chest
> festering under the zippers, the waterproof armor,
> you sit here, on the hill, a vantage point, at this X or scuffling
> in the earth, which they call a nest. Who chose that word? (137)

In later lines, the poet similarly questions the literal meaning of "life," "justice," "annunciation," "mercy," "killing," and "death," pointing clearly to the inadequacy of language in most human situations. The trope of war is only one extreme. Tonally, then, Atwood's "new poems" are continuations of the work she selects from the previously published books *Two-Headed Poems*, *True Stories*, and *Interlunar*.

Atwood's choice of poems for the second *Selected* collection shows something of her confusion about how to define "poem." Omitting the five-part "True Romances" prose poem from *True Stories*, she similarly underplays the contradictory imagery of the work from *Two-Headed Poems*. Missing are the despairing "Burned Space," "Foretelling the Future," "Nothing New Here," "The Man with a Hole in His Throat," "Footnote to the Amnesty Report on Torture," "The Right Hand Fights the Left," and the Daybook series, among others. More than half the poems from *True Stories* have been omitted, including "The Arrest of the Stockbroker," "French Colonial," and "Last Poem." Whether Atwood felt that the didacticism of some of the more outspoken of these was inappropriate, or whether she faulted them as poems, she made choices that left *Selected Poems II* gutted of much of her most interesting work. There was no representation at all from *Murder in the Dark*.

Good Bones

NINE YEARS after her enigmatic *Murder in the Dark* and five years after *Selected Poems II*, Atwood returned to what had become the useful form of the prose poem for her deepest, most biting expression. In the 1992 *Good Bones* she returned as well to the trope of language honed to its core, to its essentials, and maintained that mocking tone of cynical, clear-sighted observation that had by now become characteristic of her writing. With *Good Bones*, she added an exclamation mark to her slow dirge of pain throughout the 1980s. As she writes in the title prose poem that concludes the book, "Flesh diminishes, giving way to bedrock. Structural principles. What you need is the right light, to blot out the wrinkles, the incidentals. The right shade, the right amount of sun, and see, out come the bones, the good bones, the bones come out like flowers" (149).

A woman's life depends on her beauty, and the consolation

that Atwood's "good bones" should have been to her in her girlhood comes late. She moves between the bones of the dead — treated wryly in "Them bones, them bones, them dry bones," and more seriously as she muses in a cemetery, and when she comforts a friend who is dying. The final segment of the five-part monologue places Atwood at the top of the stairs, rejoicing in her physical ability to climb, praising her bones for keeping her moving — a glimpse of realistic life at the close of yet another surreal voyage.

Good Bones is another of Atwood's imaginative triumphs. In this collection she begins with parodic versions of the Cinderella story, of Hamlet (from Gertrude's point of view), and of the Little Red Hen (who in this voicing becomes a convincing masochistic female sufferer), and moves to the imaginative rhapsodies from a key image or idea that so pleased readers in *Murder in the Dark*. "Stump Hunting" is the fantasy that all water-logged stumps are really animals, and treated as such, will provide food for the hunter. "Making a Man" poses five propositions for the creation of a human being, with a woman persona empowered to make the figure. "Epaulettes" fantasizes that the world order must respond to male competition in costume rather than on battlegrounds. "My Life as a Bat" projects a life story from the mammal's perspective. "Poppies: Three Variations" gives Atwood the chance to create a text that reifies the words from "In Flanders fields the poppies blow," not once but three times. "Homelanding" is a monologue spoken by an earthling to a listener from another planet. "The Female Body" is a seven-part sequence of description, beginning with the personal ("I get up in the morning. My topic feels like hell. I sprinkle it with water, brush parts of it, rub it with towels, powder it, add lubricant"), charting its necessary accessories, and describing its many uses.

Atwood's cynicism in *Good Bones* is more playful, less traumatic, even in a selection like "Hardball" where she describes the future as "a meteorite, a satellite, a giant iron snowball, a

85

two-ton truck in the wrong lane, careering downhill with broken brakes" (93). Pathos also occurs in the voiced dialogue of "Death Scenes" and "Unpopular Gals," while the outright satire of "Let Us Now Praise Stupid Women" (who fuel most literary fictions) breaks into the deeper cynicism of much of Atwood's writing.

In short, *Good Bones* seems less serious, less intentional, than much of Atwood's poetry during the past fifteen years. It could be that she has finally convinced herself of the efficacy of play, and has found ways to accomplish a playful threnody rather than only talk about doing so. It could be that she has become willing to join with the speakers of her satires rather than poke fun at them, as she seems to in "We Want It All," stating with earnest in the midst of irony: "we still find the world astounding, we can't get enough of it; even as it shrivels, even as its many lights flicker and are extinguished (the tigers, the leopard frogs, the plunging dolphin flukes), flicker and are extinguished, by us, by us, we gaze and gaze. Where do you draw the line, between love and greed? We never did know, we always wanted more" (142).

It could be, too, that Atwood has finally come to terms with the world around her, and has realized that her very talents as a poet and a writer create their own limitations: she can affect only those who read her, and many who read her probably do so for pleasure. *Good Bones* is a pleasure; it is markedly less stern than *Two-Headed Poems* or *Interlunar* — or even *Murder in the Dark*. True to form, Atwood continues to write provocative texts that avoid being what her readers expect: and in this, her agile effusion of imagination, may lie the key to her real and continuing poetic achievement.

NOTES

1. Margaret Atwood, *Second Words: Selected Critical Prose*, 14.

2. Ibid 191. See Atwood's "Great Unexpectations," her autobiographical foreword to Van Spanckeren and Castro, xiii-xvi, where she discusses

being "scared to death" by deciding to be a writer, sure that she was doomed "to the garret and the T.B." because of gender politics.

3. *Second Words* 15.

4. Ibid 172.

5. *Two-Headed Poems* 172.

6. In her interview with Christopher Levenson (Ingersoll, *Conversations*), Atwood states that she hears poetry "as a voice" (23). The integrity of oral speech, of voicing, then, must be preserved, and the deaf would be incapable of such understanding.

7. Despite the pervasive tone of despair in *Two-Headed Poems*, the book was critiqued as if it were a positive statement about culture, probably because of the several poems to Atwood's daughter ("A Red Shirt," "Today," and in some ways the Daybooks and grandmother poems). George Woodcock comments on the book as a "strange oasis of relative calm," calling it "tender" (in Grace and Weir 134); Cheryl Walker sees it as concerned with "issues of language" (in Mendez-Egle 161); Lorna Irvine views it as a testimony to feminine continuance (in Davidson and Davidson 95ff.) while Frank Davey reads most of Atwood's poetry as a complaint about women's situation (Davey 108); and Jean Mallinson describes the book as a series of "occasional, reflective lyric or lyric series, adapted from the model of the Romantic poets" (Mallinson 38). For Barbara Hill Rigney, the collection is the transition from *Surfacing* to *The Handmaid's Tale* (Rigney 117–18).

8. In the Levenson interview (*Conversations*), Atwood corrects his assumption that poetry expresses emotion. "It evokes emotion for the reader, and that is a very different thing" (22).

9. *Two-Headed Poems* 26.

10. *Second Words* 335.

11. Ibid 346.

12. In a later interview (*Conversations* 65), Atwood describes writing as "play" and in her interview with Joyce Carol Oates (73) she explains that the ideal poem "acts like a lens, or like a thread dipped in a supersaturated solution, causing a crystalization." Whatever means the poet finds to create that effect is suitable.

13. *Murder in the Dark* 30.

14. Earl G. Ingersoll, ed., *Margaret Atwood: Conversations*, 32.

15. *Selected Poems II* 117.

WORKS CITED

Atwood, Margaret. *Good Bones*. Toronto: Coach House Press, 1992.

———. *Murder in the Dark*. Toronto: Coach House Press, 1983.

———. *Second Words, Selected Critical Prose*. Toronto: Anansi, 1982.

———. *Selected Poems II: Poems Selected and New, 1976–1986*. Boston: Houghton Mifflin, 1987.

———. *True Stories*. New York: Simon & Schuster, 1981.

———. *Two-Headed Poems*. Toronto: Oxford UP, 1978.

Davey, Frank. *Margaret Atwood: A Feminist Poetics*. Vancouver: Talonbooks, 1984.

Ingersoll, Earl G., ed. *Margaret Atwood: Conversations*. Princeton, NJ: Ontario Review Press, 1990.

Irvine, Lorna. "One Woman Leads to Another." *The Art of Margaret Atwood: Essays in Criticism*. Eds. Arnold E. Davidson and Cathy N. Davidson. Toronto: Anansi, 1981. 95–106.

Mallinson, Jean. *Margaret Atwood*. Toronto: ECW Press, 1984.

Rigney, Barbara Hill. *Margaret Atwood*. New York: Macmillan, 1987.

Van Spanckeren, Kathryn, and Jan Garden Castro, eds. *Margaret Atwood: Vision and Forms*. Carbondale: Southern Illinois UP, 1988.

Wagner, Linda W. "The Making of *Selected Poems*, the Process of Surfacing." Davidson and Davidson, 81–94.

Walker, Cheryl. "Turning to Margaret Atwood: From Anguish to Language." *Margaret Atwood, Reflection and Reality*. Ed. Beatrice Mendez-Egle. Edinburg, Texas: Pan American UP, 1987. 154–71.

Woodcock, George. "Metamorphosis and Survival: Notes on the Recent Poetry of Margaret Atwood." *Margaret Atwood: Language, Text, and System*. Eds. Sherrill E. Grace and Lorraine Weir. Vancouver: U of British Columbia P, 1983. 125–42.

announced that the United States had invaded Grenada" (*xii*). Their answer is to investigate the "making and consuming of images of the non-Western world" (*xii*) in the West, an investigation anticipated by Atwood's *Bodily Harm*. It would be no defence to say that Atwood uses Caribbean characters as props (in the way that Conrad uses Africans) in order to reveal the white soul. What she does is more complicated: she reveals not only how this use of people of other races and cultures as props is typical of her own culture's "worlding" and "soul-making" (Spivak, "Three Women's Texts"), but also how this image-making process works to obscure, deny, and justify their exploitation.

Like feminism, postcolonial criticism is usually an engaged criticism concerned with theorizing the agency of oppressed peoples. But whereas feminism addresses discrimination on the basis of gender, postcolonialism interrogates a wider range of economic and political domination that has been partly justified and supported by a complex interrelation of imperialist definitions of race, class, caste, and nation, in addition to gender. These imperialist definitions, and the assumptions on which they are based, have been supported by the development of academic disciplines designed for knowing the other, and they have been popularized and made familiar through literature. Currently, the postcolonial is a contested field, composed of several different lines of investigation, most of which converge only in their efforts to move beyond the colonial. I believe, along with Stephen Slemon, Helen Tiffin, and Alan Lawson, that the study of settler-invader societies such as Canada can bring an important dimension to our understanding of imperialism and postcolonialism in their various manifestations around the world. And I believe it will be impossible to fully appreciate Atwood's artistic achievement and its limitations without accounting for the postcolonial contexts of her vision.

These contexts are multiple, but all derive from Atwood's experience as an aspiring Canadian writer growing up and learn-

Diana Brydon

Atwood's Postcolonial Imagination: Rereading *Bodily Harm*

POSTCOLONIAL CRITIQUE HAS EMERGED
major new force in theory and criticism in the decade follo
the publication of *Bodily Harm* in 1981. This new mode of rea
enables different insights into how we are to understand Re
Wilford's ill-fated trip to the Caribbean. Like Joseph Con
Heart of Darkness, *Bodily Harm* risks dismissal as inadequ
resistant to Eurocentric formations and as insufficiently c
terdiscursive in the critique of imperialism that it provides.
dismissal would be unfortunate, however, for *Bodily Harm*
vides compelling insights into the representations of other
available to North American readers in our time.

Bodily Harm records its central character's efforts to con
terms with her repressive Canadian childhood and her b
cancer in the context of a Caribbean holiday disrupted by
interference in local politics. The novel asks why North An
cans feel justified in ignoring Caribbean sovereignty to me
in the region. In posing this question, Atwood anticipates s
arly studies in the postcolonial mode, such as *Reading Nat
Geographic*, by Catherine Lutz and Jane Collins.

Lutz and Collins locate their interest in writing their s
in their efforts to understand how university students ir
United States in 1983 could "burst into cheers as a TV newsc

ing about literature and the world in what was still, in the postwar period of the 1940s, a colonial environment. *Survival* (1972) not only details Atwood's understanding of how Canada's status as a colony informed and continues to inform Canadian literature, but the book also outlines an action plan for decolonizing our imaginations. This early critical work shows Atwood attempting to intervene in the making of decisions about what literature gets taught as well as the way literature is spoken about in her country. It reveals her awareness of the role of literary institutions and the educational system in promoting colonialism, as well as her belief that they could be altered to help develop a national sense of identity in opposition both to the paternalistic British imperialism of our past and the economic and cultural imperialism promoted by the United States in our present. It was a short step for Atwood and most of her generation who cared about these issues to move from the Canadian cultural nationalism of the 1960s, as expressed in magazines such as *Canadian Forum* and *This Magazine* and in the House of Anansi Press, to involvement with international organizations such as PEN and Amnesty International that were combatting human rights abuses around the world. Although it would be difficult to determine the ways in which Atwood's postcolonial commitments shape her writing, we can read her work from the particular vantage point that postcolonial reading strategies provide.

Postcolonial critique involves a double focus. It examines the writing produced in formerly colonized parts of the world, or by writers from these places; but attention to this new subject matter is insufficient on its own. More importantly, the colonial habits of mind that have been promoted by colonialism and that have supported its ascendancy require decolonization by a postcolonial critique that deconstructs, questions, or rejects those perspectives. This is the real challenge of postcolonialism. It suggests that every modern discipline of knowledge, every institutional structure for knowing the world, and even every "commonsense" assumption about the world, at least in the West and in those parts of the world touched by contact with the West, is implicated in imperial habits of mind. Clearly study of that complicity is in order. But finding a ground and a method untainted by imperial assumptions is not easy. There probably is no cleared space outside conquered territory from which to survey the field anew. The best we can do is to work comparatively, balancing attempts in one postcolonial country against those of others in the hope of finding holes in the imperial straitjacket of the imagination. Here rereading, reading "contrapuntally," as Edward Said suggests in *Culture and Imperialism*, and reading comparatively across colonized cultures without always referring back to an imperial centre, as Helen Tiffin and I argue in *Decolonising Fictions*, remain our best options.

Study of countries like Canada can also be useful, for they disturb and upset any simplistic postcolonial models based on dualistic oppositions between "us" and "them," "First World" and "Third World," "advanced" or "developing" nations, "colonized" and "colonizer." As Atwood noted in *Surfacing*, for her Canadian protagonist the home in northern Quebec where she grew up was inescapably both "home ground" and "foreign territory" (11). As an anglophone of European descent, Atwood's narrator is perceived as "*maudit anglais*" by the Québécois, and as invader by the First Nations peoples that her presence has displaced, but like most white South Africans she has nowhere else to go. She thinks of this place as home, but she remains aware that others see her as a conqueror and intruder. Her identity, then, is inescapably multiple and mixed. She is an other when she is most herself. Although Atwood's text posits this identity as pathological, almost psychotic, echoing her statement in the "Afterword" to *The Journals of Susanna Moodie* that the Canadian identity is necessarily schizophrenic, this diagnosis also suggests that to move beyond the "sanity" that colonized this continent and waged the Second World War might ultimately prove liberating, enabling nonrepressive alternatives to emerge.

All of Atwood's work would be illuminated by a rereading from this kind of postcolonial perspective, interrogating its representation of the fractured Canadian subject and the peculiar anxieties of a people simultaneously marginalized and privileged. My interest here is more narrowly focused on the specific dynamics of *Bodily Harm*, one of Atwood's few texts that can be seen as ostensibly and openly about postcolonial concerns, although it has not always been interpreted in this way. Indeed, despite several Canadian reviews addressing the novel as postcolonial in its scope (Blaise, Brydon, Davey), the majority of articles in the decade following the book's publication argued instead, with Roberta Rubenstein, that the novel was "a truly feminist existential text" (121). Perhaps the turning point came with the publication of the debate between Helen Tiffin and Jennifer Strauss about the aesthetic value of *Bodily Harm*'s engagement with the postcolonial field, published in 1987. Certainly by 1992 Marilyn Patton felt confidently able to reverse the earlier critical consensus about the primacy of the novel's personal dimensions to assert instead that "*Bodily Harm* is a tale of politics first and personal interaction second" (171). A postcolonial critique would reject that division and its implied hierarchy, to consider the ways in which all notions of the personal are constructed through the political. Nonetheless, Patton's statement seems to reflect the centrality that studies of imperialism and its aftermath now enjoy in both the academic establishment and, filtered down, commodified, and refitted to suit capitalist agendas, in the popular media.

Rereading *Bodily Harm* in the light of these developments can help us understand the current debate about the future of postcoloniality and Canada's torn position within it. A 1993 article in *Time* exemplifies the mass media tendency to turn postcolonialism into the kind of "lifestyle" piece once favoured by Rennie Wilford. *Time*'s language is the dominant language, so apparently natural and sure of its assumptions that it seems to write itself. Rennie lives and breathes this language. When it fails her, the results disrupt our expected experience of narrative continuity and our assumptions about the book's participation in received patterns of representation, including those of realism and of romance, of Harlequin, thriller, travel fiction, and travelogue. The ending calls all these formulae for packaging experience into question, leaving Rennie and the reader destabilized, literally "up in the air," and held up only by "luck." Whereas Iyer, in the *Time* article, hails transnational migrations and traveling fictions as the essence of the new postcolonialism, *Bodily Harm* reminds us of the human costs, betrayals, and material suffering on which these apparent freedoms are built. This focus links Atwood's vision more closely to that of critic bell hooks than to the critics and writers quoted by Iyer.

In responding to the postmodern play Edward Said and James Clifford have brought to postcolonial notions of travel, bell hooks warns of the need to "expose the extent to which holding on to the concept of 'travel' as we know it is also a way to hold on to imperialism" (173). *Bodily Harm* valuably explores this insight, exposing the inevitable investment of contemporary tourist travel in imperialist and capitalist domination. But it reveals the imperialist participations of traveling almost exclusively through the mind of a character who registers these links without understanding them. The reader must make the logical connections that Rennie, and Atwood's text, fail to make. A reader bringing postcolonial questions and an awareness of colonial history to the text can learn much about Canada but little about the Caribbean other than the way some Canadians see it. From the African-American perspective, hooks complains of just this tendency in current postcolonial work, where she finds "much writing that bespeaks the continued fascination with the way white minds, particularly the colonial imperialist traveler, perceive blackness, and very little expressed interest in representations of whiteness in the black imagination" (166). Helen Tiffin has applied such a critique to *Bodily Harm*. On the other hand, as Marlene Nourbese Philip points out, writing as a Caribbean-Canadian woman of African descent who is concerned about Canadian racism, "in a racist, sexist and classist society, the imagination, if left unexamined, can and does serve the ruling ideas of the time" (278). In focusing on Rennie, *Bodily Harm* provides the materials for the kind of examination that Philip calls for.

Bodily Harm shows us how the dominant language of a racist, sexist, and classist society writes Rennie far more consistently than she is able to write it. Even when she seeks to escape it, or at least distance herself from it, it returns to shape her perceptions and even her actions, as when she automatically scores Paul on the meals he produces. The stories she produces are generic, not individualized; they are written to a formula with which she becomes increasingly dissatisfied, but which she cannot escape. Without that formula, she cannot write at all. She can only abandon the stories investigating the hidden life of the happy judge and the "playful" side of pornography, and she cannot write her tourist piece on St. Antoine and Ste. Agathe; she cannot find a language for communicating what she sees when she begins these stories because they exceed the frames she brings to them.

Bodily Harm addresses this phenomenon of the contemporary packaging of reality through its manipulation of irony in several dramatic situations: Rennie's encounters with her editor; her relationship with Jake; and her rejection of the tourist brochures and formulaic thriller fiction she reads in Paul's house. Implicitly, the novel invites the reader to consider its own formulaic nature as a constructed fiction through its dislocating use of the future tense.

Helen Tiffin argues that *Bodily Harm* is ultimately far too complicit with Eurocentric attitudes to colonized places. My reading sees the reproduction of Rennie's Eurocentric outlook as part of a necessary exposure and exorcism of a Canadian identity — as racist, sexist, and classist — that Canadians are loathe to recognize. For Tiffin, *Bodily Harm*'s "content is subverted by form" (130), largely because there is insufficient distance between Atwood and her central character (121). Tiffin concludes that there is a "tension between apparent condemnation of colonialism (and neo-colonialism) and the implicit ratification of a monocultural perspective" (121). Atwood seems to anticipate this response by having Rennie articulate her ambivalent feelings about her infatuation with Daniel as being like "soft-core gossip masquerading as hard-nosed research and exposé" (33). Tiffin accuses *Bodily Harm* of playing a similar masquerade. But it is also possible to argue that this novel reworks the emotional and intellectual appeals of both gossip and exposé in tribute to the ambivalences of its topic: Canada's conflicted identity as simultaneously imperialist power, aid giver, peace broker, Commonwealth partner, and secret sharer in *both* repression and revolutionary aspirations within the Caribbean. *Bodily Harm* is monocultural in its exclusion of the Caribbean perspective, but its enunciation of Canadian ambivalences is more complicated than Tiffin suggests.

Marilyn Patton bases her disagreement with Tiffin on her reading of the archival evidence of earlier drafts and research for the novel, which suggest that Atwood intended to criticize imperialism, yet this alone is insufficient evidence of her success in realizing this objective. From my point of view, Tiffin allows insufficient scope for the role of the reader as cocreator of the meaning of the text, and she is too hasty in conflating Atwood's views with those of her character. Furthermore, I would qualify her argument that "Rennie's is the controlling consciousness throughout" (121). It would be more accurate to suggest that the dominant language (of Eurocentric privilege) that writes Rennie is also writing most of this narrative. Nonetheless, Tiffin's reading points convincingly to problems in *Bodily Harm*'s realization that weaken its effectiveness as a counterdiscourse to imperialism while making it an important document of Canada's ambivalent positioning within the "home ground/foreign territory" of imperialist Eurocentrism or, in its racially inflected manifestation, of "white cultural discourse."

In using this term I am extrapolating from Dean MacCannell's lucid analysis of what he terms "White Culture": "the structural (that is, social, linguistic, and unconscious) pre-condition for the existence of 'ethnic' groups" (129); "The culturally unmarked term of a binary opposition" (131); "a metalanguage for the global dialogue" (165); and a discourse that "imagines itself to be neutral, transparent, universal, and principled as the rightful 'container' of that which is 'nonwhite,' 'coloured,' 'slanted,' or otherwise marked by specificity" (170). MacCannell connects this discourse with tourism, claiming that "Ethnic tourism is the mirror image of racism" (170). This is a language system that does not necessarily depend on white people alone to enforce its hegemony. MacCannell explains:

> If a revolution were to succeed in dislodging white males from positions of power, no change will necessarily have taken place as long as authority itself continues to be represented as "white," or "transparent," and "colourful" ethnic groups are represented as "something to see." Within the white cultural totalization, a military general, though black, can be white, and a Prime Minister or a Supreme Court Justice, though a woman, can be a man, but only a man in the sense that white bureaucrats are men. (171)

Bodily Harm can be seen as Atwood's indictment of the tourist mentality and the media who promote it. That indictment works satirically to imply that Rennie's approach to her Caribbean escape is part of a larger pattern of late twentieth-century "white culture." That pattern is built on denial.

Denial connects Griswold to Toronto and to St. Antoine and Ste. Agathe; it links cancer to pornography and to the development of underdevelopment. *Bodily Harm* considers the kind of world that shapes our decisions as we deal with the many different kinds of bodily harm (effected through disease, violence, poverty, capitalism, and advertising images of bodily perfection) that define our sense of normality under capitalism. Rennie is conscious of the specific forms of her denial, particularly of Griswold and her cancer, but she cannot see the larger patterns of "white culture" that link these personal denials to her culture's denials of genocide, slavery, and oppression. Even at the end of the novel, her resolve to be a reporter is limited to focusing on the visible results of abuses of power rather than on the networks that enable and facilitate such abuses.

For Rennie, the Caribbean is never fully real as a place in its own right, as a "here" equal to the Canadian "here" she carries with her in her memories. Although she resents Torontonian dismissals of Griswold, she treats St. Antoine and Ste. Agathe with a similar disrespect. She refuses to admit responsibility for breaking the laws of St. Antoine, because she doesn't take the law as seriously there as she would at home. Atwood blurs moral judgement of Rennie's law-breaking by stressing Rennie's sense of innocence, her lack of intention, and her vulnerability to the manipulations of others. The Canadian government either does not know or does not care about Rennie's smuggling of a gun to Prince. To them, her imprisonment is just "a regrettable incident" (294). But to the reader who notes these dismissals of Caribbean sovereignty, the collusion between Rennie and her government's representative in assuming that as Canadians they are above the laws of the Caribbean shows only too clearly the consequences of Eurocentric white cultural assumptions, promoted through damaging media portrayals of the Caribbean as a place designed for Canadians to act out their transgressive dreams.

The only alternative to the tourist's voyeurism that Rennie can imagine is that of the reporter. Rennie decides to cover political events and inform audiences back home of injustices overseas, injustices their own government and charities may well be involuntarily perpetrating. Ironically, this role as she envisions it is only barely distinguishable from that of a secretary, who records the dictated words provided by others. To be mistaken for a secretary is Rennie's greatest fear. The obvious class bias of this fear cannot disguise her more troubling half-awareness that in a world of mass media monopolies the two jobs may justifiably be confused. Yet the novel continues to believe in the value of reporting as bearing witness, implying that although the role is limited, it can help safeguard the work for change undertaken by local citizens within a foreign country, without repeating the interferences of direct imperialist intervention. Dr. Minnow offers this role to Rennie, who, too late to help him, decides to take it on in the novel's ambiguous conclusion.

To understand the novel's postcolonial position, we need to consider how Rennie (and through her, how the reader) is prepared for the shift in position from tourist to reporter through the course of the novel, and then to ask if this is enough to counter Tiffin's charges. Minnow shows Rennie abuses of power in the present, but these problems are never contextualized or analysed in a way to make their causes comprehensible. Rennie is clearly out of her depth here, and unable to link effect back to cause in any convincing way. Instead, she falls back into what can only be seen as narrowly provincial, even racist, assumptions. She quotes Paul as her guide to the idiocies of the local culture, remarking that "Paul says some people here think that because it says LONG LIFE on the carton, you'll have a long life if you drink it" (238). This is the kind of half-truth that ideological justifications for exploitation of other peoples thrive on. The reader has no way of knowing whether the statement is true, or what it might mean about local thinking if it were true, but it seems offered here as validation for the poverty and violence being inflicted on people who don't share North Americans' consumer literacy. The framework of the novel as a whole discredits Paul as a source of information, yet Rennie's trust in him can carry an unobservant reader along into a sharing of this kind of colonial justification: subscribing to the belief that these people are primitive, other; therefore, they don't count. If the reader has been carried along with Rennie into this kind of prejudice, the shock of realizing that she has been wrong in all her pat judgements can perhaps prompt a salutory reconsideration by the end of the novel.

While recognizing that Rennie is portrayed as unwittingly participating in the Eurocentric prejudices of dominant North American mentalities the postcolonial critic must consider a further question: why does the novel *Bodily Harm* never ask why there is no library and no doctor on the island, why nothing works, why there are constant shortages, or why so few people can read? (One wishes that Jamaica Kincaid's *A Small Place* could be prescribed reading alongside *Bodily Harm* to draw out the implications of these absences.) Samir Amin identifies one feature of Eurocentrism as its belief that colonized societies "can only progress to the extent that they imitate the West" (107). "This prescription," he notes, "assumes the superiority of the capitalist system" and assumes that "the European West has little to learn from others" (108). In his view, this vision of the world rests on two erroneous formulations: "that internal factors peculiar to each society are decisive for their comparative evolution," and "that the Western model of developed capitalism can be generalized to the entire planet" (109).

Through Rennie, *Bodily Harm* dramatizes the consequences of such thinking. Rennie implicitly blames the local people for following their own leaders instead of taking the American drug and arms trader Paul's advice. When they start their revolution,

Paul laments "I told them not to do that" (252). At first, it seems by their failure that they did indeed need a white man to tell them how to run their revolution (on the pattern most Hollywood movies produce). Paul identifies the new CIA agent as someone from within their own community whom they have trusted. Later, however, that appears to have been a deliberate misidentification to deflect attention away from himself. At that point, all of Rennie's earlier reasoning is called into question. Whether or not Paul is the new CIA agent, it is clear that the real terrorists here are Americans and Canadians propping up a corrupt comprador government. This realization enables an important reversal in Rennie's unconscious racial stereotyping. In *Black Looks: Race and Representation*, bell hooks observes that

> one fantasy of whiteness is that the threatening Other is always a terrorist. This projection enables many white people to imagine there is no representation of whiteness as terror, as terrorizing. Yet it is this representation of whiteness in the black imagination . . . that is sustained by my travels to many different locations. (174)

Although *Bodily Harm* fails to present indigenous voices to balance Rennie's, it does throw into question her automatic assumption "that the threatening Other is always a terrorist," and it shows her the falsity of her smug belief in her own innocence.

Similarly, when Rennie dismisses the uprising as "Windowbreaking, juvenile delinquency, that's all it is, this tiny riot" (253), there is little in the text that *explicitly* contradicts her. By this time, however, the alert reader may well have identified a pattern in which Rennie's judgements about people on the island have been proved consistently wrong. In that case, we will have been conditioned to read a statement like this against the grain, and to see the event as politically motivated. For the postcolonial reader, the question then becomes: is that kind of readerly suspension of assent to Rennie's normalized white cultural judgements enough to move the text as a whole beyond complicit colonialist discourse into the postcolonial?

Even Rennie can see that imperialist patterns of exploitation survive in this region and contribute to its underdevelopment. To this extent, the novel acts as exposé. *Bodily Harm* makes visible certain patterns of exploitation and abuse: misuse of foreign aid, human rights violations, U.S. involvement in the drug trade, in the supply of arms to unstable "Third World" countries, in the propping up of corrupt dictatorships, and in the "development of underdevelopment" through the encouragement of cash crops, high unemployment, environmental pollution, and censorship of any opposition, all to discourage autonomous local economies and maintain dependency. These are all referred to, as are the presence of Canadian banks in the Caribbean, but the links between them and a history of slavery, a plantation economy, and contemporary World Bank and International Monetary Fund policies are never made.

These elements of exposé function mostly as background, but are twice linked directly to Rennie's understanding of the personal. At this level, the novel appeals to a shared sense of humanity, inviting the First World reader to care more directly about the fate of colonized peoples through their recognition of the basic human need for shelter and food.

But *Bodily Harm* never questions the hierarchical relation between First and Third Worlds; it only suggests that exploitation should be replaced by charity. The power to exploit or help is still assumed to rest entirely within the First World. When Rennie tells Dr. Minnow that she cannot write his political story because she does lifestyles, he responds: "You might say that I also am concerned with lifestyles . . . What the people eat, what they wear, that is what I want you to write about" (136). The scene is repeated when Rennie meets the "multiculturalism functionary" (189) from the Canadian High Commission at the bar. When she tells him that she just does food, he replies: "What could be more important?" (190). These scenes mark Atwood's endorsement of the 1970s feminist contention that the personal is political and her belief in a fundamental sense of justice and decency in her readers, which can be activated if only her words can make them see what is wrong with the present arrangement of their world.

We are now in a better position to see the flaws in such appeals, largely because of the contributions of postcolonial and African-American critics to these debates. The kind of feminism that *Bodily Harm* was able to assume has been enormously complicated, fractured, and enriched by women of colour pointing out its inherent systemic racism and participation in the dominant white discourse of imperialism. This is a more complicated issue than the novel's blindness to the Caribbean point of view. It points to the larger pattern of assumptions in which Canada and the Caribbean are constructed as norm and variation from the norm through their economic and racial relations. Tiffin astutely notes that "the interaction of sexual and political themes in *Bodily Harm* is in itself disturbing because it glosses over any sense of qualitative difference" (125). Specificities suffer here. The novel works symbolically, treating the Caribbean as her Canadian's "heart of darkness," blurring it with similar symbols such as Malcolm Lowry's literary Mexico in *Under the Volcano*,[1] the tourist's Mexico, and even India. *Bodily Harm* doesn't even try to be cross-cultural, and for the cross-cultural critic this is certainly a disappointment. It gives the book a claustrophobic feel. We are trapped for most of the narrative in Rennie's mind, in the naive, unthinking, Upper Canadian racism analysed so painfully by Marlene Nourbese Philip in *Frontiers*.

Atwood's decision to examine the limitations and strengths of Rennie's imagination reflects back on the audience she assumes she is addressing. Just as Rennie thinks her lack of courage connects her to her audience at home, making her a better travel journalist than those who are more adventurous, so Atwood appears to have made Rennie unaware of Caribbean history and politics and unaffiliated with any group in order to appeal to Atwood's conception of her audience as similarly situated. *Bodily Harm* does more than merely document the gap between rich and poor, powerful and powerless; it makes visible the language and logic of imperialism that glosses over these differences, simultaneously justifying and obscuring the ways things are. Because this language is all pervasive, it infects the text of *Bodily Harm* even as the novel tries to expose it and find some distance from it. This language is part of our thought as surely as Rennie's cancer is part of her.

Sometimes *Bodily Harm* highlights the biases of the language it uses; other times it does not. When Rennie writes about drain-chain jewellery achieving "the slave-girl effect" and women shaving their heads "with an Iroquois fringe running down the middle" (24), she demonstrates that for her and her fashion readers the painful histories of European imperialism in the Americas have been reduced to just another fashion effect, divorced from any acknowledgement of the material effects of slavery, dislocation, and violence. Yet "slave-girl" and "Iroquois fringe" remain markers, traces, of that history and its denial, demanding further unpacking from the informed and attentive reader.

Rennie's unconscious language is implicitly racist. One of Jake's sadistic games, in which she participates, involves pretending to be "a slave girl" (207). She thinks to herself of "[t]heir blacks" in comparison to "our blacks" (39) and describes Daniel as being "like a Patagonian in Woolworth's, he was enthralled by trivia" (141). She cannot deal with English beyond the intonations of her own group. She has difficulty understanding the educated Dr. Minnow as well as other local people, and cannot even catch the name of the official with the Canadian High Commission because "it's something Middle European . . . a multiculturalism functionary" (189). Her sphere of experience has been very narrow.

When the Abbots tell her about the international parrot smuggling business, Rennie's reaction is complicated: "From the horror in their voices, they could be talking about a white-slave ring. Rennie concentrates on taking this seriously" (188). The macabre humour here is multidimensional. Rennie sees nice people identified as CIA agents worrying about environmental destruction as they contribute to U.S. manipulation of the local economy and government. Rennie is so out of place in the Caribbean and so self-centred that in the heat of a region violently shaped by a slave trade in African people, she can think of white slavery as the ultimate, titillating abomination without even being conscious of the irony in her reaction. The obscenity of her response is signaled by her pornographic sexualization of slavery in those references to slave girl and white-slave ring, made in the very place built on the basis of African slavery.[2] A complex fantasy of bondage and transgressive freedom through union with the other, along the lines constructed in the popular Hollywood movie *The Sheik*, seems to be invoked here. White slavery created conditions in which the white woman, apparently enslaved because of her gender, remains culturally privileged because of her race: she could defy her culture's sanctions and gain some measure of economic freedom, while denying her own agency in that achievement. At a time when there is a holiday trade in white Canadian women traveling to the Caribbean to buy sex with black men, this exploitation can be simultaneously acknowledged and denied through the trope of white slavery.

White slavery enacts a double displacement, displacing anxiety about unresolved power relations across racial and gender boundaries in the present and guilt about African slavery in the past. Yet that unnamed history of black slavery continues to proclaim its absence in the circumlocutions of the tourist brochure, which notes that "the Spaniards were through here, once, along with everyone else. 'Leaving a charming touch of Old Spain' is how they put it" (69). Without being at all specific, Atwood does suggest through these means that there is much more to this Caribbean country than Rennie is capable of seeing or understanding, but her focus falls on the process of Canadian denial rather than on the substance of what is being denied.

Atwood seems to have assumed that her readers were not ready to venture far from Rennie's perspective. Certainly most Canadians (at least those not originally from the Caribbean themselves) probably do think of the Caribbean in terms of the brochures that Rennie finds in St. Antoine (67–68).[3] Atwood may have believed that to go further into the historical causes and political intricacies of the country behind the glossy tourist facade would have been to lose her readers. To make the critique more explicit would have labeled her venture too quickly, exposing it to the kind of easy dismissal, the "glazed eye" response that Rennie reserves for anything challenging. Rennie asks some of the questions that need asking: "Who cares?" (129), and "If this man is so terrible . . . why does he keep getting elected?" (185). For Rennie, these are rhetorical questions whose answers are already implied, but for the reader of Bodily Harm they necessarily take on greater resonance, pointing to everything Rennie remains blind to.

Nonetheless, some of Atwood's narratorial decisions suggest that she shares her character's ambivalence about political analysis and involvement. Her epigraph from Berger's subtly analytic account of "ways of seeing," like her text itself, separates symptom from cause, thus implying (as he never does) an essential difference between men and women, colonizer and colonized, rather than a historically determined and situated and therefore alterable state of affairs. Ildiko de Papp Carrington points out that "Atwood slightly misquotes this passage" (62), leaving out the crucial middle two sentences suggesting that "presence" may be "fabricated." This omission, in addition to the absence of contextualization, twists the Berger quotation to imply that women invite their own violation, and through the kind of extension the novel invites, that colonies also must take equal responsibility with their colonizers for what is done to them. This kind of false sharing out of responsibility for oppression, this equation of victim and victimizer as actually equal participants in a chosen dynamic, surfaces early in Rennie's thinking, as she theorizes that two people are always "involved in boredom, not just one: the borer and the boree" (19). In this way, hierarchical relations get misrepresented as horizontal ones. Only an attentive reading of the entire novel can persuade the reader that *Bodily Harm* finally contests rather than endorses this view, by leading the reader through Rennie's various experiences of its falseness. Like Rennie, the novel needs to explain to its readers how it got "here," into a world where exploitation and bodily harm pass for normalcy.

For Canadian readers, this opening phrase carries an added cultural specificity, well known to Atwood readers from her use of it in *Survival*. Northrop Frye wrote in *The Bush Garden* that Canadians' postcolonial identity was "less perplexed by the question 'Who am I?' than by some such riddle as 'Where is here?'" (quoted in *Survival* 10). *Bodily Harm* is still trying to answer Frye's riddle. Today, postcolonial critics are questioning the colonialist ideology implicit in Frye's ideas and in Atwood's adoption of them (Cavell). In 1994, Canadians are more interested in addressing questions of how we get out of "here"[4]: questions of cultural appropriation, the shortfalls of multiculturalism, and the social reorganization necessary for creating an inclusive, nonracist and nonsexist community if the nation is to survive. But in *Bodily Harm*, Atwood's "here" refers literally to the prison cell in which Rennie and Lora are trapped after the abortive rebellion, and figuratively to the prison cell of the mind that has led Rennie to underestimate St. Antoine and Ste. Agathe, ignore its history, and trivialize its present.

In many ways, "here" is within the heart of MacCannell's white cultural discourse. When Rennie is "turned inside out, there's no longer a *here* and a *there*" (290), the distinctions between Canada and the Caribbean, safety and danger, seem less important than the power relations that structure language and life in both places. On the one hand, this can lead to useful insights into the way Canadians' wealth and safety are built on the underdevelopment of the Caribbean, but this fact can also easily be twisted by the metaphysically inclined reader to imply that such economic inequalities are less important than the moral complicities of everyone everywhere in systems of exploitation. Although *Bodily Harm* works hard to draw our attention to the specifically material underpinnings of Rennie's privilege, the celebration of her "luck" (301) in the closing passage obscures these yet again.

Like Raymond Williams, Atwood sees imperialism as an extension of the country/city hierarchy into territory beyond the boundaries of the colonizing nation, creating a centre/periphery dynamic. Rennie is partly prepared to appreciate the damaging perspective she brings to the Caribbean, if she can learn to draw analogies between her own experience and theirs, because of her childhood experiences in Griswold:

> People from bigger places, Jake in particular, think that Griswold has an exotic and primitive charm. Rennie doesn't think this. Mostly she tries to avoid thinking about Griswold at all. Griswold, she hopes, is merely something she defines herself against. (18)

Rennie goes to the Caribbean, planning to celebrate its "exotic and primitive charm" in order to pay for her trip, demonstrating the same kind of thinking that allows *Time* to celebrate the wild, colourful energies of writers originally from colonized parts of the world. What she seems to find is everything she fled when she left first Griswold, and then Toronto.

There is a danger here, as Helen Tiffin notes, of forming "easy identifications" (124) between an exoticized Griswold and an exoticized Caribbean, which reinforce rather than challenge the universalizing imagination of imperialism. Atwood takes this risk, consistently using the language of excess to describe both St. Antoine and Rennie: both are characterized through adjectives modified by "too." This is the language that imperialism (gendered masculine) assigns to women within its own culture as well as to the colonized, usually racialized, other. Rennie thinks of the colonized island in these terms. Before she even begins, Rennie knows that her day will be "too long, too hot" (63) after a breakfast of jelly "too sweet" (62). Yet she herself is here partly because she has the reputation for being "too picky" (65). Later, Paul explains how he knew that she wasn't CIA: she was "too obvious," "too nice," "too naive," "too easy," and she "wanted it too much" (245). This seems to be an American assessment of the Canadian. Here Rennie learns the lesson of the colonized, that it hurts to be on the labeled side of the equation, denied the freedom and power of the bestower of labels.

But this equation of woman and island is exceedingly problematic. In "Woman Is an Island: Femininity and Colonization," Judith Williamson demonstrates the continuities linking contemporary advertising, tourism, and classic narratives of cross-cultural encounter in their deployment of the island/female conflation. Williamson argues that "Our culture, deeply rooted in imperialism, needs to destroy genuine difference, to capture what is beyond its reach; at the same time, it needs *constructs* of difference in order to signify itself at all" (101). *Bodily Harm* enacts this double process in its own narrative even as it critiques its operation on other levels of contemporary discourse, in tourist advertising, T-shirts, and popular romance. The title itself embodies the conflation of body politic, female body, and colonized space/tropical island that generates the double narrative of Rennie's cancer and Ste. Agathe's revolution. Cancer is real, yet as metaphor it runs the risk of naturalizing the exploitation that Rennie sees but fails to understand in the Caribbean.

Atwood seems to have taken this risk of equating Rennie's social construction as female to the island's political construction as colony to help her North American readers imagine themselves in a position they are usually encouraged to reserve for others. Atwood notes that "Rennie dislikes having . . . assumptions made about her, she dislikes being lumped in with a fictitious group labelled *people like you*" (90). Rennie never fully realizes that other people feel the same way about her labeling of them (as in her comparing of "our blacks" to "their blacks"), but the reader sees the irony in her offended response when her own labeling techniques are cast back at her. In this light, her inability to think of a title for the report she plans to write on her return seems a positive sign of a growing maturity.

If we compare the novel's report on Rennie's Caribbean experience with the work on pornography prepared within the text by the Toronto artist called Frank, we can see how the novel subtly directs the reader beyond Rennie's limited point of view. Rennie finds Frank's work just as pornographic as the pornography he parodies through his own documentational repetitions. Frank describes his work in terms very similar to those used by Atwood elsewhere: "What art does is, it takes what society deals out and makes it visible, right? So you can *see* it. I mean, there's the themes and then there's the variations" (208). Rennie and the reader find this justification for the apparent objectivity of an art that merely makes visible, without passing judgement, inadequate. In rejecting Frank's approach, *Bodily Harm* seeks to go beyond that kind of documentation into the kind of art that celebrates an imagining of genuine alternatives to exploitation. But to create that imagining, it relies on a shift away from political analysis into religious imageries (Jones) and what Larry Mac-Donald astutely terms "psychologism." As MacDonald explains, psychologism assumes "that history is essentially determined by consciousness, and that a change in individual consciousness (a quasi-religious rebirth) is the only legitimate history-making activity open to us" (142). Postcolonial criticism, on the other hand, explicitly seeks alternative history-making activities in communal and national movements for social change. With Rennie, *Bodily Harm* appears suspicious of such activity, preferring a personal transformation and the reporter's authority to describe events as she sees them to any kind of interactive dialogue.

Yet although *Bodily Harm* offers the kind of rebirth of an individual consciousness critiqued by MacDonald in its ending, it simultaneously denies its readers full satisfaction in such a limited imagining of human possibility. The ending is unsatisfying and ambiguous. Throughout the book, Rennie has longed for completion/healing through union with the other. She expresses this longing through her need for a (white) male body, but seems to achieve it, vicariously, through Lora, the white woman who sleeps with most of the black men presented in the text. The epiphany once more recalls the sequence of references to white slavery, problematizing merely spiritual or feminist readings of the union achieved here. The book unleashes problems that demand a rethinking of the history-making activities that are open to both Rennie and its readers within the assumptions of psychologism and its frame of Eurocentric white cultural discourse. *Bodily Harm* raises questions about Canadians' relations with other cultures, and the ways they have been distorted by our own "racist, sexist and classist society" (Philip). In providing no answers, it implies that there are none within the assumptions accepted by Rennie. But that recognition of one dead end can open up new avenues for the reader, setting her on her own quest for understanding what remains a puzzle for Rennie.

By the end of the novel Rennie has abandoned her sureties and her glibness; she exists in a state of receptivity in a world defined by paradox. We are told that "She's paying attention, that's all"

(301). I read this description of Rennie's final state as advice to the readers of *Bodily Harm*. Paying attention to this narrative includes puzzling through its contradictions, conflations, ambivalences, and absences. *Bodily Harm* is neither counterdiscursive nor cross-cultural, but it locates some gaps in the apparently seamless web of white cultural discourse. This is the kind of novel that challenges postcolonial critics to refine their terminologies and rethink their methods. *Bodily Harm* exposes the limitations of simple distinctions between resistant and complicit narratives, just as its settler-invader context leads critics away from a rhetoric of subversion towards what Gayatri Chakravorty Spivak has described as "un-learning our privilege as our loss" ("Criticism, Feminism, and the Institution" 9). This project makes *Bodily Harm* important for white North Americans and for white feminists seeking a ground for forming genuine coalitions across racial and class barriers, and yet may make the novel seem less relevant to people fighting a colonial heritage under different conditions, such as those in the Caribbean. Many postcolonial readers believe that the universality once assumed to be a property of a great work of art is itself a powerful, interested specificity in disguise. Rereading *Bodily Harm* from this perspective, we can see that what the great West Indian poet Edward Kamau Brathwaite called "the terrible terms meted out for universality" (20) have also had their particularly Canadian repercussions.

NOTES

1. Recalling a week with Jake in Mexico, Rennie invokes one of the most famous scenes in Lowry's *Under the Volcano* when she remembers finding "a sign in a little park that read, *Those found sitting improperly in the park will be punished by the authorities*" (*Bodily Harm* 71).

2. The history of concern over "white slavery" seems inevitably caught up in imperialist definitions of the sexualities of "good" and "bad" white women and of racial others. See Donna J. Guy, "'White Slavery,' Citizen-

ship and Nationality in Argentina,"and Abdul R. JanMohamed, "Sexuality on/of the Racial Border: Foucault, Wright, and the Articulation of 'Racialized Sexuality.'" Rennie's fascination with white slavery seems complexly linked to her own problematic sexuality, selfhood, and relation to racial others.

3. In "Mass Media Worldviews: Canadian Images of the Third World," Eleanor O'Donnell explains that "The images Canadians have of the rest of the world (and to a large extent of ourselves) tend to come from the mass media, not from direct experience" (288), and these images are produced for us in images that obscure causal relationships (278). In *The Caribbean Connection*, Robert Chodos argues that "Canadians have long harboured a touchingly romantic and often dangerously naive view of their own role in the Caribbean" (22).

4. In *We gotta get out of this place: poplar conservatism and postmodern culture*, Lawrence Grossberg suggests that "A spatial model of culture and power seems somehow tied, both to diaspora populations and to nations founded as settler colonies. The latter (e.g. America, Canada and Australia) all have origins involving genocidal campaigns. To different degrees and in various ways, each of them actively represses this history (which doesn't mean it is not there but that its effects are articulated in different ways). Each of them constructs its identity in spatial rather than temporal terms, erecting billboards rather than monuments" (27). This is what I see happening in *Bodily Harm*'s attention to spatial metaphors of body/island, here/there, surfaces/depths, and in its actively produced denial of histories of slavery, racism, and capitalism.

WORKS CITED

Ahmad, Aijaz. *In Theory: Classes, Nations, Literatures.* London and New York: Verso, 1992.

Amin, Samir. *Eurocentrism.* Trans. Russell Moore. London: Zed; New York: Monthly Review, 1989.

Appiah, Kwame Anthony. *In My Father's House: Africa in the Philosophy of Culture.* New York and Oxford: Oxford UP, 1992.

Ashcroft, Bill, Gareth Griffiths and Helen Tiffin. *The Empire Writes Back: Theory and Practice in Post-Colonial Literatures*. New York and London: Routledge, 1989.

Atwood, Margaret. *Bodily Harm*. Toronto: McClelland & Stewart, 1981.

———. *The Handmaid's Tale*. Toronto: McClelland & Stewart, 1985.

———. *The Journals of Susanna Moodie*. Toronto: Oxford UP, 1970.

———. *Surfacing*. Toronto: McClelland & Stewart, 1972.

———. *Survival: A Thematic Guide to Canadian Literature*. Toronto: Anansi, 1972.

Bhabha, Homi K., ed. *Nation and Narration*. London and New York: Routledge, 1990.

Blaise, Clark. "Tale of Two Colonies." *Canadian Literature* 95 (1982): 111–12.

Brathwaite, Edward Kamau. *History of the Voice*. London: New Beacon, 1984.

Brydon, Diana. "Caribbean Revolution and Literary Convention." *Canadian Literature* 95 (Winter 1982): 181–85.

———. "Margaret Atwood: *Bodily Harm*." *Westerly* 1 (March 1982): 98–100.

———. "No (Wo)man Is an Island: Rewriting Cross-Cultural Encounters within the Canadian Context." Forthcoming in *Kunapipi*.

——— and Helen Tiffin. *Decolonising Fictions*. Denmark: Dangaroo, 1993.

Cavell, Richard. "Where Is Frye?: Theorizing Postcolonial Space." Forthcoming in *Postcolonial Theories and Canadian Literatures: Testing the Limits*. Ed. Diana Brydon. *Special Issue of Essays on Canadian Writing*.

Chodos, Robert. *The Caribbean Connection*. Toronto: James Lorimer, 1977.

Davey, Frank. "Life After Man." *Canadian Literature* 95 (1982): 29.

de Papp Carrington, Ildiko. "Another Symbolic Descent." *Essays on Canadian Writing* 26 (1983): 45–63.

Goodwin, Ken. "Revolution as Bodily Fiction — Thea Astley and Margaret Atwood." *Antipodes* 4.2 (1990): 109–15.

Grossberg, Lawrence. *We gotta get out of this place: popular conservatism and postmodern culture*. London and New York: Routledge, 1992.

Guy, Donna J. "'White Slavery': Citizenship and Nationality in Argentina." *Nationalisms and Sexualities*. Ed. Andrew Parker et al. London and New York: Routledge, 1992. 201–17.

Hansen, Elaine Tuttle. "Fiction and (Post) Feminism in Atwood's *Bodily Harm*." *Novel* 19.1 (1985): 5–21.

hooks, bell. *Black Looks: Race and Representation.* Boston: South End, 1992.

Humm, Maggie. "Going through the green channel: Margaret Atwood and body boundaries." *Border Traffic: Strategies of Contemporary Women Writers.* Manchester: Manchester UP, 1991. 123–59.

Irvine, Lorna. "The Here and Now of *Bodily Harm.*" *Margaret Atwood: Vision and Forms.* Ed. Kathryn Van Spanckeren and Jan Garden Castro. Southern Illinois UP, 1988. 85–100.

Iyer, Pico. "The Empire Writes Back." *Time* 141.6 (February 8, 1993): 68–73.

JanMohamed, Abdul R. "Sexuality on/of the Racial Border: Foucault, Wright, and the Articulation of 'Racialized Sexuality.'" *Discourses of Sexuality: From Aristotle to Aids.* Ed. Domna C. Stanton. Ann Arbor: U of Michigan P, 1992. 94–116.

Jones, Dorothy. "'Waiting for the Rescue': A Discussion of Margaret Atwood's *Bodily Harm.*" *Kunapipi* 6.3 (1984): 86–100.

Kincaid, Jamaica. *A Small Place.* New York: Penguin, 1988.

Lawson, Alan. "A Cultural Paradigm for the Second World." *Australian-Canadian Studies* 9.1–2 (1991): 67–78.

Lucking, David. "In Pursuit of the Faceless Stranger: Depths and Surfaces in Margaret Atwood's *Bodily Harm.*" *Studies in Canadian Literature* 15.1 (1990): 76–93.

Lutz, Catherine A., and Jane L. Collins. *Reading National Geographic.* Chicago: U of Chicago P, 1993.

Lynch, Denise E. "Personalist Plot in Atwood's *Bodily Harm.*" *Studies in the Humanities* 15.1 (1988): 45–57.

MacCannell, Dean. *Empty Meeting Grounds: The Tourist Papers.* London and New York: Routledge, 1992.

MacDonald, Larry. "Psychologism and the Philosophy of Progress: The Recent Fiction of MacLennan, Davies and Atwood." *Studies in Canadian Literature* 9.2 (1984): 121–43.

McDougall, Russell, and Gillian Whitlock, eds. *Australian / Canadian Literatures in English.* Melbourne: Methuen Australia, 1987.

O'Donnell, Eleanor. "Mass Media Worldviews: Canadian Images of the Third World." *Conflicts of Interest: Canada and the Third World.* Eds. Jamie Swift and Brian Tomlinson. Toronto: Between the Lines, 1991. 275–94.

Patton, Marilyn. "Tourists and Terrorists: The Creation of *Bodily Harm*." *Papers on Language and Literature* 28.2 (Spring 1992): 150–73.

Philip, Marlene Nourbese. *Frontiers: Essays and Writings on Racism and Culture*. Stratford: Mercury, 1992.

Rubenstein, Roberta. "Pandora's Box and Female Survival: Margaret Atwood's *Bodily Harm*." *Journal of Canadian Studies* 20.1 (Spring 1985): 120–35.

Said, Edward. *Culture and Imperialism*. New York: Knopf, 1993.

Slemon, Stephen. "Unsettling the Empire: Resistance Theory for the Second World." *World Literature Written in English* 30.2 (1990): 30–41.

Smith, Rowland. "Margaret Atwood and the City: Style and Substance in *Bodily Harm* and *Bluebeard's Egg*." *World Literature Written in English* 22.2 (1985): 225–64.

Spivak, Gayatri Chakravorty. *In Other Worlds: Essays in Cultural Politics*. New York and London: Methuen, 1987.

———. "Criticism, Feminism, and the Institution" (interview with Elizabeth Grosz). *The Post-Colonial Critic: Interviews, Strategies, Dialogues*. Ed. Sarah Harasym. Routledge: London and New York, 1990. 1–16.

———. "Three Women's Texts and a Critique of Imperialism." *Critical Inquiry* 12 (1985): 243–61.

Strauss, Jennifer. "Being There, Being Here." McDougall 111–19.

Suleri, Sara. *The Rhetoric of English India*. Chicago and London: U of Chicago P, 1992.

Tiffin, Helen. "Voice and Form." McDougall 119–32.

Williamson, Judith. "Woman Is an Island: Femininity and Colonization." *Studies in Entertainment: Critical Approaches to Mass Culture*. Ed. Tania Modleski. Bloomington: Indiana UP, 1986. 99–118.

Wilson, Sharon R. "A Note on Margaret Atwood's Visual Art and *Bodily Harm*." *Antipodes* 4.2 (1990): 115–16.

———. "Turning Life into Popular Art: *Bodily Harm*'s Life-Tourist." *Studies in Canadian Literature* 10.1–2 (1985): 136–45.

Hilda Hollis

Between the Scylla of Essentialism and the Charybdis of Deconstruction: Margaret Atwood's *True Stories*

MARGARET ATWOOD'S POETRY AND NOVELS, because they question a single, dominant version of the truth, have frequently been identified with deconstruction or postmodern irony. While there is justification for this identification, Atwood's stance differs from some postmodern theorists in her insistence on the possibility of *bearing witness*. She deconstructs oppressive structures of power, but stops short of undermining *all* positions. Atwood recognizes the constructedness, and hence indeterminacy, of language and the impossibility of living outside it, or without an interpretive system. Yet she insists on a physical knowledge of existence apart from any constructed system. The powerful may play with and manipulate interpretation, but Atwood writes that "The facts of this world seen clearly / are seen through tears" ("Notes Towards a Poem That Can Never Be Written" 1–2). Brenda Higgins articulates the difficult path that must be charted by those sympathetic both to feminism and postmodernism as they find their way

> between the Scylla of univocal readings and the Charybdis of
> infinitely proliferating indeterminacy. The possibility of rape
> [and other forms of oppression] makes it especially urgent that
> we avoid both positions; a theocracy of a Single Truth is pro-
> foundly antidemocratic; on the other hand, real people (nearly
> always women) get raped, and they do not want to hear that rape
> is only one among an infinite number of possible meanings of
> their experience. (305)

This essay will explore how Atwood deals with the issue of
truth in her ninth collection of poetry, *True Stories*. Charting a
difficult course, she disputes universalizing moral and social
interpretations, but simultaneously recognizes corporeality, a
phenomenon that exceeds Western metaphysics. By insisting on
a temporal and physical reality apart from artificial constructions
of time and being, Atwood is able to halt proliferating indeterminacy. The limitations imposed on *true stories* by a common
physical existence, which, it should be emphasized, does not
minimize difference, enables a political, although not party,
stance. Atwood can therefore say, regarding suffering and pain,
"Witness is what you must bear" ("Notes Towards a Poem That
Can Never Be Written" 16).

Jacques Derrida's critique of Western metaphysics is based on
his rejection of the "constant of a presence" (*Structure, Sign, and
Play* 960). This does not simply lead him to reject an external
hypothesis, such as God, but anything that can offer some ground
for positionality. He includes in his list "*eidos, arché, telos, energeia,
ousia* (essence, existence, substance, subject), *aletheia*, trans-
cendentality, consciousness, or conscience, God, man, and so
forth" (960–61). Although Derrida bundles all these terms together and seems to imply that if God is rejected then the others
necessarily fail also, it is not clear that this follows. A concept of
existence is valid without a belief in God, and the retention of
any one of these terms undermines the absolutism frequently

associated with the deconstructive project. The result of Derrida's rejection of a centre is the extension of "the domain and the interplay of signification *ad infinitum*" (961).

Derridean freeplay disturbs not only the literary text, but also social structures, because Derrida extends this freeplay by arguing that nothing is not text (*Living on: Borderlines* 83–84). Gayatri Chakravorty Spivak comments that any careful reader of Derrida will realize that "he does not claim that there is *no* intention, *no* reference, *no* practice, *no* world. He attempts to 'situate' them and claims that they are never self-adequate, never (except strategically) altogether distinct from their political opposites" (22). But, we can never *know* intention, *know* reference, *know* practice, *know* world, according to Derrida. Since all is text, and therefore indeterminate, there is no point of stability. The merits of an irony that renders all positions — including those that advocate social justice — meaningless through too much meaning is ambiguous. Atwood, like many thinkers with social and political concerns, uses some insights of deconstruction, but rejects its extremes.

Linda Hutcheon, in her recent book on Canadian ironies, *Splitting Images: Contemporary Canadian Ironies*, celebrates postmodern irony's power of deconstructing "isms," but admits that its power of contestation is limited: "it questions the very act — and authority — of taking a position, any position, even an oppositional one that assumes a discursive situation exterior to that which is being opposed" (140). She writes that

> The single most problematic issue surrounding the postmodern use of irony is not its efficacy or its interest as a means of political consciousness-raising or deconstruction; it is whether this "lightness of thoughtfulness" can go beyond the destabilizing and dismantling to construct something new. This is the issue raised by many feminists as well as Marxist critics. If your agenda is action, where can irony fit in, especially if it is seen as a rhetorical

> weapon of the smug dominant culture, used to keep you in your
> place? (153)

Hutcheon seems to be searching for a limited irony, which is very different from the sort of irony proposed by Derrida or his American counterpart, Paul de Man. The latter is moving in a very different direction than Hutcheon, and is more devoid of political possibility than Derrida. Michael Ryan comments that "the Yale school can be held guilty of shunting aside the social and political (latent and overt) possibilities of Derrida's text" (125). A limited irony is rejected by these powerful male philosophers because it must inevitably subscribe to some form of presence, no matter how confined. Instead, they push irony to the limit, where it becomes impossible, or pointless, to act politically, as the "impossibility of our being historical" is recognized (de Man 211). Atwood extricates herself from this problem of utter indeterminacy by observing a physical reality that places limits. She questions the idea of a single true story but finds political power in the presence of *true stories*. In a review of *True Stories*, Ann Mandel writes that the "power of these political poems . . . comes from their insistence that torture is not abstract but physical, that *bodies* are flayed, beaten, burnt, sliced, torn" (248).

The title poem begins with an imperative, "Don't ask for the true story" (1), which is subverted by the question that follows immediately, "why do you need it?" (2). The final lines of the third part of this triptych contain the same imperative and question, but reverse their order, thus providing a firm closure for the poem. While the question initially subverts the imperative, it is eventually shut down by the dictatorial "Don't ever ask" (iii 10–11). This rejection of the search for the true story seems to echo the poststructuralist concept of the impossibility of arriving at a single truth, but this position is also mocked. Although its emphasis is the destruction of the metaphysical, deconstruction ironically sets up an incontrovertible metaphysics of contradiction. Derrida recognizes the inevitable irony of his own position but continues to operate within it (*Structure, Sign, and Play* 961). Atwood, however, undermines deconstruction's imperative in a truly deconstructive or subversive gesture (but one not used often enough by deconstructors) when she asks why true stories are necessary. This question haunts the collection of poetry as it becomes increasingly evident why this search is important.

Navigating the course between Scylla and Charybdis, Atwood shows that while a single, all-determining, true story may not be found, this does not preclude the existence of true *stories* that testify to the inhumanity of humanity. In an interview with Elizabeth Meese, Atwood explains this distinction:

> There isn't just one story; there are lots of stories. It's the same thing that black women writers complained of early in the [feminist] movement. . . . You are trying to tell us that our experience is like this, and it is *not* like this. It's like that. (Ingersoll 184)

A single true story is constantly subverted by other stories, but true stories can be true only because they are based on reality as it is experienced by individuals.

The speaker of the title poem expresses the difficulty, even the impossibility, of arriving at "*the* true story," a universally accepted truth. Truth is always complicated by history and distorted by story:

> Don't ask for the true story;
> why do you need it?
>
> It's not what I set out with
> or what I carry.

> What I'm sailing with,
> a knife, blue fire,
>
> luck, a few good words
> that still work, and the tide. (3–8)

The second of these stanzas denies an originary or portable truth that can be universally applied. The next two stanzas, without creating an absolute definition, depict truth as it is reconstructed by Atwood. Truth both is and is not what she sails with. She does not sail with the true story, but she sails with true stories in process. Truth is death and life, and the luck that mediates between the two. A *knife* can be used to take and/or to sustain life. The story depends on which side of the knife you are on. Similarly, the hot sun, *blue fire* from the sky and off the water, is essential for life, but can also dehydrate and burn. Yet, although story is suspect, some truth is found in those "few good words that still work." Atwood comments on the general failure of language, but suggests that it contains a *trace* of the physical world. This *trace* is stronger than that which Derrida presents, for it has the possibility of being related to the material world and is not necessarily only derived from another trace of a trace of a trace.

Finally, truth is found in the tide, symbolic of a nonchaotic and expressed temporality outside of language. The tide, like the female body, is related to the moon and its cycles. It is a present that can express the present, since it, without mediation, speaks time. This concern with the expression of temporality lies at the centre of poststructuralist discourse. Derrida's project is directed against the privileging of the present, which must always contain absence; the present is always already past in its utterance. De Man expresses the dilemma:

> Irony divides the flow of temporal experience into a past that is
> pure mystification and a future that remains harassed forever by

a relapse within the inauthentic. It can know this inauthenticity but can never overcome it. It can only restate and repeat it on an increasingly conscious level, but it remains endlessly caught in the impossibility of making this knowledge applicable to the empirical world. It dissolves in the narrowing spiral of a linguistic sign that becomes more and more remote from its meaning, and it can find no escape from this spiral. (222)

By focusing on the tide, and as she does later in the collection, on the winter solstice, the sunrise, and the body, Atwood attempts to close this temporal gap that becomes so problematic for de Man and Derrida. Although neither the tide nor the body can become a language system, they can arrest the otherwise ever-spiraling irony through a complete identification of signified and signifier. Atwood, as will become clear in this essay, distinguishes between this immediate expression of experience and a temporally separate interpretation that imposes meaning upon experience. There are some truths knowable in the present, even though none of them may be known perfectly, and though they will all be filtered, with varying results, through the interpretation of language systems.

The second part of the poem continues Atwood's exploration of temporal issues. She acknowledges the mystification of the past: "The true story was lost / on the way down to the beach . . ." (1, 2). Returning to the origin of humanity, the ocean, does not reveal a single originary truth. Atwood is not saying that there is no truth, but that it is not something perfectly grasped by anyone: "it's something / I never had, that black tangle / of branches in a shifting light" (2–4). She does not follow Derrida's path and reject all truth because she cannot return to an originary one. Rather, truth is a black tangle of branches, facts sorted out with difficulty, whose interpretation varies with the "shifting light" or with a shifting perspective.

In part three, Atwood states that the "true story lies / among the other stories" (1, 2). This seems to imply that the true story exists, but that it is plural and contextual, and only found in fragments. Atwood's mode appears to be ironic: "The true story is vicious / and multiple and untrue / after all" (7–9). True and untrue seem to be elided in a multiplying indeterminacy as they are caught in an undecidable relativism. It is, however, possible to derive a more stable interpretation of these lines: there are multiple versions of the true story; many people have been brutalized and subjected to viciousness; the true story is about people being untrue to others. Both readings are simultaneously possible, and I question the absolute privileging of the indeterminate one, so that all meaning is erased from the stable one. Engaging in such double reading is important, but should the *lisible* be termed only *provisional* and be utterly destroyed by the indefinite reading? Is it possible to take a path between a totalizing reading and one that empties meaning through its proliferation?

In her interview with Geoff Hancock, Atwood poses a series of rhetorical questions:

> Is there such a thing as knowing it [reality, for example a piece of granite] directly without language? Small babies know the world without language. How do they know it? Cats know the world without language, without what we would call language. How are they experiencing the world? (Hancock 134)

In the midst of these questions, Atwood makes some important assertions. She finds a reality beyond metaphysics that can be known directly without the structure of language. A level of being exists in contrast to one of interpretation. Although "truth" can be imposed by language, there is a truth related to existence that is independent of words. At the same time, Atwood warns, "There's something tricky about 'reality,' let alone language. Insofar as language relates to a cultural experience of reality, to what extent is that transmissible?" (135).

In "Landcrab I" and "Landcrab II," Atwood deals with understanding reality apart from language. She probes perceptions of reality, *true stories*, from the perspective of a human speaker and a landcrab. In the first poem, the landcrab is hunted down by the speaker who looks at the crab in an attempt to understand herself. Truth becomes relative as the speaker dismisses an originary truth in the reflection of the landcrab: "A lie, that we come from water. / The truth is we were born / from stones, dragons, the sea's / teeth, as you testify, / with your crust and jagged scissors" (1–5). The crab is described metaphorically, and in the second stanza the long line of unflattering comparisons ends with "the husk of a small demon" (13). The speaker then moves onto a more empirical reflection upon the life of the crab:

> Attack, voracious
> eating, and flight:
> it's a sound routine
> for staying alive on edges. (14–17)

The end of this stanza recognizes the hypocrisy of language, and how it can be used to hide violence:

> For mammals
> with their lobes and tubers,
> scruples and warm milk,
> you've nothing but contempt. (24–27)

The scruples of the speaker, conveyed by her initial contempt for the crab, seen in the metaphoric description, are deconstructed in the next stanza, when the speaker takes on the same physical actions as the crab when she attacks and eats it. Those scruples are of no use to the crab and operate within a particular humanistic system. Again, confined to metaphor as "a frozen scowl," it mysteriously, and without voice, disappears: "Here you are, a frozen scowl / targeted in flashlight, / then gone: a piece of what / we are" (28–31).

This poem should be read intertextually with a passage from Atwood's *Bodily Harm*, published the same year as *True Stories*. Although the purpose of targeting the crab in a flashlight is written over or obscured in the poem, it is spelled out in the novel:

> "What lives in the holes?" says Rennie.
>
> "Landcrabs," Paul says. "Big white buggers. They only come out at night, you hunt them with a flashlight and a big stick. You shine the light in their eyes, that stops them, and then you pin them down with the stick." (99)

Language and scruples can cover up and hide violence and truth, but violence does not need to be reported for it to have taken place. The crab shares a common physicality with the speaker; it is *a piece of what we are*, sharing life — eating, procreation (coupling) — and death, but also literally becomes, through engorgement, *a piece of what we are*. It insists on becoming a mirror, forcing the speaker to see the possibility of her own nightmarish activity: "my stunted child, my momentary / face in the mirror / my tiny nightmare" (32–34). Through language, the speaker tries to distance herself from her action, and perhaps even achieves this goal by turning the crab into a metaphor for her potential violent deeds, rather than looking at her actual devouring of the crab.

In the sequel poem, the crab is not simply a reflection, but there is an acknowledgement of her distinct (even female) subjectivity as the speaker and crab interact, watching and smelling each other in an effort to interpret. The crab faces a situation of life or death when she attempts to discern whether the speaker is "food or a predator" (13). As in the previous poem, the speaker has the power of naming. Within her linguistic system, she depicts the crab as alien: "working those martian palps" (17), and in a colonizing move, she describes the crab in words more fitting to a fashion show: "seawater in leather" (19). Figurative language keeps invading the words of the speaker: "Old fingernail, old mother" (24). Yet, in this poem, the speaker recognizes that her "truth," or interpretation, is not the only one. The crab has a nonverbal metaphysics and can assess reality outside of human language: "I'm a category, a noun / in a language not human" (20, 21). Her life is independent of the speaker's words: "you're no-one's metaphor / you have your own paths / and rituals" (27–29). A very real world of life and death exists on the beach outside of language: "The beach is all yours, wordless / and ripe once I'm off it" (32, 33). This multiplicity of understanding, however, does not undermine existence, only interpretation. Is it this recognition of a distinctive subjectivity that results in a very different outcome for this second landcrab?

In *The Postcard*, published in French only a year before *True Stories*, Derrida questions the existence of his correspondent. Some parallels and differences are worth pursuing in a comparison of this work with Atwood's poem "Postcard." Derrida, in one of a series of postcards, writes,

> I ask myself occasionally quite simply if you exist and if you have the slightest notion of it. . . . Sometimes I tell myself that you are my love: then it is only my love, I tell myself interpellating thus. And then you no longer exist, you are dead, like the dead woman in my game, and my literature becomes possible. (*The Postcard* 29)

In this excerpt, Derrida plays with the problem of recognizing exterior subjectivities; his lover might not exist except as a construction of his desire. Later in this postcard, he contradictorily suggests that his lover exists but that she is "quite alive outside of me. Out of reach" (29). He continues, "isn't this

somewhat what I was just saying? Unless it is the opposite . . . "
(29). These two positions are quite different, but they both
recognize the problem of distance. The gap represented by the
post, and which Derrida here finds between people, is a factor
in all communication. He argues that all texts are radically
undecidable because language cannot represent presence. All
reading, and all relations with other human beings, are indeterminate because of an unavoidable distance. Gayatri Spivak inter-
prets: "The chain [of substitutions] is constituted by the
possibility of non-arrival, first because the idea of arrival cannot
otherwise emerge, and secondly (and more 'radically') because
all arrivals are irreducibly askew" (30).

Atwood's "Postcard" poses some similar questions regarding
existence and signifying constructions. It shows that there is no
absolute, direct link between signifiers and signified, between
existence and essence. The picture on the postcard is itself fictive:
"The palm trees on the reverse / are a delusion" (2, 3). The
nonhuman, but oral, sign of the rooster is misleading: "The
roosters crow / for hours before dawn" (16, 17). Time, not as
existence, but as something that moves forward, is shown to be
a construct: "Time comes in waves here . . . I move up, it's called
/ awake, then down into the uneasy / nights but never / forward"
(11–16). The printed word is untrustworthy; "a clipping / about
democracy from the local paper" (26, 27) seems to imply a
different world from the impoverished island.

With all these illusory and meaningless signs, the writer is led
to distrust her correspondent's existence:

> . . . A universe that includes you
> can't be all bad, but
> does it? At this distance
> you're a mirage, a glossy image
> fixed in the posture
> of the last time I saw you. (31 36)

She questions whether the memory of her lover is as false a sign as the delusive image on the postcard. In her exploration of her memory of her lover she explores his love. Initially it sounds romantic, coming "in waves like the ocean" (40), but the image becomes increasingly violent: "sickness . . . filling & pounding, a kicked ear" (41–43). The "lover" exists and there is tangible proof — a kicked ear, but is he that which could make the world not "all bad"? The final image does not, as some critics have contended, refer to the intensity of love, but to the violence of so many relationships. Read in the wider context of this volume of poetry, this interpretation is clear. In "A Women's Issue" the word *love* is shown to be divorced from a feeling of affection.

An awareness develops in Atwood's "Postcard" of the disjunction between signifier and signified. Atwood, however, is demonstrating the distortive possibilities of language, not infinitely proliferating indeterminacy. Deconstruction rightly points out that not only are the images that the correspondent describes distorted, but her own words are also inevitably subject to the distortion of language. Does this, however, imply that Atwood is suggesting that the situation of this island is indeterminate? I would suggest not. Reality can be distorted from different angles, but the point is that there is a physical reality to distort. Atwood is not leading us into an *aporia*, but showing the powerful manipulative possibilities of signification. Derrida, in *The Postcard*, does not question only the interpretation of his correspondent, but her existence. Atwood questions the image, but the existence of a person is not in doubt. It is the interpretive gap between existence and signification that is problematic. Limits are placed on the truth of signification by existence. The picture on the postcard cannot erase the polluted beaches, nor does the word "love" erase the "kicked ear." Atwood insists that women, and more generally those in oppressed positions, cannot afford the luxury of seeing existence as indeterminate: "And I think a lot of the speculation about the void and things like this are very male.

Why? Because they could afford to do that, again. I think women are much more grounded in the world because they have had to be" (Ingersoll 187). Atwood emphasizes that she is "Not saying this is gender-specific that women can't think abstractly" (187).

In the section *Small Poems for the Winter Solstice* Atwood continues to explore the gap between interpretation and physical reality. In the first of these poems, she distinguishes between physical reality and the way it is seen or interpreted: "To put your hand / into the light reveals / the hand but the light also: / shining is where they touch" (13–16). The way a light shines on a particular fact creates interpretation. This discussion of the constitution of facts is continued in the tenth poem in which the speaker admits that she is a teller of mundane lies: "Such as: / I can fly. I wish I could believe / it. Instead I'm stuck / here, in this waste of particulars, / truths, facts. Teeth, gloves & socks. / I don't trust love / because it's no shape or colour" (8–14). Atwood distinguishes between material reality and an emotion. While love is not stable, particular physical items possess that *presence* that so eludes Derrida. Material existence, not an external deity or any interpretative truth, takes on the role of transcendental signifier.

Poem Nine plays with the opposition *presence / absence*, a concept of privileged difference that is strongly rejected by Derrida. In considering the *luxury* of holding hands, the speaker wonders "How can I justify / this gentle poem then in the face of sheer / horror?" (11–13). Her response is to say that it is an important assertion of difference:

> Still, if there were nothing
> but killing or being killed then why not
> kill? I know you by your
> opposites. I know your absence. (20–23)

Holding hands makes a statement against killing and a gentle poem stands against horror. Yet, in this poem, irony is at work, questioning a strictly dichotomous relationship that privileges one term over the other. Some call writing a gentle poem "collusion" (2). If the poem we are reading is *this gentle poem*, while it does not advocate violence, can it really be termed gentle? The deconstructive gesture is important because it questions the complacency of the "fat" (19). Sherrill E. Grace writes of Atwood that

> Beginning with the dominant Western system of hierarchical dichotomies which support economic and class structures and encode a society's political, cultural, and psychological values, she continually explores the evils of that system, forcing her readers to recognize their blindness and responsibility. (13)

Grace argues that Atwood is looking for a third way beyond victor/victim dichotomies. Although Atwood subverts the distancing of the powerful from their responsibility for systemic injustice, she is not simply seeking to plunge us into an irresolvable text of *différance*. When the two terms, *being skewered* and *holding hands* are juxtaposed, the latter is the term that is privileged and desired by the body; the other causes the body to shudder. Insisting on physical polarities and also on the complex interplay of culpability, Atwood engages in a delicate balance.

The most disturbing section of *True Stories* is embedded in its centre, "Notes Towards a Poem That Can Never Be Written." The title is, itself, clearly ironic, for poems have been written. This title resembles Derrida's first words of *The Postcard*, "You might read these *envois* as the preface to a book that I have not written" (3). Both Atwood and Derrida deny the possibility of the written text capturing the complete text. Yet just because the word is not a perfect representation, does it have no value at all? While Derrida allows his irony to extend to the point where he can doubt the existence of his correspondent, Atwood focuses on the reality of suffering and pain, and the way a body can become a universal sign.

In "Torture" Atwood describes a woman whose mouth is sewn closed; she is "a mute symbol" (11). There is also

> a flayed body untangled
> string by string and hung
> to the wall, an agonized banner
> displayed for the same reason
> flags are. (32–36)

Atwood writes that "power / like this is not abstract, it's not concerned / with politics and free will, it's beyond slogans" (21–23). These signs work outside the linguistic system, but they universally convey the idea of unutterable pain. Different interpretations of this pain are possible — victory, submission, revenge — but the bodies are displayed because they are understood, "for the same reason / flags are" (35, 36).

Atwood continues to make a distinction between physical facts and the multiple possibilities of language and interpretation in "Spelling." The poem moves from the play of language to its power. The first image is of the speaker's daughter:

> My daughter plays on the floor
> with plastic letters,
> red, blue & hard yellow,
> learning how to spell,
> spelling,
> how to make spells. (1–6)

Even these childish letters are unmalleable. Learning to spell involves using man's hard alphabet — being formed by a language and simultaneously forming it. The young girl is not only learning conventional spelling, but how to make spells, an alternative way of achieving power.

The third stanza is complex, bringing together a number of

issues in the seemingly simple question of the relation between a child and a poem:

> A child is not a poem,
> a poem is not a child.
> There is no either/or.
> However. (12–15)

The first lines seem to invoke mutual exclusivity. The third line, however, rejects any type of contradictory positioning; no choice should exist between poetry and children. They are distinct, but connected. Atwood is both discussing the choices women have had to make between bearing children and writing poetry, and the relationship between aesthetics (a poem) and the ethics involved in real human lives (a child). She argues that women should not have to make a choice between children and poetry, and goes on to show that the production of both has been controlled by men. While Atwood is in this stanza specifically discussing the choices women must make, her words recall Kierkegaard's famous two volumes, *Either/Or*, in which the reader is implicitly asked to choose either the life of an aesthete (poetry), or the life of an ethically responsible family man within a universalized moral system (children). Kierkegaard seems to reject both, and Atwood here does the same: "There is no either/or" (14). In response to Hancock's question about whether art needs to be moral, Atwood replies that it is moral

> whether the artist tries to be or not. Even Oscar Wilde was making a moral statement when he said, "Morality is boring, and what I'm after is the beautiful". . . . you [can] say *what I'm after is pure form*. By saying that, you imply the moral dimension is not important to your art. Or you can say, *the social conscience is innate, therefore spit on the bad guys*. However, the closer you get to that view, the closer you get to propaganda. (129)

Atwood rejects both the *either* and the *or*, bringing both together in her work. The final enclosed *however* encapsulates the limited irony that Atwood supports. Morality, *social conscience*, is not innate and fixed, and yet it is not subject to an infinite shifting because the living, breathing child, of the first stanza, vulnerable to the hard letters of language, cannot be written away.

Atwood draws the two issues together through a discussion of power. Prohibitive control has been exerted by patriarchal society over women's production of children and poetry:

> I return to the story
> of the woman caught in the war
> & in labour, her thighs tied
> together by the enemy
> so she could not give birth. (16–20)

The story of the burning witch similarly tells how her linguistic production has been controlled: "her mouth covered by leather / to strangle words" (22–23). Both the woman dying in the violent prevention of childbirth and the burning witch speak through their suffering bodies. At "the point where language falls away. . . . the body / itself becomes a mouth" (26–35). Their bodies tell a truth outside language.

When the body becomes both signified and signifier, the gap that allows infinite indeterminacy is closed. There is no temporal gap between intention and meaning. Derrida dismisses such a mark that disallows indeterminacy because it cannot be cited:

> This citationality, duplication, or duplicity, this iterability of the mark is not an accident or an anomaly, but is that (normal/abnormal) without which a mark could no longer even have a so-called "normal" functioning. What would a mark be that one could not cite? And whose origin could not be lost on the way? (*Signature Event Context* 321)

Atwood writes of such a mark: "when the bones know / they are hollow & the word / splits & doubles & speaks / the truth" (31–34). The doubling that is a part of communication occurs without a gap when it is the body itself, a nonlinguistic word, speaking. The word is one with its origin. Atwood, however, recognizing the inherent distance in language, identifies her own words as "metaphor" (36), because she cannot fully represent this body in pain. Through her aphoristic statement about metaphor, she implicitly contrasts the suffering body to language. In acknowledging the *aporia* of language, she attempts to draw us beyond language to a recognition of pain. This body speaks in a way that can be understood by all because of a shared physical or material reality. Such a concept of a body writing or speaking should in no way be confused with Hélène Cixous's identification of women's writing with "white ink" (339). Atwood is not engaging in an essentialism of this nature.

The truth that the dying body utters is not a "truth" that constructs authoritative systems. The speaker comments that "A word after a word / after a word is power" (24–25). Interpretation is formed through a complex relation of words and it is this imposition of meaning that has the power to distort and control. This is what Atwood deconstructs.

Barbara Blakely, in a study of Atwood's phenomenology, argues that she recognizes the imperialist male colonization of language. Women are constructed as a reflection of men. However, Blakely posits that Atwood finds a possibility for breaking out of this circle when women recognize their own bodies and move into a more liquid speech:

> When words become no longer the "syntax of chained pebbles / but liquid" (*PU*, p. 69), man and woman can also "Take off the signatures" (*PP*, p. 50), the lies, alternate versions, and verbal reifications. Words will not speak in the lying double voice of the oppressed. They will pour forth from the power of brokenness

> in a leap toward a primal existence before language, toward the
> revelation of the body's plenitude before speech. . . ."(46)

Unlike Blakely, Atwood does not conceive of an escape into a liquid linguistic world, for she recognizes the impossibility of leaving the indeterminate world of language and form. The spiral of irony, however, is halted from reaching an extremist position of meaninglessness by her acknowledgement of an existence exterior to language. Duplicity is an inherent part of language, but Atwood posits the *possibility* of a correlation with that which is exterior to the linguistic text. She does not demand a perfect repository in order to posit *a* truth. Marxist critic Frank Lentricchia points to what many theorists with social concerns view as an unacceptable implication of unlimited irony. He comments that "deconstruction can show that representations are not and cannot be adequate to the task of representation, but it has nothing to say about the social work that representation can and does do" (50). In Atwood's equivocating, yet assertive, rejection of a divide between poetry and children ("There is no either/or. However."), she finds a link between language and that which exists outside it.

The title poem of "Notes Towards a Poem That Can Never Be Written" is divided into six parts. In the first, a place is described that will both "defeat you" (5) and that cannot be imagined (4). Far from being a construct of desire, it insists on entering into consciousness from the outside. That is the place we would rather not know about, which stops us from wanting to seek for truth. Here language is able to reflect reality: "the word *why* shrivels and empties / itself. This is famine" (6, 7). The fact, not the interpretive "why," is the only thing that counts. In the next poem, dead bodies become an incontrovertible text: "the un-endurable / pain still traced on their skins" (4, 5). The speaker does not allow this pain to be dismissed as *pure mystification*, but insists on an immediate present: "This has been happening, / this happens" (8, 9). Despite this temporal immediacy, there is a spatial distance in the poem's perspective that results in a *we / them* dichotomy:

> We make wreaths of adjectives for them,
> we count them like beads,
> we turn them into statistics & litanies
> and into poems like this one. (10–13)

The *we* attempts to change the reality of *them*. By imposing descriptive language, those who are not suffering attempt to obliterate, ignore or contain the suffering, but the speaker comments sadly, "Nothing works. They remain what they are" (14, 15). The suffering body exists outside of discourse. It is a sign that does not lose its origin.

The image of the writing body continues in the third poem "It is her body, silent / and fingerless, writing this poem" (8, 9). The woman is not similar to Derrida's "dead woman" who enables him to write, or to the writer who "dies" in the act of sending the card (*The Postcard* 28). Here the distinction between dead and alive becomes clear. Teresa de Lauretis comments that while a signifier for Ferdinand de Saussure refers to another signified, and for Derrida only to another signifier, for the feminist scholar it must have a reference to the physical world. Discussing Michel Foucault's theory in terms of family violence, de Lauretis argues that violence can exist before it is understood or named: "It seems to me that of the three — the concept, the expression, and the violence — only the first two belong to Foucault's discursive order" (246). De Lauretis's argument can be extended to any form of oppression. Violence to the body, which can be spoken through the body, must place a limit on interpretation. Atwood's view accords with that of de Lauretis; the physical is not of the same order as the interpretive. Violence may be ignored, (mis)labeled and variously interpreted, but the act nevertheless exists. Even though Atwood fully endorses the deconstruction of the text of language and culture, of "uniformity" (Lorraine York), a limit is placed on questioning by the assertion that there is a reality that is not part of this text and cannot be fully contained by it.

The question of an inherent morality in art is raised in the fourth poem in the description of an operation of torture: "Partly it's a job, / partly it's a display of skill / like a concerto / . . . Partly it's an art" (5–10). The aesthetic life only concerned with the execution of a work of art and not with suffering (Kierkegaard's *Either*) is seen in this poem. The terms by which the operation is discussed, "done badly / or well" (8, 9), are a frightening reflection of evaluative judgements devoid of concern for humanity. If torture can be complicit with art, then the reverse is also possible. Susanne Kappeler comments that "the conception of the literary as separate, as aesthetic, as non-political sanctuary, as the pure field of desire, is a political conception, an ideological cornerstone of patriarchal culture" (136). Atwood deconstructs this artificial separation.

Poststructuralist theory argues that the way we see is created by a metaphysical system. In the fifth poem, Atwood defies this rejection of a natural bodily perception in her statement that the "facts of this world seen clearly / are seen through tears" (1, 2). Although visual testimony can be rejected by those who do not wish to see it, Atwood is relentless in her questioning, in her search for truths:

> What is it you see then?
> Is it a bad dream, a hallucination?
> Is it a vision?
> What is it you hear? (9–12)

This series of rhetorical questions seems to demand agreement — torture is no more than a bad dream. Yet, in the next stanza, sight is given more substance: "The razor across the eyeball / is a detail from an old film / It is also a truth" (13–15). While this picture of torture is an image from film, from a piece of artwork, its presents a truth. Existence within a reflected mode implies distance, yet Atwood claims that it is a truth that is seen. Finally this poem ends with an imperative: "Witness is what you must bear" (16). This witness implies political action and the possibility of at least limited communication.

In the final poem of this section, Atwood delineates the difference between a quietistic poststructuralist philosophy and her own. She argues that in this country "you can try to write / the poem that can never be written, / the poem that invents / nothing and excuses nothing, / because you invent and excuse yourself each day" (3–7). The construction and deconstruction of subjectivity to which Atwood alludes is the essential tenet of deconstructive philosophy. Derrida writes: "You substitute yourself for yourself all the time, I forget you in order to fall in love, with you, from the very next second" (*Postcard* 180). He goes further in his claims: "Thus I have *lost my life* writing in order to give this song a chance . . . " (143 my emphasis). In the face of physical death, Derrida's posings become irrelevant.

The we/they dichotomy of the second poem is continued as *this country/elsewhere*. The anaphoric *elsewhere* is insistent throughout the second half of the poem: "Elsewhere, this poem is not invention" (8). A deconstructive reading would suggest that this statement is subverted by its being made by someone *here* who invents and excuses herself each day. It is, however, also possible to read this poem so as to give credit to the reality of elsewhere that can reflect upon the self-indulgent self-creation of this country. Why should the meaninglessness derived from deconstruction authoritatively impose a meaning of meaninglessness on elsewhere? Why shouldn't the meaning of elsewhere impose demands on this country?

In the concluding pages of *Bodily Harm*, Rennie finds that

"there's no longer a *here* and a *there*" (290) when she realizes the existence of violence and victimization in both Canada and the small West Indian island. A similar manoeuvre is made in this collection of poems. Atwood concludes this poem by saying that "Elsewhere you must write this poem / because there is nothing more to do" (16, 17). In a poem about a friend dying from cancer, Atwood writes "Because there's nothing more I can do I do nothing /. . . Each poem is my last and so is this one" ("Last Poem" 25–29). The sense of futility created by death draws together *here* and *there*, and creates a commonality of vision in the understanding of suffering or oppression. In *The Postcard*, Derrida laughs at the privileging oppositional tactics of opposing here and there: "They want to *oppose fort* and *da*!!! There and here, there and there" (41). In German da contains the possibility of both here and there. Atwood undermines the separation of here and there, not only to point to indeterminacy, but also to suggest a common, though different, experience of the physical and of death.

Atwood's poetry is concerned with the injustice and suffering of real life. She refutes Derrida's comment that "*il n'y a pas de hors-texte*" (*Of Grammatology* 158), and the implication that all existence possesses the indeterminacy of language and culture. Despite this assertion, with few exceptions, Derrida apparently focuses primarily on what would commonly be perceived as literary textuality and not on issues of the real world. But, in his Mandela essay, Derrida comes face to face with apartheid. While saying that such a question is "not only theoretical or philosophical" (41), he is unable to find an *hors-texte* and a ground from which to oppose these *evils* (I italicize not because of my own discomfort with the application of the term in this context, but to acknowledge the unease of those who believe we should move beyond this term).

Derrida poses this question about Mandela: "Why does he *seem* exemplary and admirable in what he thinks and says, in what he does or in what he suffers?" (13 my emphasis). He answers that

Mandela is "admirable for having known how to admire" (15). Mandela reflects the Western moral law which is in practice ignored by those of European descent in power:

> He presents himself in his people, before the law. Before a law he rejects, beyond any doubt, but which he rejects in the name of a superior law. . . . And sometimes we think we hear Rousseau's accent in these confessions, hearing a voice which never ceases to appeal to *the voice of conscience*, to the immediate and unfailing sentiment of justice, to this law of laws that speaks in us before us, because it is inscribed within our heart. (27)

Given Derrida's other discussions of Rousseau, in which he positions him in a "privileged place . . . in the history of logocentrism" (*Of Grammatology* 97), the introduction of Rousseau's name and ideas in connection with Mandela appears to undermine that voice to which Mandela appeals. Mandela, Derrida argues, is "the captive of his admiration" (41), and he suggests that Mandela's past actions can be understood as the result of an imprisonment by Western laws. Yet, Derrida maintains that this alone is too narrow an understanding of Mandela, whose witness also has a possible future aspect: "the promise of what has not yet ever been seen or heard, in a law that has not yet presented itself in the West, at the Western border, except briefly, before immediately disappearing" (38). This possibility — "this arch-ancient thing that had never been present, as the future even — still now invisible" (37) — does not become fully present. Despite his admiration, Derrida concludes that Mandela is still hidden from our sight (42). Throughout the essay, no firm ground for opposing apartheid is adduced. Because of his concern with deconstructing all forms of presence, Derrida is only able to discuss why Mandela *seems* admirable — not why he is so.

The limits Atwood imposes on irony are physical. She recognizes that language, culture, morality, and conscience are subject to irony, but that physical referentiality imposes a limit on the questioning of deconstruction. Her poems show that not everyone hears the voice of conscience and that the *sentiment of justice* is not unfailing. But rather than absolutely deconstructing these ideas, Atwood insists that conscience and justice cannot be abstract; they must be related to the physical. Atwood recognizes the "long bone lying in darkness / inside my right arm: not / innocent but latent" ("Trainride, Vienna-Bonn" 10–13). A latent law will not rescue us from inhumanity, but only the incessant recognition of common physical needs and sensations. Artists, says Atwood, make squawking noises: "They protest. They insist on some kind of standard of humanity which any such [monolithic] regime is going to violate" (Ingersoll 183). Atwood attempts, through her poetry, to create a very basic metaphysical system — the imposition of suffering and pain on other people is wrong. This story, however, is not simplistically true. Indeterminacy regarding culpability and circumstance circles endlessly, but this circling pales into insignificance when juxtaposed with the horror of torture or famine.

It is finally worth contrasting Atwood's insistence on humanity to the philosophy of Heidegger, the most influential thinker in de(con)structive philosophy. Arnold I. Davidson, in his introduction to a *Symposium on Heidegger and Nazism* in *Critical Inquiry*, critiques Heidegger's rejection of humanity in his rejection of metaphysical humanism. He asks where the horror has gone in Heidegger's utterance in a 1949 lecture regarding the progress of technology:

> Agriculture is now a mechanized food industry. As for its essence, it is the same thing as the manufacture of corpses in the gas chambers and the death camps, the same thing as the blockades and reduction of countries to famine, the same thing as the manufacture of hydrogen bombs. (423)

Davidson argues that human beings cannot be spurned simply because the divine is rejected. The physical experience of suffering is more than a metaphysical construction. He writes,

> Hannah Arendt associated Heidegger with Paul Valéry's aphorism, "*Les évènements ne sont que l'écume des choses*" ("Events are but the foam of things"). I think one understands the source of her intuition. The mass extermination of human beings, however, does not produce foam, but dust and ashes; and it is here that questioning must stop. (425–26)

Atwood makes a similar argument in *True Stories*. While rejecting a totalizing metaphysics — a single true story, she insists on recognizing individual people and asks us to see the horror that Heidegger misses. The written body of a physically dead woman is a very different type of text than the one I am writing now. Atwood shows us how to sail between the hard rock of Scylla and the circling whirlpool of Charybdis, by recognizing both the problems inherent in language's creation of "reality" and the reality of our physicality. She neither founders in an *aporia*, nor is constrained by an imperialist metaphysics, but sails on:

> What I'm sailing with,
> a knife, blue fire,
>
> luck, a few good words
> that still work, and the tide.

WORKS CITED

Atwood, Margaret. *Bodily Harm*. Toronto: McClelland & Stewart, 1981.

———. *True Stories*. Toronto: Oxford UP, 1981.

Blakely, Barbara. "The Pronunciation of the Flesh: A Feminist Reading of Atwood's Poetry." *Margaret Atwood: Language, Text, and System*. Eds. Sherrill

E. Grace and Lorraine Weir. Vancouver: U of British Columbia P, 1983. 33–51.

Cixous, Hélène. "The Laugh of the Medusa." *Feminisms: An Anthology of Literary Theory and Criticism*. Eds. Robyn Warhol and Diane Price Herndl. New Brunswick: Rutgers UP, 1991. 334–49.

Davey, Frank. *Margaret Atwood: A Feminist Poetics*. Vancouver: Talonbooks, 1984.

Davidson, Arnold E. "The Poetics of Pain in Margaret Atwood's *Bodily Harm*." *American Review of Canadian Studies* 18 (1988): 1–10.

Davidson, Arnold I. "*Symposium on Heidegger and Nazism*: Questions Concerning Heidegger: Opening the Debate." *Critical Inquiry* 15 (1989): 407–26.

de Lauretis, Teresa. "The Violence of Rhetoric: Considerations on Representation and Gender." *The Violence of Representation: Literature and the History of Violence*. Eds. Nancy Armstrong and Leonard Tennenhouse. New York: Routledge, 1989. 239–58.

de Man, Paul. "The Rhetoric of Temporality." *Blindness and Insight: Essays in the Rhetoric of Contemporary Criticism*. (2nd ed.) Minneapolis: U of Minnesota P, 1983.

Derrida, Jacques. "The Laws of Reflection: Nelson Mandela, in Admiration." *For Nelson Mandela*. Eds. Jacques Derrida and Mustapha Tlili. New York: Seaver Books, 1987. 13–42.

———. "Living On: Border Lines." *Deconstruction and Criticism*. Eds. Harold Bloom, et al. London: Routledge & Kegan Paul, 1979. 75–176.

———. *Of Grammatology*. Trans. Gayatri Chakravorty Spivak. Baltimore: Johns Hopkins UP, 1974.

———. *The Postcard: From Socrates to Freud and Beyond*. Trans. Alan Bass. Chicago: U of Chicago P, 1987.

———. "Signature Event Context." *Margins of Philosophy*. Trans. Alan Bass. Chicago: U of Chicago P, 1982. 307–30.

———. "Structure, Sign, and Play in the Discourse of the Human Sciences." *The Critical Tradition: Classic Texts and Contemporary Trends*. Ed. David Richter. New York: St. Martin's Press, 1989.

Grace, Sherrill E. "Articulating the 'Space Between': Atwood's Untold Stories and Fresh Beginnings." *Margaret Atwood: Language, Text, and System*.

Eds. Sherrill E. Grace and Lorraine Weir. Vancouver: U of British Columbia P, 1983. 1–16.

Hancock, Geoff. "An Interview with Margaret Atwood." *Canadian Fiction Magazine* 58 (1986): 113–44.

Higgins, Brenda. "Screen/Memory: Rape and Its Alibis in *Last Year at Marienbad*." *Rape and Representation*. Eds. Higgins and Brenda Silver. New York: Columbia UP, 1991. 303–21.

Hutcheon, Linda. *Splitting Images: Contemporary Canadian Ironies*. Toronto: Oxford UP, 1991.

Ingersoll, Earl, ed. *Margaret Atwood: Conversations*. Willowdale: Firefly Books, 1990.

Kappeler, Susanne. *The Pornography of Representation*. Minneapolis: U of Minnesota P, 1986.

Kierkegaard, Soren. *Either/Or*. Parts I & II. Eds. and trans. Howard Hong and Edna Hong. Princeton: Princeton UP, 1987.

Lentricchia, Frank. *Criticism and Social Change*. Chicago: U of Chicago P, 1983.

Mandel, Ann. "Review of *True Stories*." *Critical Essays on Margaret Atwood*. Ed. Judith McCombs. Boston: G.K. Hall & Co., 1988. 245–51.

Ryan, Michael. *Politics and Culture: Working Hypotheses for a Post-Revolutionary Society*. Baltimore: Johns Hopkins UP, 1989.

Spivak, Gayatri Chakravorty. "Love Me, Love My Ombre, Elle." *Diacritics* 14 (1984): 19–36.

Weir, Lorraine. "Atwood in a Landscape." *Margaret Atwood: Language, Text, and System*. Eds. Sherrill E. Grace and Lorraine Weir. Vancouver: U of British Columbia P, 1983. 143–53.

York, Lorraine. "The Habits of Language: Uniform(ity), Transgression and Margaret Atwood." *Canadian Literature* 126 (1990): 6–19.

Sherrill E. Grace

"Franklin Lives": Atwood's Northern Ghosts

What should we have taken
with us? We never could decide
on that; or what to wear,
or at what time of
year we should make this journey

so here we are, in thin
raincoats and rubber boots

on the disastrous ice, the wind rising

"PROVISIONS" 1[1]

IN EARLE BIRNEY'S 1947 POEM "Can. Lit." he
mocked what he saw as the poverty of the Canadian imagination.
As far as Birney was concerned "it's only by our lack of ghosts /
we're haunted."[2] About the ghosts, of course, Birney was dead
wrong. Canada has always had plenty of ghosts, and Margaret
Atwood knows how to call them up better than most of our
writers. Her poems, stories, and novels are often haunted by

revenants, ghosts, or gothic presences of one sort or another, and the speakers in her poems, like the characters in her fiction, are almost always surrounded by the warning voices and unfulfilled desires (not to mention the dead hands) of the past. Sometimes that past is buried within a character where it lies repressed until the pressures of the present force it to surface. At other times, that past is represented in a historical figure whom Atwood reinvents and reanimates as a potent sign in a cultural semiotics of peculiarly Canadian significance. The protagonists in *Surfacing*, *Lady Oracle* and *Cat's Eye* all suffer from repressed personal pasts that erupt as ghostly presences in the present of their lives. "Susanna Moodie," however, haunts us all; Atwood brings her back from the dead to tell us a story about who we are as Canadians — and how we should behave. In her 1991 collection of short stories, *Wilderness Tips*, Atwood is again calling up ghosts, one of whom is particularly important to the Canadian imagination, Sir John Franklin.

Atwood is on record as liking ghost stories. In her 1972 interview with Graeme Gibson she described *Surfacing* as a ghost story in the tradition of Henry James.[3] In that novel, the ghosts the narrator sees (her father, her mother) are parts of herself that have split off: they are *doppelgänger*. In *The Journals of Susanna Moodie*, the ghost of Mrs. Moodie, while representing a historical figure, can also be seen as part of the Canadian self, if by "self" we can accept a generalized notion of the Canadian self or psyche. Certainly Atwood constructs a Moodie who is meant to represent an archetypal immigrant double-think about the country. And she, too, is double; she sees and speaks with a double voice.[4] Atwood's treatment of Franklin is similar and, as with *Surfacing* or *Susanna Moodie*, her formal method for dealing with his ghost is important. It seems to me that Atwood has reinvented (or revivified) Franklin as a part of the contemporary Canadian psyche that has split off and been repressed within the national consciousness, and that in bringing him back to life she offers us a mirror in which we can contemplate a profoundly disturbing self-image.

Ghosts, mirrors, shocks, self-image — all this is familiar Atwood territory that I have previously designated as a topography of "violent duality," where she uses a "poetics of duplicity" to map a "space between" either/or dichotomies in a semiotic system that permits other choices, other meanings.[5] Here I want to explore how Atwood brings Franklin back to life in "The Age of Lead," and why that story, which I see as occupying an important position in *Wilderness Tips* and in her oeuvre, recapitulates her persistent concern with the aesthetics of doubling and the semiotics of the "space between." But first, like the speaker in "Provisions," with which I began this journey "on the disastrous ice, the wind rising," I must begin with "small white filing-cards / printed with important facts."

Who was Franklin and why should he matter to Atwood or to us? The historical-biographical answer to this question is simple enough. In May 1845, at the ripe age of fifty-eight, John Franklin (1786–1847), a career sailor with the British Royal Navy, veteran explorer in the Canadian Arctic, former British governor of Van Dieman's Land (Tasmania), popular hero and highly respected naval officer, left England as the leader of a major British expedition in search of the Northwest Passage. Many previous attempts had been made to find a shipping route through the ice of the Arctic archipelago that would link England and northern Europe with the Pacific. The primary impetus for these expeditions was economic, but economic motives included, of course, imperialist pride, power, and domination. The search for the Northwest Passage, however, was driven by other, less tangible forces. Even by the time of Franklin the passage, together with the high Arctic, the polar sea, and the North Pole itself, had acquired the status of a fabled territory, a mythic landscape that lured men with the promise of spiritual, as well as personal, economic, and national, reward. To Victorian England, the search for a Northwest Passage was a romantic adventure that rivaled our late twentieth-century fascination with space exploration. Since the time of Franklin the high Arctic and the search for the passage have become inextricably associated with his name. Moreover, it is still possible to arouse the old dream of adventure, challenge, and discovery by speaking that name. The word "Franklin" has become a sign in a semiotic system of complex, shifting significance.

Franklin's expedition consisted of two bomb vessels specially adapted for their assault on the Northwest Passage. They bore the extraordinary names of *H.M.S. Erebus* and *H.M.S. Terror*. The commanding officer of *Terror* was Captain Francis Crozier, an experienced arctic sailor, and the captain of *Erebus* (the ship Franklin himself sailed in) was Commander James Fitzjamcs. The expedition carried 134 carefully selected officers and men, three years' worth of food supplies preserved by the latest technology, every conceivable scientific instrument for navigation and research, libraries holding almost 3,000 volumes (including *The Vicar of Wakefield*!), silver, china, writing desks, medicines, and the means for mounting theatricals and other diversions to see them through the cold, dark, Arctic wintering-over periods. *Erebus* and *Terror* were little worlds unto themselves with the full apparatus of Victorian British ideology, culture, and a considerable degree of self-sufficient comfort (or so they thought). Despite all this, Franklin's ships were last seen in Baffin Bay in late July of 1845. Since that time, and in spite of numerous searches that continue to this day, surprisingly little has been learned with certainty about the fate of the Franklin expedition. An official document called the "Victory Point Record," found in 1859, tells us that Franklin died on June 11, 1847, that the ships were beset and abandoned, and that the survivors were heading south to the mouth of Fish River on the Canadian mainland. However, Franklin's grave (possibly on King William

Island) has never been located, the wrecks of the *Erebus* and *Terror* have never been found, neither the graves nor the remains of a majority of the men, and the causes of this disaster are still debated. Rumours of cannibalism and survivors have reached us through the Inuit, but accounts of the former were passionately denied in England (by no less a personage than Dickens) and the latter have never been traced.[6]

What we know for sure is that Franklin's men began dying early in 1846. There are three graves on Beechey Island (off the northwest coast of Devon Island) with headboard inscriptions "sacred to the memory of": John Torrington from *Terror*, aged twenty, who died on January 1, 1846; John Hartnell, from *Erebus*, aged twenty-five, who died on January 4, 1846; and William Braine from *Erebus*, aged thirty-two, who died on April 3, 1846. The traces of Franklin's 1846 winter camp can still be seen on Beechey, as can the remains of his garbage dump. The trail of the lost expedition, however, is not picked up again until King William Island, where the Victory Point Record was discovered and where searchers found skeletons, a ship's boat, piles of possessions of a most unlikely kind (clothing, silver, furniture, soap, a copy of *The Vicar of Wakefield*, etc.), and a scatter of bones as the trail thins southward and east, and finally disappears at Starvation Cove on Adelaide peninsula.

What really happened to Franklin and his men remains a mystery, and in the nineteenth century it was important to solve the mystery by discovering the facts; the facts mattered to Lady Jane Franklin, the British Admiralty, and the public. But it is the idea of mystery itself that has continued to fuel twentieth-century retellings of the Franklin story and has led to renewed searches for clues to the cause and meaning of the disaster. Franklin has gradually become a mystery story told for the story's sake, and that story has taken a fascinating array of forms that inscribe a complex, shifting array of meanings.[7] Margaret Atwood first articulated her interest in Franklin in a 1991 Clarendon lecture at Oxford University that was subsequently published as "Concerning Franklin and His Gallant Crew" (the title taken from a nineteenth-century ballad that can be traced back to broadsides from the 1850s).[8]

This lecture, as well as summarizing the Franklin history, reveals Atwood's familiarity with a major research expedition carried out in 1984 and 1986 by a team of scientists led by Canadian forensic anthropologist Owen Beattie, who exhumed the corpses on Beechey Island and concluded that lead poisoning from food preserved (by Victorian state-of-the-art technology) in lead soldered cans had played a critical role in sealing Franklin's fate. The lecture also demonstrates her interest in Canadian literary treatments of Franklin and the relationship, as she sees it, between Franklin's story and the broader category of "mystic-North imagery" in Canadian culture (history, painting, song, poetry, etc.). She traces the Canadian northern line through poets Robert W. Service, E. J. Pratt, D. C. Scott, A. M. Klein, and Al Purdy to Gwendolyn MacEwen's radio verse-play *Terror and Erebus* (1974) and, finally, to Mordecai Richler's "most 'Canadian' book," *Solomon Gursky Was Here* (1989), which is a major parodic reinvention of Franklin as Canadian national narrative.

What Atwood does in this (I think, important) lecture is to map Canada as a northern territory in which the key *topoi* are: death by drowning, frozen corpses, humans going mad or becoming "lost" in an alluring but uncompromising wilderness, or else on rare, brief occasions, becoming one with nature. "To sum up" she says:

> popular lore, and popular literature, established early that the North was uncanny, awe-inspiring in an almost religious way, hostile to white men, but alluring; that it would lead you on and do you in; that it would drive you crazy, and, finally, would claim you for its own. (22)

This is, of course, familiar Atwood subject matter and landscape. It sums up one of the most profound and pervasive discursive doublings of her work: the creation of a wilderness that both attracts and terrifies us, that is both our main source of salvation and the arena of our destruction. It should come as no surprise, therefore, to discover her saying at the end of this lecture that "even as we speak, another major Canadian novelist [besides Richler] is writing about the Franklin expedition; though I've been forbidden to say who it is" (26).

That novelist was Atwood herself. The writing about Franklin is "The Age of Lead," now part of *Wilderness Tips* (although it might be argued that other stories in the collection, notably "Death by Landscape," participate in the mystic northern *topoi* that Atwood finds so provocative). On the copyright page of the collection she acknowledges that the "factual material about the Franklin Expedition" is from *Frozen in Time* (1987), the narrative account, by Owen Beattie and John Geiger, of their research on Beechey Island, but she goes on to note that although "there was a television program on the subject; the one in this story is imagined."[9] Be that as it may, a television program showing the exhumation of the Franklin graves on Beechey Island is essential to the story, and a CBC documentary film constitutes a crucial intertext in "The Age of Lead," forming one half of the doubled narrative.

Through her re-presentation of the documentary representation of *Frozen in Time* (the title of both book and film), Atwood dialogizes her narrative and gives voice to a highly problematic otherness that lives within her text and that also haunts the cultural context within which her story asks to be read. Our reading of "The Age of Lead" is thereby doubled: we read it in the present simultaneously with the chief character's watching of the program (which, for many Canadians at least, may actually recall our own viewing of the program), and we read it retroactively as part of a much larger story about the past, about

Canadian history, and about the future. We, in fact, read two very different stories in the same narrative while Atwood executes an ironic turn on the experience of déjà vu.

A brief description of these two narratives is necessary at this point before I examine the ways in which Atwood aligns them. In "The Age of Lead," a middle-aged woman called Jane (an appropriate name, after all, for the heroine in a story about Franklin) is mourning the recent death of a longtime friend called Vincent. She sits alone in her Toronto home with the television on, unable to sleep and finds her attention drawn to the program because it "is so unlike what she usually sees" (160). As one image follows another on the screen — melting ice, John Torrington's "astonished snarl," "tea-stained eyes," coffin and nameplate, bare white feet, ankles tied together, shirt, trousers, buttons, excited scientists with "earnest mouths . . . twitching" (174) — Jane reflects on her childhood, her mother, her friendship with Vincent and his aloof, ironic personality. As the story advances and the television program draws towards its close, Jane's memories circle more insistently around Vincent's death which crept up on him without warning or medical explanation. Although he has been dead for many months, and although "John Torrington, recently thawed after a hundred and fifty years, probably looks better than Vincent" (172), it is Vincent in the hospital that Jane recalls with a vividness inspired by the television images of Torrington. She sees him in his wintry white room, his pale cold feet protruding from the sheet, packed in ice for the pain caused by some unknown virus creeping up his spine to kill him. No one knows what is killing him, and it is this mystery, like the lure of a whodunnit, that haunts Jane now.

Unlike the documentary that locates its villain in the lead solder used by Goldeners, the London firm that supplied the Franklin expedition, Jane's mystery remains unsolved when the story ends. Instead of answers, closure, she (and we) are left (abandoned, stranded?) like "purposeless objects adrift in the physical world" (175). Instead of answers, Atwood's text sets up more questions, doubts, and anxieties that will haunt us beyond the end of a story in the form of the familiar detritus that we, like Jane, pick up from the sidewalks today only to find dropped there again tomorrow.

Both book and film versions of *Frozen in Time* recount the scientific search for hard evidence that might explain the failure of the Franklin expedition. Both follow the activities of Beattie and his team from their initial investigations on King William Island in 1981 to his first expedition to Beechey in 1984 when he exhumed John Torrington, to his final major research trip in June 1986 when he exhumed John Hartnell and William Braine. The film, aired in 1987 on the CBC program "The Nature of Things," with voice-over by David Suzuki, concentrates on the 1986 visit and reconstructs in detail the scientific activities of the team as they dig through the iron-hard permafrost; exhume, thaw, and x-ray the bodies; and label and discuss their findings.

Atwood was quite precise in her acknowledgements for "The Age of Lead": the documentary in her story is *not* the CBC documentary. In fact, her story follows the film closely but conflates it with the book by choosing the presence of John Torrington as the appropriate ghost instead of Hartnell or Braine. Images of Torrington appear only fleetingly in the film, but colour photographs of the young sailor figure prominently in the book. They are, quite simply, stunning — and haunting (see figure 1). By the time one reaches the book's colour plates of Hartnell and Braine, the face to face visual impact is less forceful. The film, however, works differently to achieve its end, and the dramatic effect of the medium serves to heighten and prolong the suspense, horror, and tension, which are then resolved/released into a final sense of safety and reassurance supplied by forensic science and technological power. Both the book and the film situate Beattie's scientific project in its historical context. The facts surrounding Franklin's ships and men are summarized, and the

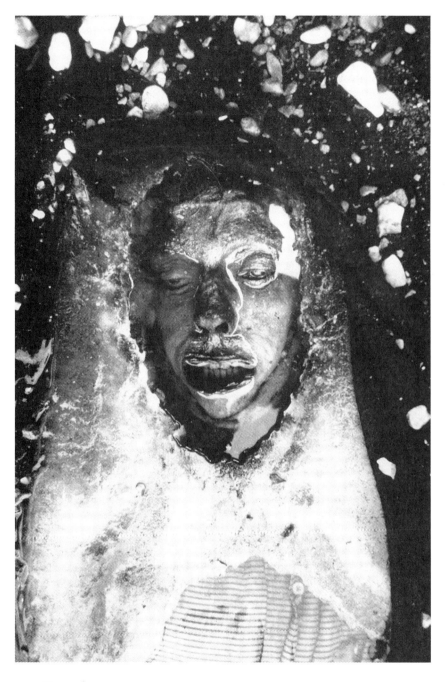

Figure 1

many subsequent searches for traces of the lost expedition are reviewed. In short, an arctic genealogy is constructed for Beattie who becomes the most recent in a long line of men obsessed with Franklin and, so the book and film imply, the most successful. Where others failed, Beattie and his team succeed. The real winner, however, is contemporary science because it is science, as the film in particular stresses over and over, that uncovers the truth buried for 140 years in the arctic permafrost.

Although both book and film end with a satisfying sense of closure, this closure is reinforced in the film by an expertly constructed visual and musical frame. The film opens with a cartoon-like series of black and white reproductions of nineteenth-century paintings and prints illustrating the Franklin story (after the events, of course). These are linked with one another by means of period music, including a rendition of "Rule Britannia," and a narrated summary of people, places, and conditions. This sequence shifts to animated maps of the Arctic, showing various routes and cairns, accompanied by the nineteenth-century ballad known as "The Franklin Expedition." Through these strategies, a simplified past is invoked/constructed as a static point of contrast with the full colour, mobile representation of Beattie in the present as he flies north, arrives, sets up camp, and works. During the main part of the film, the all-seeing, powerful camera lingers voyeuristically over the exhumed bodies as the shrouds and layers of clothing are slowly folded back to reveal the evidence — or what is being constructed for the viewer (Jane and us) as revelation. These moments serve as codes for the entire narrative movement and purpose of the film: to bring us face to face with the past, with ourselves, with the truth. When we are returned to the black and white static images at the end of the film, we know we have penetrated further than the men of that Victorian world could have dreamed possible. We have reached beyond them, as the Stan Rogers song says, "to find the hand of Franklin reaching for the Beaufort Sea."[10]

"Frozen in Time" is what Leo Braudy would call a "closed" film.[11] The present scientific search for answers is framed by a static construction of history. By the end of the film, the question posed by the past has been answered; the scientists can meticulously cover all traces of their presence, pack up their equipment and samples, and fly south to warmth, safety, and fame. Effectively they have closed a chapter in history and obviated the need for anyone to revisit the place or the problem. All this is not to say that the film (like the book) is unaware of the transgressive power and mythic resonance of the story. The film medium is particularly effective in constructing an illusion of presence and revelation, both of which are dramatically established through camera shots angled up from inside Hartnell's grave at the legs and downturned faces of the twentieth-century men crowding around the edge of the grave, and by shots focusing tightly on Hartnell's emerging face, then cutting immediately to a similar shot of the dead sailor's descendant, Brian Spenceley. Spenceley, a Canadian physics professor and the team's forensic photographer, is captured literally face to face with an ancestor who has been brought back from the grave — from the dead as it were — to answer his questions. Thanks to the miracle of technology we can watch a man staring at the dead face of his personal past, his own genealogy, ghost, or *doppelgänger* made manifest — and seeming to return his stare. The film frame serves to contain and control these moments. It holds them in place, and then puts them neatly away. Atwood's story, however, refuses such tidiness. Her purpose is not to answer but to ask again, to re-visit, to re-view, to re-present.

The titles of story and film are instructive here. Where the metaphoric "Frozen in Time" points directly to *what* — What is frozen in time? corpses, therefore, answers — the metonymic "The Age of Lead" sets up a complex chain of *whys* — Why is this the age of lead? Why is lead a defining characteristic? Why is lead a useful synecdoche? Then, as the story unfolds, we are left asking why "the" age of lead (the nineteenth century) is relevant today. Rather than framing her narrative, Atwood establishes two parallel narrative situations focalized through Jane who both watches the television in the present of 1991 (she thinks of Torrington as dead for 150 years) and remembers her life and friendship with Vincent from some time in the 1960s to the present. Her attention shifts back and forth between the images and voices on the screen and the images called up by remembering her own past.

A particular film image is thereby transformed in Jane's mind, and by the discourse of the text, into a remembered image of Vincent from the distant or more immediate past. For example, it is Torrington who stares at Jane from the television with his "indecipherable gaze, innocent, ferocious, amazed, but contemplative, like a werewolf meditating, caught in a flash of lightning at the exact split second of his tumultuous change" (160); but it is Vincent whom she remembers joking about Franklin in history class (162), Vincent who was "hollow-eyed even then" and resembled "a very young old man" (163). Very quickly Vincent becomes the contemporary embodiment of John Torrington; Torrington haunts the present in Vincent's "ancient, jaunty . . . smile of detachment, of amusement" (173). The "indecipherable gaze" and "tumultuous change" that Jane sees in the face of Torrington are the signs to be read in the evidence of the present, in Vincent's sudden death, in the poisonous detritus of contemporary life.

In order to read these signs, to decipher the dead man's gaze, Atwood sets up a dialogue, focalized through Jane's wandering attention, between past and present, between the Franklin mystery and Vincent's death, between the high Arctic and Toronto, between the simulacra of the television and the (represented) "real appearances of purposeless objects" (175) in Jane's kitchen or on the sidewalk in front of her house. The two texts, presented in separate passages, must be followed, first this one, then that, back and forth, like a conversation between two speakers who seem to be discussing different things, until gradually we realize that they are struggling to negotiate a gap in understanding, what Atwood called in *Surfacing* "a failure of logic," and trying to articulate a common, shared meaning.[12]

That meaning, however, can only be recapitulated by the reader who listens carefully to the two voices (one from the TV, the other inside Jane) and creates the alignment of the two texts in the last two sections of the story. It is the reader who must move from the *what* to the *why*. On the television we are told that the Franklin expedition suffered from lead poisoning, but that "Nobody knew it. Nobody could taste it" (174). They were sabotaged by their own technology, from within, secretly, ironically by "what they'd been eating" (174). In Jane's kitchen, however, we are told almost nothing except that it "looks ownerless" in its sophisticated modernity. It is Vincent, lying on his deathbed of ice, who reaccentuates the remark: "It must have been something I ate" (173).[13] The warning signs are there, however, in the plastic, aluminum, and styrofoam garbage on the sidewalk, and it is in the final paragraph that Atwood shifts our focus outside her doubled text and beyond the end of the story to a point where we can begin to decipher another meaning in the Franklin lesson and another significance in Beattie's research.

Although it is never stated as such, we are positioned to perceive that the moral of the texts and the story is that we, like Franklin and his men, are being poisoned by what we eat or by what we are doing to the environment upon which we depend for food. And yet only a moment's further reflection will open other possibilities in Atwood's text. Just as Jane (and we) are surrounded daily by devices (ovens, microwaves, espresso machines) and convenient supplies (throwaway cups, cans, and take-out plates), so were Franklin's men. If they could not read the signs connecting their destruction with the conveniences of their world in time to save themselves, why should we? If

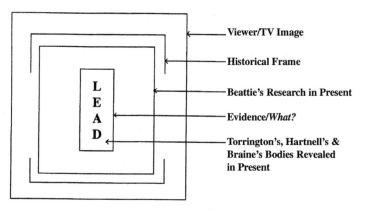

Frozen in Time

- Viewer/TV Image
- Historical Frame
- Beattie's Research in Present
- Evidence/*What?*
- Torrington's, Hartnell's & Braine's Bodies Revealed in Present

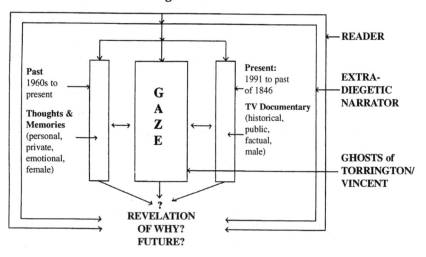

The Age of Ice

READER

EXTRA-DIEGETIC NARRATOR

GHOSTS of TORRINGTON/ VINCENT

Past 1960s to present

Thoughts & Memories (personal, private, emotional, female)

GAZE

Present: 1991 to past of 1846

TV Documentary (historical, public, factual, male)

? REVELATION OF WHY? FUTURE?

Figure 2

they were not safe in their science and technology, why should we be safe? Perhaps the moral of Atwood's doubled narrative and open text, in sharp distinction from "Frozen in Time," is that we cannot and are not. Perhaps "The Age of Lead" provides a mirror, with its carefully represented film, in which we come face to face with the "tea-stained eyes" and "indecipherable gaze" of our own ghosts that only serve to remind us that we can never know — in time. In any case, the semiotics of Atwood's narrative, by reaccentuating "Frozen in Time," problematizes the Franklin story, opening it out into a new set of urgent questions, not about what happened to them, but about what we can learn from them and about why they continue to haunt us.

A diagrammatic summary of the semiotic systems in "Frozen in Time" and "The Age of Lead" demonstrates the different representations of Franklin in the two texts and clarifies the distinct use that Atwood makes of her intertext (see figure 2). The social-semiotic meaning of "Frozen in Time" includes the following claims: that the past lies embedded in and fully accessible to the present; that discoveries in the present link present with past to confirm continuities, validate identities and activities, and establish genealogies; that the truth can be discovered, revealed, brought to the surface and its signs read; that science has the ultimate power to make these discoveries and to solve mysteries and, therefore, the authority to claim solutions, answers, truths — even Truth; that the transgressive act (here of exhumation and undressing the corpse and also of the gaze) facilitates a claiming of the Arctic and the past that grants us, as listeners, viewers, readers, writers, scientists, power over time and space, that makes this northern history with all its secrets ours. By the end of "Frozen in Time" we have laid claim to a story, from beginning to end, taken possession of it.

The semiotic system of "The Age of Lead" inscribes a different meaning that includes but goes beyond a deconstruction of the film. Although it also affirms that the past is accessible through the present (the ghosts are much more *present* in Atwood's story) and that present and past are linked to confirm, validate, and establish, just as they are in the film, Atwood questions notions of truth and belief in the accurate reading of signs, in the power of science, and the necessity for transgressive acts that lead to the possession of bodies, knowledge, or texts. Instead of asserting such ideas or claims, the dialogized narrative of her story puts them into question. These are our ghosts all right, this is our history and our territory; but, the story reminds us, there are other stories and other questions that intersect with "Frozen in Time" and exceed the frame of its telling. Franklin, in Atwood's hands, becomes a supplementary discourse that cannot be controlled by science or narrative or the gaze. After the autopsies, the X rays, the analyses, comes the fear of death and of the unknown — the fear we are wise to feel when we recognize that the meditating werewolf gazing back at us was human, a part of ourselves.

Atwood's "The Age of Lead" is a lesson in Canadian history (for those who, like Vincent and Jane, make jokes in history class) with the ghosts written in but left largely unexplained. The Franklin expedition, as she tells it, is living history with John Torrington back from the dead, like Susanna Moodie, to warn us. What he is saying, however, is not simply that he died of lead poisoning, but that we must acknowledge and learn from the past. Like Vincent, however, his most troubling warning is that there are some secrets, mysteries, truths that will always escape our desire to possess, label, and control.

At the end of her essay, "Concerning Franklin and His Gallant Crew," Atwood insists: "Make no mistake about it: Franklin lives" (26). She means, of course, that Franklin lives in the Canadian imagination, in the work of playwrights, poets, novelists, filmmakers, and scholars who are drawn to construct and participate in a myth of the North. But there is another way in which Franklin lives, the way that Torrington is trying to warn us about and that Vincent dies resisting; he lives in our continuing, insistent demand for answers, our rapacious need to uncover and possess, our transgressive, objectifying gaze, our continued search for the Northwest Passage to origins and truth. Like Atwood's progressively insane pioneer, Franklin lives in us and we may not be able to kill him before the story ends. Like the speaker in her poem "The Revenant," we may be left writing our own names "over and over in the snow" and wondering:

> Mirror addict, my sickness
> how can I get rid of you.[14]

NOTES

1. Atwood begins *The Animals in That Country* with this poem. I start with it because of its obvious relevance to a discussion of Atwood's treatment of the Franklin expedition, but also because the date of the poem provides a sort of *terminus a quo* for Atwood's interest in a configuration of ideas about the North, exploration, ghosts, and the multiple ironies of human ignorance portrayed in the language and form of duality and doubleness. Another journey might map this particular Atwood country in detail, but for my present purpose "The Age of Lead" must serve as my *terminus ad quem*.

2. The last verse of Birney's poem reads:
   > the wounded sirened off
   > no Whitman wanted
   > it's only by our lack of ghosts
   > we're haunted.

   The poem was written in 1947 and has been frequently reprinted and anthologized. See, for example, Birney's *Ghost in the Wheels: Selected Poems* and Atwood's edition of *The New Oxford Book of Canadian Verse in English*.

3. The interview was first published in Graeme Gibson's *Eleven Canadian Novelists* (Toronto: Anansi, 1973), and it is reprinted in *Margaret Atwood: Conversations*, ed. Earl G. Ingersoll, 17–18.

4. This doubleness is dramatized most emphatically in the last poem of

"Journal II," called "The Double Voice." However, the ghostly presence of Moodie is apparent throughout the volume in the illustrations and the verbal images, and Atwood describes her Moodie explicitly as "the spirit of the land she once hated" in her "Afterword" to the first edition; see *The Journals of Susanna Moodie*.

5. I began my exploration of Atwood's landscape in *Violent Duality: A Study of Margaret Atwood* and continued it in "Margaret Atwood and the Poetics of Duplicity," and "Articulating the 'Space Between': Atwood's Untold Stories and Fresh Beginnings."

6. The story of cannibalism among Franklin's men was brought back to England in the winter of 1854 by Dr. John Rae who had explored the Arctic on behalf of the Hudson's Bay Company and who investigated the Franklin mystery in 1853–54. Rae, who was experienced in arctic survival and prepared to listen to Inuit testimony, became convinced of the gruesome fate of the expedition. He entered into a heated debate about his findings with Charles Dickens in the pages of *Household Words* in the winter of 1854–55. For a superb reassessment of the evidence, see David C. Woodman, *Unravelling the Franklin Mystery: Inuit Testimony* (Montréal: McGill-Queens UP, 1991).

7. I have discussed these meanings in a paper called "Reinventing Franklin" presented at the 1993 "Aux Canadas" Conference in Montréal. This paper is part of a larger project on the semiotics of the North.

8. A condensed version of the Clarendon lecture called "Concerning Franklin and His Gallant Crew" was published in *Books in Canada* (May 1991): 20–26. All subsequent references are to this version and are included parenthetically in the text.

9. All references to Atwood's "The Age of Lead" are to *Wilderness Tips* 157–75. Beattie and Geiger's *Frozen in Time: Unlocking the Secrets of the Franklin Expedition* contains several full-colour photographs taken by Beattie of the exhumation process and the bodies, and I would like to thank Dr. Beattie for his kind permission to reproduce his photograph of John Torrington. CBC television showed a dramatic documentary film about Beattie's research, also called "Frozen in Time," in 1987.

10. Stan Rogers's song "Northwest Passage" provides a haunting refrain in

the film. At the end of Atwood's lecture on Franklin (26), she cites Rogers's song, describes his death, and inscribes the man and his text within her northern myth. The lines from "Northwest Passage" used in the film are as follows:

> Ah, for just one time, I would take the Northwest Passage
> To find the hand of Franklin reaching for the Beaufort Sea
> Tracing one warm line through a land so wide and savage
> And make a Northwest Passage to the sea.

See the compact disc notes for *Stan Rogers Northwest Passage* (Dundas, ON: Fogarty's Cove Music, 1981).

11. Braudy sets forth the characteristics and effects of the "open" and the "closed" film in *The World in a Frame: What We See in Films*. See, in particular, pages 44–65 where he notes that, among other qualities, closed films are voyeuristic, tightly framed and controlled, schematic and self-reflexive, and that they "impose structures of perception" that resolve meanings, often in so-called happy endings.

12. *Surfacing* 166.

13. As Bakhtin explains, reaccentuation of this sort facilitates dialogism at the level of the word or phrase, while the intertextuality of "Frozen in Time" and the doubled narrative of the story operate dialogically at structural levels. Together, these strategies contribute to the "double-voiced discourse" of the text. See Mikhail M. Bakhtin, *Speech Genres and Other Late Essays*, and *Problems of Dostoevsky's Poetics*.

14. "The Revenant," *The Animals in That Country*, 52.

WORKS CITED

Atwood, Margaret. "The Age of Lead." *Wilderness Tips*. Toronto: McClelland & Stewart, 1991. 157–75.

———. *The Animals in That Country*. Toronto: Oxford UP, 1968.

———. *The Journals of Susanna Moodie*. Toronto: Oxford UP, 1970.

———. *The New Oxford Book of Canadian Verse in English*. Toronto: Oxford UP, 1982.

———. *Surfacing*. New York: Simon and Schuster, 1972.

Bakhtin, Mikhail M. *Speech Genres and Other Late Essays*. Trans. Vern W. McGee.

Eds. Caryl Emerson and Michael Holquist. Austin: U of Texas P, 1986. 87–93.

Beattie, Owen, and John Geiger. *Frozen in Time: Unlocking the Secrets of the Franklin Expedition*. Saskatoon: Western Producer Prairie Books, 1987.

Birney, Earl. *Ghost in the Wheels: Selected Poems*. Toronto: McClelland & Stewart, 1962.

Braudy, Leo. *The World in a Frame: What We See in Films*. New York: Anchor Press, 1977.

Emerson, Caryl, ed. and trans. *Problems of Dostoevsky's Poetics*. Minneapolis: U of Minnesota P, 1984. 181–99.

Grace, Sherrill E. "Articulating the 'Space Between': Atwood's Untold Stories and Fresh Beginnings." *Margaret Atwood: Language, Text, and System*. Eds. S. Grace and L. Weir. Vancouver: U of British Columbia P, 1982.

———. "Margaret Atwood and the Poetics of Duplicity." *The Art of Margaret Atwood*. Eds. C. and A. Davidson. Toronto: Anansi, 1981. 55–68.

———. *Violent Duality: A Study of Margaret Atwood*. Montréal: Véhicule Press, 1980.

Ingersoll, Earl G., ed. *Margaret Atwood: Conversations*. Willowdale, ON: Firefly Books, 1990. 17–18.

Glenn Willmott

O Say, Can You See:
The Handmaid's Tale
in Novel and Film

VOLKER SCHLONDORFF'S FILM VERSION of *The Handmaid's Tale* could not easily have opened with the same scene as the novel by Margaret Atwood, which begins with the sentence . . . "We slept in what had once been the gymnasium" (3). Perhaps this sentence seems harmless enough to read, but try to *picture* it. It would be difficult, in film, to convey the tenses at work here in the writing, which offer us an image but take it away again, which offer a time, also, but take it away again. "We slept" is the past tense of a present situation about which we know nothing, and "what had once been" indicates a past that is even more anterior. But the film image has no such conjugations, so that translated to film, an image of mere *sleeping* would convey a wrongly present tense. And it would be difficult to frame this image in the past without giving away something of the present — something the writing does not do.[1] Worse, an image of a *gymnasium*, that place which did not even exist during this *sleeping* but during a time previous to it, would be contradictory; "we slept in what had once been the gymnasium" and is no longer.

Atwood's complex and subtle transformation of this opening space, sustained and developed in the first "Night" chapter, renders a darkness illuminated only by time, or times:

We slept in what had once been the gymnasium. The floor was
of varnished wood, with stripes and circles painted on it, for the
games that were formerly played there; the hoops for the
basketball nets were still in place, though the nets were gone. A
balcony ran around the room, for the spectators, and I thought
I could smell, faintly like an afterimage, the pungent scent of
sweat, shot through with the sweet taint of chewing gum and
perfume from the watching girls, felt-skirted as I knew from
pictures, later in miniskirts, then pants, then in one earring,
spiky green-streaked hair. Dances would have been held there;
the music lingered, a palimpsest of unheard sound, style upon
style, an undercurrent of drums, a forlorn wail, garlands made
of tissue-paper flowers, cardboard devils, a revolving ball of
mirrors, powdering the dancers with a snow of light. (3)

The narrative originates in darkness. The narrator dims or
suppresses physical space from view in order to evoke a temporal
function, a play of time and memory, which is the founding
moment in the narrative. Thus it begins in darkness, in a nighttime which dissolves its own location in ambiguity and un-
nameability. Nothing may clearly be seen. Or what is seen is not
what is actually present, but what is past — all the *afterimages* of
the place. Indeed there are multiple pasts — from felt skirts to
miniskirts to pants to punk — and remembered with these pasts
are *past futures*:

> There was old sex in the room and loneliness, and expectation,
> of something without a shape or name. I remember that yearn-
> ing, for something that was always about to happen and was
> never the same as the hands that were on us there and then, in
> the small of the back, or out back, in the parking lot, or in the
> television room with the sound turned down and only the
> pictures flickering over lifting flesh.

> We yearned for the future. How did we learn it, that talent for
> insatiability? It was in the air; and it was still in the air, an
> afterthought, as we tried to sleep, in the army cots that had been
> set up in rows, with spaces between so we could not talk. (3–4)

The relationship between these pasts and futures is remembered
in sensual romantic terms. Yearning, expectation, desire tie these
times and time relations together. And this "expectation" somehow takes us beyond visual categories, to "something without a
shape or name." In the darkness of night Atwood's narrator,
Offred, perceives a scent that triggers a series of memories,
images, and desires — both her own, and not her own — which
have no final shape or name, and which exist almost as *images of
times* only, that is, of relations in time: yearnings for the future
lodged between the memories and experiences of people and
places that are, that were, and that were no longer what they had
been.

Schlondorff did not open his film of *The Handmaid's Tale* with
this night scene. Faithfulness to the text could have led him to
begin with five minutes of a screen plunged in darkness, with a
voice-over intoning Offred's night thoughts and with, perhaps,
scratch and sniff cards provided to simulate the "sweet taint of
chewing gum." But that would not have been satisfactory realism.
It would only have plunged the film itself into darkness, filling
its absence with the book. Of course, one immediately asserts,
film and novel are different forms of text, like different languages, and translation between them will always be partial and
difficult. But this is so not simply because such media are different forms of language. Rather, I will argue, media are different
forms of power as well — and in a story about power, such as
The Handmaid's Tale, one is concerned about how power will be
communicated in both the medium and its massage.

The formal powers of media are what Marshall McLuhan

wished to illuminate when he told us to dim the lights on the content, for the *medium* is the message — and further, emphasizing the unconscious impact of these powers, the medium is the *massage*. I will demonstrate how this formal power of the medium is able to intersect with its message. *The Handmaid's Tale* is exemplary, for it is a story about power whose message is clearly grounded both in the *presentational* power of its media and in the *representational* power of its narrative events; it is a story in which it is important, before all else and before your very eyes, that the medium be one with the message. Such a demonstration has pedagogical value, I believe, in helping us to grasp the feminist project in Atwood's ironic play with language, and in the politics of form and language generally.

⟪◉　◉⟫

THE FIRST "Night" locates us in a prison-like school where the narrator is trained to be a handmaid. It is the most conspicuously militaristic and oppressive place in the novel — other locations equally, only less conspicuously, so. A barbed-wire fence encloses the centre, armed soldiers patrol the outside, and authorities with cattle-prods patrol the inside, strictly supervising every utterance and gesture. The entire physical space of the school, every inch of every corner, is ordered and controlled — right down to the regulation spacing between army cots designed to limit conversation.

By the light of day this place would resemble a prison, the very image of control, the exercise of power over freedom. But the writing begins not with the image of this prison; it begins at night, when all this space is plunged into darkness — a darkness that allows other images to arise. The present reality of the prison-school persists as an afterimage and mingles with after-images of the same space in other times. In this sense,the space is freed into its own history. Not that the past was necessarily better, but in the darkness the present reconfigures itself according to its pasts, and even recalls the futures of its pasts, the lost or forgotten fantasies, the desires.

At night the training centre also captures an image of the future. It does not have to be what it is. It has been many things in the past; it has been many things wanting to be something else in the future. Only at night, when space and spatial order scatter in the dark, do the images of the centre's history arise, allowing the present to half-dissolve, as the narrator puts it, in an "expectation, of something without a shape or name." Night plunges this place into *possibility*. Night is a time not only of history but of historicity, a time of relative freedom. At least a certain kind of freedom.

It should be evident why Schlondorff could not begin his film with Atwood's night. Not only are her complex time and tense relations so clear in writing but so difficult in film, they are at the heart of her novel's message about freedom and power. In Atwood's opening, time is the *dimension* of freedom. The power of memory and recall — whether the "afterimages" arise out of personal memory or, as the narrator recalls, from exterior media such as photographs — is a kind of temporal power.[2] It is a power of more-than-subjective reflection, which escapes its material condition at that moment. As the story evolves out of "Night," it moves constantly back and forth between this temporal power of the heroine and the spatial powers exerted upon her by her oppressive milieu.

This dialectic is the mainspring of the narrative and is analogous to the actual freedom, and the constraint, of the reader of a novel — who may stop and reflect, think ahead or recall, or even reread, at any time. The reader is always bound within a set of details fixed in place by the written text, a linear series of details of times and places, persons and things and events, sounds and colours and scents. The text is for the reader a spatial "condition," an ineluctable set of givens provided by the reading of pages of the novel. Reading along, we are bound by this unfolding conditionality; we step forward, as it were, from detail to detail, defining and redefining what *is* in the story. But we are also free to stop reading, to dim the lights on the text before us and allow other possibilities to arise, to remember other moments in the text that echo the present. At the margins of reading, the page fills with ghosts, echoes, afterimages, memories, knowledge, desire, and expectation.[3] Only the spatial reality of the written text is fixed as our unavoidable condition. For the novel reader, as for Atwood's narrator, time is the dimension of freedom.[4]

The film, however, reverses this condition of the novel medium. Time is not free in film, but is absolutely conditioned by the medium. If there is any time made for reflection in film, it is precisely that — *made* by the film, not by the reader. As such, time is built-in as another condition, something exactly measured out and unavoidable. If there is any freedom in film-viewing comparable to that in reading, it belongs to the freedom of the eye to travel across, and the freedom to integrate as it will, the space of the film screen. While the novel presents the reading eye with one thing at a time, in linear fashion, film presents the screen-viewing eye with a whole visual field all at once. It is true that the viewer also encounters the film image as a condition, comprising a determined set of details, but there is less constraint upon the visual encounter of these details; there is in film more "room" for interpretation. I will follow the instinct of Roland Barthes and emphasize, as part of the *essence* of film, that aspect of the photographic field which escapes or defies its conditioning as a visual semiotic space, which is beyond it.[5] There is a limited freedom in film space, a freedom in how and what you see.

Schlondorff opens his film with a scene that will return throughout the film as a kind of originary moment proper to his own medium.[6] It is set in daylight, in a forest in winter. The heroine, her husband, and child are trying to escape the Republic of Gilead on foot over a remote snowy border. In a sequence of shots, they trek through the snow, they approach the border, they are seen by the border patrol, the husband is killed, and the heroine and her child become separated. A final image of the child, isolated in the snowscape and bewildered by loss, will recur in the film. So the film begins with the most conspicuously free moment in the story, the moment when the as-yet-uncaptured, unsundered family is about to escape. This moment is most conspicuous because it is the most visual, the most obviously spatial and thus spectacular. If space is the main "dimension" of freedom in film, then landscape — which is simply unbounded, outer, physical reality — can provide a kind of filmic equivalent to the temporal *night* in the novel. Instead of dimming the lights on space in order to open up moments of free time, as a novel may do, the film landscape must extend, slow down, or even arrest time in order to open up a spatial dimension of freedom.

Of course a film cannot really arrest time, any more than a novel can throw reality into darkness. But film can manipulate space to divert or multiply or ambiguate time. And in so doing film can open up spaces for things to be other than what they are, calling up for the viewer the afterimages and echoes of things, equivalent to the afterimages called up for the reader when free of the conditions of novelistic space. Schlondorff's film begins in an isolated, snowy wilderness. This location appears as a margin of nature apart from civilization — that is, on the margins of human space, of articulated or controlled space, thus on the margins of human power.[7] We soon learn that this margin lies between different civilizations, or at least the possibility of different civilizations. The fact of winter in film suggests this marginality and possibility; the striking visual appearance of bright, white snow making up so much of the physical landscape conveys a blankness in space, a visual equivalent of the "something without a shape or name" that will grow out of it, or from under it, or from just beyond it. This sense of possibility or desire gives meaning to the image of the child in the field of snow recurring in the film, and explains why, moreover, the final images of the film are those of the protagonist herself, somewhat in the place of that child, located in a wild, whited-out landscape. The image represents to the film-viewer a margin of freedom from her condition. Snowscape is one visual extremity in the narrative dialectic of freedom and constraint. We never see winter in Gilead.

Even so, in neither film nor novel does the heroine absolutely escape, for to escape *from*, one must be able to escape *to*. The last sentence of the novel, for example, returns the reader to the original night on the free margins of her condition, which is figured by the open, black-hued vehicle of what might be the Mayday underground: "And so I step up, into the darkness within; or else the light" (295). The last image of the film returns the viewer to the original landscape of wilderness and snow, which not only symbolizes a kind of freedom, but also looks free in a way particular to the spatial dimension of film. For the viewer is abandoned there, with the heroine, as the watcher of a kind of bright, vivid space of "not yet" — which is the same great body of unformed future possibility as herself, or as the child. From all the potentialities of this final space, the viewer must exit his or her own darkened theatre into the daylight of actual conditions.

☙ ❧

THERE ARE many other signs of freedom in the story, however limited or fenced-off from one another: the Scrabble game, the romance with Nick, the energy of Moira, the transgressive memories valued by the Commander and the heroine, the Mayday resistance and, of course, the telling of the story itself. The story clearly emphasizes certain kinds of power and constraint associated with a sexual politics: the conditions imposed by the state of Gilead in its ordering everyone into categories of sexual being (wives, Handmaids, husbands, rapists, homosexuals, heterosexuals, prostitutes, or whatever) and its enforcement of strict sexual and social roles, codes of behaviour, and ethics for them. The dimension of space to be considered here is not so much geographical — the freedom to escape Gilead for another part of the world — but bodily. The terrain of sexuality, when struggled over by an individual, another person or group, a culture or a state, is not in a general, actual, or possible place, but in a general, actual, or possible body.

In Atwood's novel, the body represents the space of sexuality in ways that we expect to play upon the time and space of the novelistic medium. The body is constructed and disintegrated and reconstructed in the linear flow of the written narrative. It is never grasped except in this piecemeal way by the reader, who has the freedom to remember the body as another kind of afterimage of the text (and not in any old way, for this freedom is linked to a responsibility, both to memory and to the text as ineluctable sets of conditions which ground the reader's remembrances). It is perfectly clear how the body is surveyed and controlled by a cultural and state power in Gilead: the symbolic clothing; the ritualized system of social as well as sexual intercourse; the confinement to territorial assignments, and to institutions, houses, and rooms; the prescribed diets; and, of course, the entire factory-like regulation of pleasure and reproduction. The narrative shows how the body is taken apart into fragments according to fertility, sexuality, age, or whatever, and controlled and monitored in each fragment; a kind of categorical dismemberment.[8] But the narrative also allows the body to be remembered by the reader as the space across which certain desires and possibilities still can play. For instance, the ambiguity of bodily expression in the Commander, when he first states his desire to the Handmaid:

> "I would like — " he says. "This will sound silly." And he does
> look embarrassed, *sheepish* was the word, the way men used to

look once. He's old enough to remember how to look that way,
and to remember also how appealing women once found it. The
young ones don't know those tricks. They've never had to use
them. (138)

We sense, with the Handmaid, that the Commander really is
embarrassed by his desire, yet also knows his bodily expression
of embarrassment will help him attain his desire. Instinctive
feeling is mixed with deliberate memory. His desire causes him
to "remember" how to be sheepish, and in so doing his body is
slightly unhinged in time — simultaneously a present and a past
thing, expressive in the present of a desire patterned in the past.
By this gesture, two signs of possibility are opened up — two
significations of freedom in the space of the body. First, the
Commander's bodily play momentarily escapes the Gileadic
body condition: he has no reason to make a sheepish gesture, for
he, just like the "young ones," no longer needs to use it. The
gesture does not signify in Gilead. Rather it signifies a desire in
the body language of another time, a past or perhaps future time
which is allowed briefly to inhabit the body of the present. And
this is as much a sign of his power, the power of a master to bend
his own rules in his favour, as it is a sign of his weakness. For the
gesture is not entirely voluntary. Nor is it entirely successful: the
Handmaid is by virtue of *her* present body free of certain conditions of the old body language. She does not say that his half-
ironic sheepishness is appealing, but that that is how "women
once found it." The anachronism does not carry its full power
over her. But her bodily reaction to his desire takes a turn as he
fully reveals his desire:

> "I'd like you to play a game of Scrabble with me," he says.
>
> I hold myself absolutely rigid. I keep my face unmoving. So
> that's what's in the forbidden room! Scrabble! I want to laugh,
> shriek with laughter, fall off my chair. (138)

She wants to laugh because the sheepishness suddenly has a present, rather than a past, referent. It now makes a kind of sense. But the laughter comes from her past body, a body that was remembering its fears and expectations in another existence. For Scrabble would have been funny in the past. It is not funny in the present, which is why she holds her body rigid. She, too, is bodily doubled or unhinged. Her own remembrances at this juncture are revealing:

> This was once the game of old women, old men, in the summers or in retirement villas, to be played when there was nothing good on television. Or of adolescents, once, long long ago. My mother had a set, kept at the back of the hall cupboard, with the Christmas tree decorations in their cardboard boxes. Once she tried to interest me in it, when I was thirteen and miserable and at loose ends. (138)

All this seems innocent enough, just a series of past associations. But there are some uncanny echoes. Scrabble was a game for old women and old men, like the Commander. It was a game for when there was "nothing good on television" — as ever in Gilead — and for "when I was thirteen and miserable and at loose ends." This last is a very specific memory, particular to her age, her sex, her modernity, and to herself as an individual. But it resonates in a defamiliarizing way with the mood of the Commander, whose desperation for the pleasures of Scrabble reveals a similar adolescent restlessness — if not also, at some deeper, unacknowledged level, a similar adolescent misery. Certainly this adolescence is behind his sheepishness and other social games which, however wily, seem to arise out of the simplicity of a childishly lording manipulativeness and an insensible naïveté. The Handmaid's first physical description of him combines these features, in another unhinging or multiple imaging of his visible, sexual body:

> The Commander is standing in front of the fireless fireplace,
> back to it, one elbow on the carved wooden overmantel, other
> hand in his pocket. It's such a studied pose, something of the
> country squire, some old come-on from a glossy men's mag. He
> probably decided ahead of time that he'd be standing like that
> when I came in. When I knocked he probably rushed over to the
> fireplace and propped himself up. He should have a black patch,
> over one eye, a cravat with horseshoes on it. (137)

The adolescent doubleness of this man combines with his unhap-
piness and his being at "loose ends" to resonate uncannily with
her own remembrances. This is the second signification of freedom in his physical bearing. In this uncanny moment over the
Scrabble board, these two individuals, otherwise so different in
Gileadic terms, attain a shared possibility. In the novel he is
clearly her equal in Scrabble and in the larger games they play
(though he is a more harmful player). But in the space of the body
and its memories and desires, they share a possibility — not love
or sensuality, of course, but a certain experience of inner dissat-
isfaction that inhabits their desires and bodily life and that tran-
scends the conditions of their Gileadic space. That shared
possibility, which never converges in the story except during the
Scrabble games, is the heart of their physical relationship.

This after-imaging or multiple-imaging of the body, its undoing into possibility, its historicization in the temporal medium of
the novel, may be considered an undoing of the "image" itself as
the ground for what I will call, following Jeanne Campbell
Reesman's borrowing from the American philosopher Richard
Rorty, an "ocular" form of knowledge. This is the traditional
"mirror of nature" epistemology which tells us that truth comes
in objective forms, standing apart from us, and may be mirrored
by appropriate images. The sign as image thereby effects an
ideological closure, an adequacy to itself, which I would extend
to mean that, in erasing its human and dialogic production, its

making and unmaking, its possibility, it is reified. The undoing or historicizing of images I have described above for the gendered body is congruent with Reesman's claim that Atwood in *The Handmaid's Tale* "resists the certainties of an ocular epistemology in favor of a conversational, hermeneutic model of knowledge," which is "open to the give-and-take of an ongoing dialogic relationship."[9] Reesman's "conversational" epistemology is concerned, as am I herein, with freedom from conditions of constraint imposed by the visualization of spatial objecthood: its "moral theme," she tells us, is "how human beings damage each other when they 'see' each other as objects to be manipulated in the service of interested designs."[10] The critical power of Atwood's Scrabble scenes lies in the ironic way in which the two players "see" each other, as pastiches, as palimpsests, as ghosts — as only partial objects.

Ironically, such an ocular epistemology seems to have led one critic to prefer the film version to the book. Quoting Atwood's detailed and defamiliarized description of a nightclub costume — a "Playboy Bunny" outfit of which the narrator has forgotten the name and function — Cynthia Baughman complains: "Of course, we are screaming 'Playboy Bunnies!' long before this passage ends, and such coyness abounds in Offred's reminiscences and social commentary. It's contrived; it's a set-up; the insights are predictable."[11] This reader sees the image and has done with it, finds closure in providing its (predictable) name. He or she may solve an "ocular" epistemological riddle, then, but not the historical or existential one: the question of how to "see" the multiple image of the body, here an assembled costume, an accumulation of masks with different grounds of meaning observed by the narrator — the erotics of nudity, the theatrics of musical comedy, the pageantry of Easter holiday, the otherness of wilderness animals — its ambivalences and possibilities as a set-up, as a made thing. The question is not what she has been forced to become, but *out of what* she has been forced to become what she appears to be, and *out of what* she might become something else — the contradictions of her freedom and constraint.

Of course, ocular epistemology belongs inescapably to cinema, and if it is to be challenged in the film of *The Handmaid's Tale* by a "conversational" form, this form must be entirely redescribed apart from the medium of the word and its temporal media. It is easy to see that Schlondorff's film could not represent the body as the kind of integrated space of remembrances and desires allowed in the writing of a novel, in which the body attains this temporal dimension of freedom. The Commander in the film, when he is sheepish, is sheepish without ambiguity — in the present tense of the visible body. The viewer does not see the ghosts and echoes that transcend and haunt the condition of his physical reality. Margins of freedom in narrative film must rely not on temporal but on spatial ambiguity, as I have suggested above. It is difficult to do this without awkward flashbacks, and the recurring image of the child is one attempt to multiply the space of the body in an ambiguous way — not so much as a symbol of love and loss (a cliché which it unfortunately resembles), but as a marker of survival and chance, a physical loose end that challenges the rest of the ordering of space on-screen. But with this exception, the episodic flashback structure of the novel — the entire night/day, reflection/action organization — is absent from the film. Baughman has called these eliminations of voice and memory, even as they are linked to a similarly eliminated female subjectivity, "unlamentable" — since "the film's subtle visual juxtaposition of the familiar and the futuristic is much more disarming."[12] For example, she says, "The Wife and Commander live in an upper-middle class suburb which is as familiar as the concrete barriers and soldiers who guard their driveway. What jars us is seeing the Colonial and the arsenal in the same frame: San Salvador meets Scarsdale."[13] Here she illuminates a spatial unhinging or undoing of the image that filmically takes over from the temporal one in the novel, but she cannot avoid the reification of the ocular, which represents no historicity or human agency in the undoing, hence no margin of freedom: the conversational ideal of dialogic knowledge is rendered in ocular terms as visual juxtaposition, but as such it remains no one's work, no one's writing or making, and the female subjectivity, which articulates the possibility, the future of the body, remains mute. The narrative so constructed is indeed more "disarming," because it is more totalitarian, more hopelessly dystopian. And my own earlier example of filmic white space as a translation of the temporal night suffers from the same closure of the image, as its signification depends upon the marginality of the referential image itself as this approaches mere white light. [14] If there is a "conversational" form of representation to be found in a stubbornly "ocular" cinema, it must resist the closure of the reified image, and insist upon the human work and relations of its always partial and "dialogic" construction.

Just so, I believe, there is at least one realization in this paradoxical form of the relatively freed, multiple body of Atwood's story. This is produced out of the representation of video and television newscasts within the film. The video screen intrudes several times upon the space of the film; it is one kind of screen within another, a screen within a screen. Focusing on people and faces, as the compactness of video dictates, this screen is dominated either by gospel entertainment or newscasts of the wars. If Schlondorff's aim had been merely to display to us that Gilead was at war — let us say to suggest that its totalitarian order was founded upon an ongoing and violent military project — then it would have sufficed for him simply to display this actual space of war in the film image, without the mediation of video screens. We would have seen how the reality of Gilead extended from the experience of the heroine in the home to the experience of others in the war, in one continuous space (in the manner of conjoining San Salvador to Scarsdale). But with the mediation of video, this other reality of war is intercepted and packaged. It is not simply continuous with the physical space of the film, but is framed and produced as an artificial reality. Not "artificial" because unreal, but because deliberately constructed or made.

An example will demonstrate the de-reifying and after-imaging effect of this use of one kind of screen within another. In a scene invented for the film, the Commander's face appears on television for an interview. It occurs very near the end of the narrative, just before the film space returns to the snowy wilderness landscape in which it began; as such it is a last view of Gilead, of the physical space of Gilead and the condition of its categorical body. Now, the viewer knew all along that the Commander was one of those persons running the war. But Schlondorff saves the visual presence of the Commander at war, and on television, for the end — and it conveys an estranging effect. Not only does he appear as a "talking head" — only the face shown in the typical frontal pose of a television interview — but his manner is strangely plastic or superficial, making him look a little unreal, not himself. And this look is not strange to television news. Indeed he is a perfect television personality; he has taken on a role that is neatly adapted to the television space that surrounds him — a kind of Television Commander. If he looks not quite "himself" as this Television Commander, it is not because he fails to be true to what we know of his personality or ideology — which is after all that of a type, the Commander — but because it is not true to how we have seen him in the space of the film.

Television and its physical space have an unreality inside film because its contextual space is only the reality of film.[15] In watching film we have already suspended our disbelief once; we "believe" in film space. We cannot suspend disbelief on two different hooks at the same time. We may tune out our living room to watch the TV placed within it, but we do not tune out a film to watch the TV placed within *it*. Our senses commit themselves to the unreality of film. Video space cannot help but appear stripped of the disbelief with which we would normally invest it. Which means that video will not appear as a simple extension of the space represented by the film, but as a very different kind of space. It appears as the artificial space of a medium fabricated within the space of the film. It plays upon or against the naturalness of film, or what our senses accept as natural in film space. It can unhinge the space of the film, as it does the body of the Commander, opening it up to possibilities inherent in its own artifice, its own quality of being made. "What I must present is a made thing," Atwood's heroine says in summoning her own powers of artifice, "not something born" (66).

The Television Commander is the filmic translation of these artificial conditions. He speaks for the physical body of Gilead in our last view of it, "naked" of the naturalness that was supposed for it by the filmic space of the story, and revealed as a set of conditions in a frame within a frame. It is not the artifice or conditionality of video, film or whatever reality that is oppressive in the way Gilead is oppressive; rather it is the patriarchal imposition of this artifice as the individual and social *nature* of others. This is the secret to the strange effect of the new body of the Commander on television. It disturbs us that he is the same on television as in the reality supposed by the film, because our senses cannot accept the continuity of the two media spaces as real. His conceit is that television reality and natural reality should be the same. But our sense of who the Commander is, and more generally of what his reality is, of the reality he attempts to father, is unhinged by the unacceptability of the naturalness of television.

The identity of the Commander is thus freed for the viewer from its own physical conditions. He is a made thing, just like the Handmaid; he inhabits possibility as much as he inhabits the conditions imposed upon him. Unlike the heroine, however, he seems to tell us: "What I must present is something born, not a made thing." He is freely self-imprisoned.

The heroine's voice-over is also saved for the end of the film, following the television sequence, where it is now clear that her part of the filmic body, herself constructed in the medium, is free to tell its differently engendered story. Free to say: "What has come before is something made, something I have made, a *story*."[16] As in the novel, the signification of power hinges on a defamiliarization effect structural to the medium, as the reconstruction and remembering of the self produces a fragile new image of the possibilities and constraints, the loves and oppressions, locked inside its present and reified form. As Atwood has said: "You have to come to terms with the fact that you are not your image."[17]

（（（Ｃ　Ｏ）））

THE HANDMAID'S TALE is about masculinist power, which means it is about certain conditions that are imposed by an exercise of power, and about the margin of freedom (narrower for women than for men) that might exist amid those conditions. In any story with a message about power — sexual, political, or individual — there must also be a story about the power of its medium — oral, written, TV, film, or whatever. For these two kinds of power, the power that is the message of the story, and the power of this message to register upon the captured and organized senses of its audience, will appear inseparable to an artist concerned with the power to communicate.

Atwood uses the temporality particular to the novel medium to free the reader from an ocular form of knowledge in which historical possibility stands outside us in an "image of things to come." In learning to say what we see, and to undo what we see in the saying — to undo it as fate — we take the first step in a historical "conversation," as a dialogic work in social knowledge or as a dialectical work in social existence, that will deconstruct a present masculinist order. In this sense, Atwood's *The Handmaid's Tale* is an important story about writing and the exchange of stories, words, and wordiness itself in the medium of the romance novel.

The translation of the novel to film empties it of the "conversational" form constructed in its temporal dimension of freedom. What we see is what we get, the visible surface of the novel, its reification into traditional romance and dystopian science fiction genres. In order, then, to reconstruct a "conversational" form in the spatial dimension of film, a sort of subplot about the film medium, its image and screen, must also be translated. This Schlondorff is able only minimally to do as a *motif* of the double screen, a sort of lyric image removed from the logic, the motivation, the represented historicity of both romance and totalitarian narratives.

Defining the demands of *The Handmaid's Tale* in different media illuminates the premise hidden in Marshall McLuhan's assertion that the medium is the message: the "message" of a medium may be considered a particular form of power, a certain imposition of conditionality and freedom.[18] This power is not a simple, self-identical thing that flows through nature like Newtonian force or through society like economic domination. Rather, power is fundamentally different in different media, hence in different times and places. It is particular to its situation. To understand power — which is something we want to understand if we concern ourselves with questions of human welfare or oppression, of human limitation or creativity — we should say that no particular power is the metaphysical key to power in general, just as no freedom is the key to freedom in general. "There is more than one kind of freedom," Atwood's Aunt Lydia tells us. "In the days of anarchy, it was freedom to. Now you are being given freedom from. Don't underrate it" (24). Of course "freedom from" should not be underrated. But must one freedom, as she suggests, replace all others? Does that not end politics in a reified image of freedom, an "ocular" totalitarianism? In Gilead, alternative powers or freedoms are coded subordinate, irrelevant or illegal. Aunt Lydia, Atwood notes, "was in love with either/or" (8). Whatever form the story comes in, *The Handmaid's Tale* must convey the disenchantment with this either/or, and enmesh the reader or viewer in the conflict of conditions and freedoms available to the presentational media in which their representational narratives unfold, and so into dialogue with the images around them. You are not your image, Atwood is saying: you were your image.

NOTES

1. It may be objected that the simple past tense is a convention of realist narrative fiction and has no represented present. But *The Handmaid's Tale* shifts to a present tense and represented present at its very end, in the appended Historical Notes, so that the past tense narrative functions triply as a represented past (of the Nunavit future), as a represented present (of the telling, or of Gilead), and as a represented future (for which our own present is the stuff of the narrator's memory).

2. Sarah Murphy discusses the reduction of free space to the "inner space of memory and desire" in merely "free time" (43).

3. This condition of freedom in reading, the structured experience of temporal reflection, has its radical possibilities forced upon the reader by the framing of Offred's entire story in the context of the appended "Historical Notes." This is implied in Patrick D. Murphy's claim that the pseudo-documentary framing of the written narrative (as a diary recording discussed in the context of an academic conference) serves to displace the reader's reception of its flow of details and images from unconscious sublimation (as belonging to another, a fantasy alterity) into cognition (as belonging to oneself, a present crisis), as the frame and its contents superimpose their images and authority upon each other — producing the experience of reflections in the margin I have described. This present-minded "cognition," produced between the frame and its personal narrative, is considered essential by Arnold E. Davidson, who argues that such a cognition forces metahistorical thinking about the patriarchal

telling or "making" of history-making itself (a thesis corresponding to my own). This frame is absent from the film version of the tale.

4. Atwood herself has insisted that "novels are about time and about what happens to you when you are living, how you use your time," and "about change, living in time." She has also affirmed that *The Handmaid's Tale* is "organized partly by the repeated 'Night' sections. . . . periods of action, punctuated by periods of reflection" (*Conversations* 223, 203).

5. Barthes 63–64.

6. Because my discussion of the film will emphasize the story's translation into visual space and spatial relations, I will refer to its (actually collective) author as Volker Schlondorff throughout this essay. Of equal interest, however, is the screenplay authored by Harold Pinter. Pinter is known for a minimalist style in which, as Atwood has put it, referring prospectively to its appropriateness for *The Handmaid's Tale*, "people don't say very much, but convey meaning anyway" (*Conversations* 217). A sparse translation curiously appealed to Atwood, perhaps as a style that might open up dramatic "space" for reflection corresponding to her night/day, reflection/action written structure; so she was quite enthusiastic about Pinter's involvement (*Conversations* 217, 232; Johnson 43). Unfortunately, however, Pinter seems to have been attracted more to the totalitarian side of the narrative, to the Foucauldian vision of constraint without the writerly rendering of freedom. In speaking of the novel's significance, he regularly emphasized its attention to "these authoritarian regimes that are not only around the corner but with us now, in fundamentalism of all kinds," rather than its articulations of possible escape (qtd. in Chase 16, similarly Johnson 45). The romance narrative disappears. And this is consistent with Pinter's preoccupation, as Joanne Klein has shown us in her study of his screenplays, with "figures who inhabit a world both outside of and condemned by time": "His worlds become sealed systems; intrusion becomes an impossible dream. Condemned to an interminable, impregnable monotony, the characters now invent and define their own oppositions. These illusions fail, however, just as the earlier illusions of security failed, when they are tested against

the phenomenal world. The attempt to inscribe the controls of fiction on the mysteries of experience is never successful in Pinter's work" (195). But this is exactly contrary to the writing of *The Handmaid's Tale*, whose form and concerns Atwood identifies *in* time and empowers by a dialectic between fiction and reality, between fiction and history. Atwood's response to having seen Pinter's translation on film remains unrecorded; but for the next film production, of the novel *Cat's Eye*, she has entrusted the screenplay to herself (Johnson 43).

7. Though the film received generally poor reviews, the *Times Literary Supplement* praised these opening scenes, "shot with an icy sweeping clarity" to "superbly [evoke] the moments just after the final calamity, the chaos and the stunned hush of the zero hour, the deracinated despair of the exile." As soon as the film moves away from this temporal and spatial margin, to be enclosed within the spectacle of Gilead, the film loses interest (Clute 1181).

8. Stephanie Barbé Hammer argues that Gilead is a Foucauldian Panopticon, in which the individual and social body are subjected to oppressive constraints regulated through their spatial visibility (45). The form of knowledge Reesman identifies as "ocular," therefore, should be understood to be grounded not only in a genre of metaphoric discourse, with epistemological consequences, but in a technology of power with existential consequences.

9. Reesman 8.

10. Ibid 8.

11. Baughman 95.

12. Ibid 95.

13. Ibid 94.

14. An example of the disappearing referent is the full-scale replica of the Berlin Wall, which Schlondorff had built for his opening scene in the mountains of North Carolina. This totalitarian wall, a symbolic backdrop to Offred's escape, became nearly invisible on film, as it was whited out — and Schlondorff was content to leave it as such — by a blizzard (Johnson 44).

15. This may suggest why the television image has been so effectively used as an element of the contemporary horror film.

16. But the effect produced by this voice is rather too long in coming. In fact reviewers found Schlondorff's visualization of *The Handmaid's Tale* (consistent with Pinter's adaption to film dialogue) so wedded to the totalitarian depiction that (with the exceptions, perhaps, that I have noted) its film images seem utterly drained of human will, emotion, conflict, or reciprocity. Freedom and empowerment are evidently eclipsed in a film that *Rolling Stone* and *Variety* each likened, for example, to *The Stepford Wives* (36, 32). One might suspect some masculinist distortion of values in this totalitarian overdetermination, drained of its heroine's reflections. "What is this? A feminist Orwell? That's the last thing I want to be in," said Aidan Quinn, when first approached for the part of the heroine's lover (Johnson 43). But "Orwell is much more optimistic than people give him credit for," says Atwood, noting that he provides — as she does — a text at the end of his dystopian story to frame it within an alternative, if ambivalent, non-dystopian context (*Conversations* 217).

17. Quoted in Kellman C5.

18. The medium, such as the romance novel or the feature film, is itself subject to a certain imposition of conditionality and freedom, in the "medium" of its historical society. It is interesting, in this regard, that the film of *The Handmaid's Tale* was much better received in East Berlin than in West Berlin, or in the West generally (Johnson 45).

WORKS CITED

Atwood, Margaret. *Margaret Atwood: Conversations*. Ed. Earl G. Ingersoll. Princeton, NJ: Ontario Review Press, 1990.

———. *The Handmaid's Tale*. Boston: Houghton Mifflin Co., 1986.

Barthes, Roland. "The Third Meaning: Research Notes on Some Eisenstein Stills." *Image-Music-Text*. Trans. Stephen Heath. New York: Hill and Wang, 1977.

Baughman, Cynthia. Review of *The Handmaid's Tale* (film). *The Pinter Review*. 1990: 92–96.

Chase, Donald. "The Pinter Principle." *American Film* 15.13 (October 1990): 16 (1).

Clute, John. Review of *The Handmaid's Tale* (film). *Times Literary Supplement* 4570 (November 2, 1990): 1181 (1).

Davidson, Arnold E. "Future Tense: Making History in *The Handmaid's Tale.*" *Margaret Atwood: Vision and Forms.* Eds. KathrynVan Spanckeren and Jan Garden Castro. Carbondale and Edwardsville: Southern Illinois UP, 1988. 113–21.

Hammer, Stephanie Barbé. "The World as It Will Be? Female Satire and the Technology of Power in *The Handmaid's Tale.*" *Modern Language Studies* 20.2 (1990): 39–49.

Howells, Coral Ann. "Free-dom, Telling, Dignidad: Margaret Laurence, 'A Gourdful of Glory,' Margaret Atwood, *The Handmaid's Tale*, Sarah Murphy, *The Measure of Miranda.*" *Commonwealth Essays and Studies* 12.1 (1989): 39–46.

Johnson, Brian D. "Returning to a New Berlin: Margaret Atwood Revisits the Wall." *Maclean's* 103.9 (February 26, 1990): 44 (2).

——— "Uphill Battle: *Handmaid's* Hard Times." *Maclean's* 103.9 (February 26, 1990): 43 (1).

Kellman, Steven G. "Atwood scoffs at sexual stereotypes, happy endings." *San Antonio Light.* February 16, 1987: C5 (1).

Klein, Joanne. *Making Pictures: The Pinter Screenplays.* Columbus: Ohio State UP, 1985.

Murphy, Patrick D. "Reducing the Dystopian Distance: Pseudo-Documentary Framing in Near-Future Fiction." *Science-Fiction Studies* 17.1 (1990): 25–40.

Reesman, Jeanne Campbell. "Dark Knowledge in *The Handmaid's Tale.*" *CEA Critic* 53.3 (1991): 6–22.

Travers, Peter. Review of *The Handmaid's Tale* (film). *Rolling Stone.* March 22, 1990: 36 (1).

Variety. Review of *The Handmaid's Tale* (film). February 14, 1990 (338.6): 32 (1).

Molly Hite

An Eye for an I:
The Disciplinary Society
in *Cat's Eye*[1]

LIKE *BODILY HARM* AND *The Handmaid's Tale*, *Cat's Eye* is set in an extreme environment, where the central concern is not merely some aspect of well-being, but survival. As in *Bodily Harm*, especially, issues of survival are mapped onto a number of ontological levels, ranging from individual physical bodies to specific ethnic- or gender-based communities to national states. The death of Elaine's brother, Stephen, at the hands of terrorists, in many respects the climactic event in the discursive structure of the novel, replays the gender-enforcing torture of the nine-year-old Elaine at the hands of her purported friends — a torture that leads at one point to their abandoning her to die and at another point to her attempted suicide. The recurrence of such incidents on different strata of the fictional universe underscores the political implications of conventionally personal events.

This environment of extremity incorporates a sense of radical contingency that increasingly characterizes Atwood's global vision. In *Bodily Harm*, people hurt other people "because they can," "because they can get away with things" ; in *The Handmaid's Tale*, Offred's story is about the mechanisms of successful oppression, "about who can do what to whom and be forgiven for it." In both these novels, the motives for malignancy are far more systemic than individual. People are manipulated, mutilated, and

killed because they occupy certain positions in the overall structure, due largely to accidental factors rather than to anything they
have done. The question of deserving, and indeed any personal
ethics of consequences, is radically reconfigured in this sort of
political reality. There are oppressors and there is evil, but
individual justice, especially the leveling of scores implied in the
Hammurabic prescription of an eye for an eye, is largely inappli-
cable as a concept.

In *Cat's Eye*, Stephen is killed because he is a representative of
the white, Western, male oppressor class, although as an abstract
and abstracted physicist he seems singularly detached from any
individual acts of oppression. In fact, he is so removed from
human concerns that he does not seem to regard himself as
vulnerable to any sort of attack and views himself as unassailable
for exactly the reason he is finally killed: as Elaine suggests
earlier, "He thinks he is safe, because he is what he says he is"
(310). Similarly, Elaine is a surrogate victim, representative of
the category "girl" and thus a stand-in for the other girls, who
use her as a scapegoat in order to displace their own suffering
as members of a patriarchy, here literalized in the authority
of their own fathers. Carol's whip marks reinforce the message
that fathers have "real, unspeakable power" (176), power that
Cordelia attempts to appropriate for herself by applying to
Elaine her own father's expressions of contempt, "Wipe that
smirk off your face!" and "What do you have to say for yourself?"
(124, 271). Elaine realizes later that Cordelia, unlike her Shake-
spearean namesake, will never please this father "because she is
somehow the wrong person" (268), but it takes her years to put
together the corollary, that she herself was nearly sacrificed as a
proxy "wrong person" in the symbolic economy of the little girls.

As a result of her experience as victim of this displaced
oppression, Elaine turns away from the ghettoized lives of girls
and women and toward the largely separate sphere of the masculine, which she apprehends as a relatively safe haven from

female machinations. She sides first with the fathers of the neighbourhood, then with the boys in her high school, then, as an art student, she arrives at an idealized image of "men" that reproduces the marks of paternal power and comes to life in the person of Josef Hrbik and his "experienced mauve bedroom" (297, 317). Finally Elaine reaches a tentative resting point with her caretaking second husband, parodically described in terms of 1950s fantasies about male protection (403).

This turn, however, also represents a deeply unsatisfying complicity with masculinist institutions that at points amounts to misogyny, prompted by an overwhelming fear that women "know too much, they can neither be deceived nor trusted" (400). In a reactive newspaper interview arranged in conjunction with the retrospective exhibition of Elaine's paintings (and reminiscent of several interviews of Atwood herself), she lashes out at the categories in which the young female interviewer attempts to contain her, finally maintaining that gender has nothing to do with either her work or its reception, although she also notes, "I am on dubious ground, and this enrages me" (95). The interview suggests what aspects of conventionally female (and mass-media feminist) identity Elaine finds constricting and threatening, and in ways amounts to an etiology of an apparently antifeminist public stance. It is a public stance that is also complicated and undermined by many factors in her retrospective account of her life — for instance, she later narrates a version of the scenario she repudiates during the interview, "Male art teachers pinching your bum, calling you *baby*, asking you why there are no great female painters, that sort of thing" (94), when she describes her near-simultaneous initiation into life drawing and sexuality (287–327) — and in particular by the descriptions of her paintings, which appear both to document and to apotheosize the female universe she still imaginatively inhabits.

Perhaps more than any other Atwood novel, *Cat's Eye* is preoccupied with detail, with a proliferation of social and cultural observations about the postwar era that, like Elaine's initial paintings of the domestic objects of her childhood, are "suffused with anxiety" (357). As these details amass, they reinforce the imputation that growing up female, even growing up as a white, middle-class female in a relatively prosperous North American country, is different only in degree from living in a police state. *The Handmaid's Tale* was built on the observation that the implications of culturally constructed femininity, even femininity as constructed by a relatively liberal society, can be used in extremity to justify organizing women into slave casts based on various roles retroactively attributed to biology. *Cat's Eye* shows the more subtle means by which the relatively liberal society both marginalizes middle-class girls as a group and individualizes each girl, making her responsible for her own marginalization.

Furthermore, the *Künstlerroman* account of the making of an artist in this novel makes the whole idea of art problematic by making art one outcome of the process of socialization that ensures the subordination of women. Elaine manages to detach herself, albeit only to a degree, from the category of "women" by substituting an abstracted, observing eye for an engaged, interdependent I. That is, she achieves a quantum of power by self-division or self-synecdoche, and *Cat's Eye* illustrates how such a mutilation is a precondition of agency in a society that maintains its identities through a rigorous separation of seeing from being seen.

This separation is at the heart of the postwar definitions of masculinity and femininity as they are depicted in this novel. "Look" is always a pun, conveying at once the gaze that judges and the process of *being* gazed at and judged, as in "How do I look?" — or as in "I look like Haggis McBaggis," "I look like the Witch of Endor," or "I'd look like an old biddy" (76, 91, 36, 19). In these instances, to be object of the look is to look *like*, the trope of simile instantly invoking stereotypes of women who have aged past the point of being rewarding to the acquisitive gaze. Women look like, while in general men only look — unless of course they are less than men, "fruity clothes horses," in Stephen's "devastating" appraisal (230). In many respects, this distinction conditions the whole gender-segregated urban landscape of the novel's 1950s, defining the female episteme in terms of the arcana of twin sets and cold waves, and locating in the shameful invisibility of female underwear a correlative to the displayed male wound (81). For women, to be seen is both to have an identity and to be identified as vulnerable: both a requirement and a stigma. Fundamental to this definition is the premise that the female object of the look is also somehow guilty of it and thus susceptible as a consequence of her own instigation, a premise that lies behind the possibility of "making a spectacle of yourself" — "as if there's something wrong in the mere act of being looked at," Elaine reflects (176) — and leads to deep unease among the girls when another girl is found "molested" and murdered in a ravine: "It's as if this girl has done something shameful, herself, by being murdered" (260). The prime female responsibility is to control the look so that it will not kill.

"Look at yourself!" Cordelia demands, handing Elaine a mirror (169), and Elaine learns to internalize the condemnatory gaze without discerning the means to "improve" herself that will remove her from the range of such judgements. Of course, the goal of improvement is part of the mechanism of condemnation and as such is unrealizable. Yet most of the women of *Cat's Eye* are obsessed with controlling how they look, with contriving all their appearances "on purpose." The adult Elaine still harbours a (not uncommon) desire to anticipate the impossible view of herself from behind (46, 314, 153). And when Cordelia falls in the snow by accident rather than by design, she needs immediately to displace onto Elaine her shame at being caught in an inadvertency and for this reason initiates an act of savage humiliation that verges on a murder attempt, demanding that Elaine go into the ravine and onto the ice of the creek to retrieve her hat, and then leaving her there (199–200). Cordelia tries, in other words, to reverse the direction of the gaze and thus the threat of attack, a tactic that she and Elaine use later as teenagers when they "outstare" strangers on the bus (4). But the tactic has only limited efficacy because it is combined with a continued concern to control an appearance that is still female, to combine the dominating gaze with an awareness of being fashionably "cool" and "[u]ltrasharp" (118). The pose begins to crumble as Cordelia succumbs to her socialization and follows up her performance of "overly bright" chatter with the anxiously jokey question "But that's enough about me. What do *you* think of me?" (273).

Elaine succeeds much better in reversing the direction of the gaze, but only by denying her inclusion in the category "women." The discovery that "boys are my allies" (175) leads her to fantasize that boys do not view her in the same way as they view other girls, that she can "walk in the spaces between" the "silent words surrounding [other girls], *stunned broad, dog, bag,* and *bitch*, pointing at them, reducing them, cutting them down to size so they can be handled" (255). Later, in the company of male art students who speak of female models as "A cow," "A bag," "What a discard," she thinks she is "an exception, to some rule I haven't even identified" (298). Josef's dicta that she is both an "unfinished woman" who needs to "be finished" and artistically "nothing. . . . We will see what we can make of you" (291, 290) suggest that insofar as she remains sexually female, she remains subject to the goal of "improvement." The difference is that she does not ultimately allow Josef to be final arbiter of her development, either professionally or sexually. The source of her ability to set limits to her desire to please him, unlike her earlier inability to say no to Cordelia, is wound up with her choice of the vocation of painter, a professionalized embodiment of the one-way gaze. As a painter, if not as a female body, she is in control of how other people look.

In other words, as a painter she occupies a position usually reserved for the dominant class of men in a patriarchal system: she can disengage seeing from being seen, and this disengagement gives her access to a key mechanism of what Michel Foucault has described as the modern disciplinary society. In such a society, power is dissociated, diffuse, and pervasive; as such, it is internalized, and thus self-policing. Foucault finds the emblem of this sort of society in Jeremy Bentham's model prison the Panopticon, designed to individualize prisoners by virtue of their physical isolation while at the same time rendering them completely visible to an authoritative viewer who himself remains unseen. The main operation of power in the disciplinary state is precisely this surveillance, this non-reciprocal seeing. The genius of the system is that while the power reinforces the existing hierarchy and institutions, the operation of power is not centralized in any one person or class of people. In principle, any member of the society can run the panoptic machinery: as Foucault notes, "in the absence of the director, his family, his friends, his visitors, even his servants" can carry on the monitory business. Eventually the prisoners internalize the gaze of the panoptic authority. They police themselves, self-surveillance becoming part of their identity as prisoners, just as in the "generalization" of the panoptic mechanism that results in the disciplinary society, surveillance, and finally self-surveillance, becomes both the origin and the definition of the citizen. The pervasiveness of the power, however, is no index of equality. People watch each other, but this watching guarantees first of all that everyone occupies a fixed place in a given hierarchy. As Linda Kauffman has noted in the case of *The Handmaid's Tale*, the invisible and omniscient institutional gaze is leveled first at gendered subjects whose visibility is by definition compulsory.

In *Cat's Eye*, as in *The Handmaid's Tale*, the subjects who are most evidently singled out for enforced visibility are female. The panoptic goal of individualizing subjects by partitioning them off in enclosures is ensured by the institution of the nuclear family and its postwar containment in the single-family house, a unit that serves the disciplinary purpose of fixing hitherto nomadic populations like Elaine's own family. In particular, such houses pin down mothers, who are supposed to occupy them continuously: "daytime is ruled by the mothers," as Elaine observes, although the real power comes with the nighttime return of the fathers (176). The function of ensuring the visibility of subjects belongs to cultural institutions, in particular the institutions of mass culture, and the subjects who are supposed to be most visible are the women. The monitory figure of the Watchbird, who appears in women's magazines like *Good Housekeeping*, *The Ladies' Home Journal*, and *Chatelaine*, is an icon of the one-way gaze, directed initially at pictures that "show women doing things they aren't supposed to do," but then turned outward, towards the female reader: "This is a Watchbird watching YOU" (148).

The role of the Watchbird is explicitly corrective, but at the same time it guarantees that correction is impossible. The women represented in the magazines, who "put germ killers onto germs, in toilet bowls; they polish windows, or clean their spotty complexions with bars of soap, or shampoo their oily hair; they get rid of their unwanted odors, rub hand lotion onto their rough, wrinkly hands, hug rolls of toilet paper against their cheeks," are fighting a losing battle; as the child Elaine sees, "there will be no end to imperfection, or to doing things the wrong way" (148). Postwar women are fixed in their place by a process that amounts to a return to infancy, a process that renders them docile bodies, in Foucault's phrase, bodies that the preadolescent girls regard with terror: "Whatever has happened to them, bulging them, softening them, causing them to walk rather than run, as if there's some invisible leash around their necks, holding them in check — whatever it is, it may happen to us too" (97). The anxiety attendant on achieving full feminine identity comes from the requirement that the adult woman internalize a permanent belief in her need for improvement, a belief essential to her primary role as consumer, as the magazine advertisements indicate. The mitigating factor is that she can align herself with the Watchbird to police other women and female children. Mrs. Smeath relegates to herself the task of attending to the spiritual improvement of Elaine, but with apparent satisfaction finally judges her unredeemable, a "heathen" (192). The most successful product of female socialization among the girls, Grace Smeath, does much of the actual surveillance of Elaine, both as an agent of her mother and as an agent of Cordelia, who invents as an image of Elaine's transgressions a stack of plates crashing noisily to the floor, a representation of female domestic failure worthy of the Watchbird and strikingly at odds with Cordelia's own character and concerns.

The obvious form of resistance to the one-way look is the look back, a version of "outstaring" that apparently establishes parity by returning an eye for an eye. "*So, Cordelia. Got you back,*" Elaine thinks near the end of the novel, acknowledging the erasure of her former tormenter from the scene of her return. But she goes on to gloss the apostrophe: "Never pray for justice, because you might get some" (436). Indeed, revenge has turned out to be as painful as the events that motivated it. The reversal that put Cordelia in the place of victim was the consequence of Elaine's partial self-erasure in substituting an observing, judging eye for a gendered body susceptible to observation and judgement.

The substitution represents an extreme form of denial, albeit a denial warranted by conditions of extremity, the tactic of a body at risk. Modeling herself on the cat's eye marble, which Susan Strehle observes is a metonym for the one schoolyard game played by both boys and girls, Elaine retreats "back into [her] eyes" (166) to avoid feeling too much of the pain inflicted by her "friends." Later she intensifies the self-splitting by learning to faint on the playground, discovering that she can watch herself lying on the ground or stand "off to the side" of her own body

(184–85). Still later, after her brush with death and her repression of her memories of the "bad time," she encounters evidence that she has separated herself from her own affective life, in the experience not only of crying for no apparent reason but of not being able to "believe in [her] own sadness," to "take it seriously" (222). But she holds on to her hard-earned status as someone who affects but remains unaffected: "I am happy as a clam: hard-shelled, firmly closed" (215).

In professionalizing this status by becoming an artist, she additionally denies her situation as a sexed female body, conventionally the object of the painterly gaze. The implications of this denial begin to come home to her when she witnesses the aftermath of Susie's life-threatening self-abortion and hears "a small, mean voice, ancient and smug, that comes from somewhere deep inside my head: *It serves her right*" (341). The judgement echoes that of Mrs. Smeath on the torture her daughter and the other girls inflict on Elaine (193) and anticipates the judgement Elaine visits on herself by painting Mrs. Smeath shortly after learning about her own pregnancy: "Whatever has happened to me is my own fault, the fault of what is wrong with me. Mrs. Smeath knows what it is. She isn't telling" (358). The assumption that misfortune is necessarily "the fault of what is wrong with" the person suffering it is intrinsic to the structure of the disciplinary society, in which the separation between watcher and watched is sign of a separation between judge and judged, and in which the physical isolation of the subjects who are watched and judged entails that guilt is individual and personal. The limitation inherent in the nonreciprocal gaze makes blaming a primary mode of interaction among people. In a disciplinary society, deserts are just, by definition.

Elaine has largely accepted this assumption. As a child, punishing herself for the unspecified transgressions the other girls darkly hint at, she peels her feet (Atwood here alludes again to Hans Christian Andersen's Little Mermaid, one of her favourite instances of the woman who suffers mutilation as a condition of entering an alien universe), bites her fingernails, and assumes confused responsibility for her lack of "backbone" (168). As a teenager she adroitly shifts the blame for the consequences of not pleasing to Cordelia, demanding with oddly impervious self-righteousness, "How can she be so abject? When will she learn?" (268). The device of blaming works for her just as it worked earlier for Cordelia, forestalling empathy, warding off any sense that the self might be implied in the other. These effects are most evident when Elaine seizes on blaming as a means to avoid information that might recall the "bad time" to consciousness: "I want to protect myself from any further, darker memories of hers, get myself out of here gracefully before something embarrassing happens." Protection succeeds because it takes the form of attack. "I harden toward her. . . . She has all kinds of choices and possibilities, and the only thing that's keeping her away from them is lack of willpower. *Smarten up*, I want to tell her. *Pull up your socks*" (277).

Here, as in many other parts of the novel, failure of "willpower" summons up slang injunctions to control appearance. Earlier, Cordelia's older sister taunted, "Pull up your socks, Cordelia, or you'll flunk your year again. You know what Daddy said last time" (224). Like the more general condition of "letting yourself go," the spectre of drooping socks that need pulling up is a figure of characteristically feminine dereliction. Such figures specify the terms in which women monitor each other and demand "improvement." In the postwar society of *Cat's Eye*, women tell other women that they are letting themselves go (294, 339, 379), that they should pull up their socks. But behind these admonishing voices is the real threat, "what Daddy said last time."

The mechanism of blaming is essential to the disciplinary society and in its ultimate effects always ensures the hegemony of the fathers. The contrary activity, forgiveness, is in many respects part of the same structure, in that only someone who is guilty can be forgiven — Cordelia sends Elaine into the ravine by urging "Go on then. . . . Then you'll be forgiven" (200). But in other respects forgiveness seems to translate subjects out of the structure, at least to some extent, by translating them out of their hermetic isolation. Most radically, forgiveness makes blame impossible by entailing comprehension of a whole context of influences and motives, as when Elaine observes, "Knowing too much about other people puts you in their power, they have a claim on you, you are forced to understand their reasons for doing things and then you are weakened (233). As this passage suggests, the mutilated self demands as its corollary a mutilated awareness of the other. In the disciplinary society, curtailment of knowledge is power.

As in *The Handmaid's Tale*, the people who can forgive are the least powerful, the most susceptible to control and judgement, the women. In *Cat's Eye* female forgiveness is embodied in the ambiguous figure of the lady. The little girls play gender-enforcing games with cutouts of women from the Eaton's catalogue and call them "my lady," and these pasted-down women serve as models of housebound 1950s femininity: like all the mothers but Elaine's own, they are fixed in place by the requirements of consumption and ownership (57) while at the same time acting as the agents of such fixity in opposition to the men, who are "the outrageous, the subversive" (134). In the girls' cryptic jumprope rhyme, the lady is victim of "an obscure dirtiness. Something is not understood: the robbers and their strange commands, the lady and her gyrations, the tricks she's compelled to perform, like a trained dog" (150). Yet the cry of "Lady" is also "the final word of appeal" when the adult Elaine encounters a drunk woman lying on the sidewalk. The word cues for her a refusal to blame, to reduce condition to culpability: "'She's only drunk,' a man says in passing. What does that mean, *only*? It's hell enough" (163).

Elaine notes, "If you want something very badly you do not say *Woman, Woman*, you say *Lady, Lady*" (162). The term seems to summon up longings for the preoedipal mother, a figure of primordial fulfillment whose gaze is not judgemental because it is not separate, the mother who is not other. Rejection by such a mother is for many women in Atwood's fictional universes the fall that is the origin of alienated individuality. "I know about you," the drunk woman says. "You're Our Lady and you don't love me" (163). The charge evokes Elaine's childhood despair when her mother returned from the hospital after a traumatic miscarriage: "It's as if she's gone off somewhere else, leaving me behind; or forgotten I am there" (178). Mothering is passionately imagined as the force that can reverse the partitioning, blaming structure of the whole society. Real mothers are inevitably failures, never enough. At the same time, the image of the lady marks the place of an alternative construction of intersubjective life, as when Elaine chooses, against the norms of the Smeath universe, to worship the Virgin Mary instead of the paternal God of the panoptic, "watchful" stars, who continually needs more "before he can be truly appeased" (106).

The Virgin Mary is important as a reversion to a preverbal era — Elaine has not "yet learned the words to her" — who provides, at least in imagination, the encompassing aura of succor and concern impossible for actual subjects of a disciplinary society: "she knows already, she knows how unhappy I am" (197). Her incarnations are the quasi-authoritative "ladies" of Elaine's experience who are salvific either in wish, as in the case of Princess Elizabeth, or in effect, as in the cases of Miss Stuart and Mrs. Finestein, whom Elaine "rewards" for their passing kindnesses in her painting entitled *Three Muses*. This Virgin Mary is above all an agent of restoration, a Virgin of Lost Things who redresses estrangement and truncation with the inaudible but somehow spoken words, "*It will be all right. Go home*" (203).

When Elaine recovers the cat's eye marble and in the process recovers her memory of the "bad time," her relation to women undergoes a change. In recognizing what happened and forgiving her mother, she seems to comprehend for the first time both the necessary failures of all individual mothers and the context that makes visible hitherto unacknowledged strengths: "Against [my father's] bleak forecasting is set my mother's cheerfulness, in retrospect profoundly willed" (418). In looking into the marble "and seeing my life entire," she seems to begin the process of relinquishing blame (420). Although women, especially in groups, continue to have the power to threaten her, she is also poignantly aware of the needs of female figures who are involved, as she is, in the reclamation of lost things, the bag ladies whom she resembles in her "collection of shreds" of time (408), the refugee woman who approaches her with the entreaty, "Please. . . . They are killing many people," a reminder of the war that "broke up into pieces and got scattered, it gets in everywhere, you can't shut it out," "the war that killed Stephen" (334). The refugee woman, especially, is a reminder of a universe of suffering that belies the disciplinary mechanisms of individuation and blaming. "Every day there's more of it, more of that silent wailing, those starving outstretched hands, *need need, help help*, there's no end" (335). Stephen was apparently killed somewhere in the Middle East, a region from which this woman apparently derives. But these appearances, connected as they are with motives of national identity and partisanship, are not reasons or causes and do not account for the logic that suddenly transforms a person into a representative, an emblem, and a victim. Families die, the lucky ones getting away to lives of begging in foreign countries, because they live on the sites of clashes that may have nothing else to do with them. Hostages die, the lucky ones rapidly, in midair, because they mark a point of disagreement between rival forces that may have nothing else to do with them. Recounting Stephen's death, Elaine asks, "die for what? There's probably a religious motif, though in the foreground something more immediate: money, the release of others jailed in some sinkhole for doing more or less the same thing these men are doing" (412–13). Motives, though inescapably hypothetical, are not inconsequential. They are necessary. At the same time, they are not sufficient. They do not ultimately make sense of such facts as the refugees or Stephen's death by locating them in an economy of guilt and punishment. On the contrary, such an economy brings about its own unintelligible catastrophes. Elaine says of Stephen, "He died of an eye for an eye, or someone's idea of it. He died of too much justice" (410).

In a world so much larger and so much more full of misery than an ethics of personal culpability can comprehend, Hammurabic justice is less to the point than the traditional feminine virtue of mercy. Giving money to the drunk woman, Elaine comments, "I'm a sucker, I'm a bleeding heart. There's a cut in my heart, it bleeds money" (163). The "cut in my heart" suggests her resemblance to the version of the Virgin Mary to whom she first decided to shift her allegiance, Our Lady of Perpetual Help, who told her it was all right, she could go home. The bleeding wound is a stigma of femininity; it is also the sign of restoration and compassion. Similarly, the "bad heart" of Mrs. Smeath, which Elaine had imagined floating "in her body like an eye, an evil eye, it sees me" (194), is not fully visualized until it is understood as also an organ of acceptance, and until Mrs. Smeath's own eyes are acknowledged not only to judge but also to reveal a suffering subject. In the paintings of Mrs. Smeath displayed in the retrospective exhibit, Elaine recognizes that the "self-righteous eyes, piggy and smug" are "also defeated eyes, uncertain and melancholy, heavy with unloved duty," and she is suddenly able to see herself through these eyes, "unbaptized, a nest for demons: how could she know what germs of blasphemy and unfaith were breeding in me? And yet she took me in" (427). The revelation supplements the original insight; it does not supplant it. Blaming falsifies vision by representing a part as a whole. Elaine sums up: "An eye for an eye leads only to more blindness" (427).

NOTE

1. This essay is part of a longer attempt to think through the implications of the disciplinary society within the questions of art and autobiography that inform *Cat's Eye*. It is not intended to be a reading of the whole novel: as a reading, it is woefully inadequate. For a somewhat different use of (Atwood's own) eye / I pun, see Wilson.

WORKS CITED

Atwood, Margaret. *Bodily Harm*. New York: Bantam, 1983.

———. *Cat's Eye*. New York: Bantam, 1989.

———. *The Handmaid's Tale*. New York: Ballantine, 1987.

Foucault, Michel. *Discipline and Punish: The Birth of the Prison*. New York: Vintage, 1979.

Kauffman, Linda. "Special Delivery: Twenty-First Century Epistolarity in *The Handmaid's Tale*." *Writing the Female Voice: Essays on Epistolary Literature*. Ed. Elizabeth C. Goldsmith. Boston: Northeastern UP, 1989. 221–24.

Strehle, Susan. "Margaret Atwood: *Cat's Eye* and the Subjective Author." *Fiction in the Quantum Universe*. Chapel Hill, NC: U of North Carolina P, 1992. 159–89.

Wilson, Sharon R. "Eyes and I's." *International Literature in English: Essays on the Major Works*. Ed. Robert L. Ross. New York and London: Garland, 1991. 226–39.

Nathalie Cooke

The Politics of Ventriloquism: Margaret Atwood's Fictive Confessions

The true story is vicious
and multiple and untrue

after all. Why do you
need it? Don't ever

ask for the true story.

"TRUE STORIES" 11

I HAVE A CONFESSION to make: I feel as though I know some of Margaret Atwood's fictional characters pretty well. Take Elaine, Offred, and Joan, for instance; I know how they think, what they value. Admittedly, they are a bit odd as people go. Unstable. Self-absorbed. Overly analytical. But I feel as though they have taken me into their confidence, admitting their all-too-human faults, divulging their weaknesses and secret fears, telling me about their family. I have sympathized with them and, yes, upon occasion, judged them as well. Of course, I know this intimacy is mere illusion, a function of artistic contrivance and

207

rhetorical skill. In fact, Atwood's narrators are quick to point this out. So I *should* read the novels differently. But I don't.

The problem, for me, is a kind of paradox: the more Atwood's narrators admit their unreliability, the more reliable they seem to become. Consequently, it is not enough for me to recognize that these "fictive confessions" — spoken by a fictional character within a fictional context — are complex (though they are). Rather, I need to explore how that complexity manifests itself. In particular, I am interested in narrative reliability as a function of the confessional communication. That is, if reliability can be seen as a potential effect on the reader rather than as a characteristic of the narrator, then how does this affect our sense of the confessional act? And, in turn, how is it helpful to think of Atwood's fictive confessions in the light of this revisionary definition?

In this essay I suggest that the confessional tradition provides a model for analysing something that is central to Atwood's oeuvre: not truth itself (Atwood would strongly deny such an essentialist assumption), but rather the dynamics of truth-telling. Consequently, I focus not on the confession — what is said, how accurate or truthful it is — but rather on the confessional act — how it is signaled and to what effect.[1] More specifically, I propose two ways of reconciling the seemingly contradictory impulses in Margaret Atwood's work: the way it enacts its fascination with the nature and politics of disclosure, inviting the reader to play the role of confidante or confessor and, at the same time, draws attention to its own duplicity.[2] By outlining two rhetorical figures which signal the confessional communication in Atwood's oeuvre, I argue that confession is a rhetorical and ethical *strategy* rather than a *category* of literature.

MY EMPHASIS ON the effect of the confessional experience is a result of both my own reading experience and the reading signaled or prompted by Atwood's work. It does not follow from the most common definitions of confession itself; for confession, as it is most often defined, fits squarely within a non-fictional context — its central characteristic being a truth claim. Put simply, confession is most often defined as "a type of auto-biographical writing which signals its intention to foreground the most personal and intimate details of the author's life."[3] Writing about poetry, Laurence Lerner argues that "Confession is something that causes shame. Real confession will cause shame because we have done wrong, confessional poetry deals with experience that it is deeply painful to bring into public, not because it is disgusting, nor because it is sinful, but because it is intensely private."[4] That is, in addition to being autobio-graphical (grounded in the subject and his/her own experience), the author of the confession promises "to reveal something unknown, something that is not necessarily verifiable through recourse to the public record."[5] It is this promise of a disclo-sure — personal, shameful — that signals the confession in poetry or prose.

When I looked at Atwood's work, and specifically at refer-ences to the term confession (many of which appear in her novel *Cat's Eye*), I did notice the same revelation of personal detail, but I noticed something else as well: a listener or reader. Confession, Atwood reminds us, depends upon the interaction between two people, not just on what the speaker reveals, or promises to reveal. Taking my clue from Elizabeth Bruss's influential notion that a genre cannot be "classified" according to characteristics, but rather "at the heart of its generic value" are "the roles played by an author and a reader,"[6] I consequently choose to define the confessional disclosure in Atwood's oeuvre in terms of the "sig-nals" of the confessional dynamic. On the part of the speaker, they seem to be as follows:

(a) First, the speaker communicates details that are intimate in nature and, in some way, shameful. For example, Elaine Risley in *Cat's Eye* admits to peeling the skin off her feet at the time she was being tormented by her playmates:

> In the endless time when Cordelia had such power over me, I peeled the skin off my feet. I did it at night, when I was supposed to be sleeping. My feet would be cool and slightly damp, smooth, like the skin of mushrooms. I would begin with the big toes. I would bend my foot up and bite a small opening in the thickest part of the skin, on the bottom, along the outside edge. Then, with my fingernails, which I never bit because why bite something that didn't hurt, I would pull the skin off in narrow strips. . . . Nobody but me ever looked at my feet, so nobody knew I was doing it. (113–14).

The information Elaine provides here for the reader cannot be verified, but the sheer detail involved in the disclosure invites the reader into the speaker's confidence.

(b) Second, the speaker creates a context of intimacy for the communication:

> "There's dog poop on your shoe," Cordelia says.
> I look down. "It's only a rotten apple."
> "It's the same colour though, isn't it?" Cordelia says.
> "Not the hard kind, the soft squooshy kind, like peanut butter." This time her voice is confiding, as if she's talking about something intimate that only she and I know about and agree on. She creates a circle of two, takes me in. (71)

The intimate context of the confessional communication provides an invitation for the listener. Here, Elaine is drawn into a conversation with Cordelia in spite of herself.

(c) Third, the intimate tone Cordelia uses in this passage, linked with intimacy of detail, activates a kind of power dynamic since the narrator appears to make herself vulnerable. Often the confession is a kind of admission of powerlessness. Confronted with her daughter's torment, for instance, Elaine's mother makes a confession:

> My mother sets down the bowl and puts her arms around me. "I wish I knew what to do," she says. This is a confession. Now I know what I've been suspecting: as far as this thing is concerned, she is powerless. (156–57)

So far, I have defined confessional disclosure, illustrating it with examples of confessions embedded in Atwood's work, specifically *Cat's Eye*. Atwood's fictive confessions are further marked by a metafictional self-consciousness which points to the orchestrated, structured aspect of the confession. In brief, fictive confessions are spoken by a fictional character who is highly self-conscious about the nature and medium of the communication. When distinguishing confessional poetry from confession, Laurence Lerner already notes what he calls "deliberate jokiness" — a kind of implicit self-consciousness that characterizes the confessional disclosure.[7] In Atwood's fictive confessions, however, this self-consciousness is made explicit by, for example, the kind of framing device that we see in Atwood's poem, "Siren Song."[8] There, the siren provides the context of her disclosure: not only what is said, but to whom and to what effect. So, too, in the novels, Atwood usually provides a context for the various embedded confessions; consequently, the roles of those involved in the confessional dynamic of the text are played out within the text itself.

That these embedded confessions are staged makes us, Atwood's external readers, acutely aware of our own role in the confessional dynamic of the fictive confession as a whole. We look to the speaker not so much for the disclosure of events as for their production. And we look within the text for models of reading.

Figure 1:
The Powerful Voice That Asserts Its Own Powerlessness

ATWOOD'S FICTIVE confessions thematize the role of speaker *and* listener in the confessional exchange. What are these roles? By way of answering, I begin with "Siren Song" because it is a clear and self-conscious illustration of such a dynamic. Most obviously, "Siren Song" makes explicit the sheer power of the siren's personal revelation: telling is tantalizing. In the first section of the poem the siren explains just how powerful her disclosure can be:

> This is the one song everyone
> would like to learn: the song
> that is irresistible:
>
> the song that forces men
> to leap overboard in squadrons
> even though they see the beached skulls
>
> the song nobody knows
> because anyone who has heard it
> is dead, and the others can't remember. (195)

From this introductory section, the siren's power seems to reside in the song's words, in the secrets they disclose. However, when the song is revealed, Atwood suggests that the power lies not so much in the words as in the intimacy of their revelation.

> I will tell the secret *to you*,
> *to you, only to you.*
> Come closer. This song

is a cry for help: Help me!
Only you, only you can,
you are unique

(emphasis mine; 196)

One of the ironies of this poem, of course, is that the siren's secret is precisely that the listener is *not* unique: like all the others he falls prey to the temptress's power. "Alas / it is a boring song / but it works every time" (196). Further, because the siren's song lies within the context of Atwood's poem, the telling is far from intimate.

Another irony is that while Atwood draws her own readers into the confession, luring them with the possibility of learning the siren's secret, instead Atwood's readers catch a glimpse of a central figure in her oeuvre, and indeed in the confessional mode more generally: the powerful voice that asserts its own powerlessness. "This song / is a cry for help: Help me!" Atwood's readers know, however, that it is the siren's victims who are truly in need of help; her song is a ruse.

In this poem what lies at the heart of the siren's disclosure is not a powerful truth at all. Rather, central to the disclosure is the intimate context of the telling and, more particularly, the paradoxical power imbalance of the exchange. That is, while the speaker seems to be powerless ("Help me"), she actually wields considerable power as the one who initiates, structures, and establishes the terms of the communication. Ironically, it is precisely in her ability to convince her listener that *he* is powerful ("Help me. Only you can . . . ") that her power resides.

"Siren Song" alerts us to the fact that disclosure is marked by an intricate balance of power: the defining feature of the confession in general, and of Atwood's fictive confessions in particular. Of course, this power imbalance is most obvious in examples of oral confession — personal, religious, and legal — where the listener is recognized both by the speaker and by the society of which they are a part, to be worthy of the role of judge or "confessor." In penitential practices of Christianity and, more particularly, Roman Catholicism, of course, the confessor is able to provide relief and forgiveness for the penitent. In the best known contemporary examples of twentieth-century confessional writing, the work of the American confessional poets of the 1960s,[9] there is again a kind of power imbalance between a speaker who articulates a sense of powerlessness and, in doing so, makes him or herself vulnerable. In this secular and poetic tradition, however, the reader comes to the text with no particular institutional authority, but is authorized to enter (as a confidante) the intimate context of the poem by the poem itself — by the immediacy of personal detail as well as by the intensity of its language.

For the word "power," as I am using it, I can provide no singular definition. Generally, though, I am not interested in physical ability or the lack of it. Although physical powerlessness may provide the starting point of disclosure (as with the siren's seeming inability to free herself, for instance), the powerlessness that signals the specifically confessional dynamic is of another kind altogether and involves the admission of personal vulnerability. Further, that my discussion focuses on Atwood's oeuvre means that I am not particularly concerned with the kind of power wielded by the priest — an institutional authority to bestow God's forgiveness on the truly penitent. In short, there are two kinds of power that are central to my discussion here, and they have to do with authority over the meaning of the text: narrative authority (the speaker's ability to frame and structure the discourse), and the authority of witness (the authority to engage in the construction of meaning, bestowed upon the reader/listener by the speaker of the confession). These are, in Michel Foucault's terms, the "local power relations" at work in the confessional exchange.[10] They are constantly shifting as the authority over the discourse, its meaning, and its implications are thrown into question.[11]

PERHAPS THE MOST obvious example of the uses and abuses of power is *The Handmaid's Tale* where the novel's heroine, Offred, seems to be without either narrative control or real power. It is also in this novel that the fictive confession's central figure is most obvious: that of the powerful voice that asserts its own powerlessness.

At first glance, it seems clear that Offred is a victim of a regime that controls women to such an extent that they are unable to voice their opinions — both because of fear and because the opinion of a single woman no longer carries authority. Indeed, her resistance to the regime consists of subversive thoughts, whispered comments to a friend. It is to this kind of subversive activity that Offred seems to be confessing. On closer inspection, however, it is apparent that she also — and more disturbingly — confesses to her reluctance to resist. Offred, as the sound of her name suggests, is afraid.

> I wish this story were different. I wish it were more civilized. I wish it showed me in a better light, if not happier, then at least more active, less hesitant, less distracted by trivia. I wish it had more shape. (279)

She is resigned, fearful. "I want to keep on living, in any form. I resign my body freely, to the uses of others. They can do what they like with me. I am abject" (298). Indeed she draws attention to her own feebleness, her temptation to play the role of the passive female heroine engaged in a demoralizing spiral of demanding and needing help.[12]

> The fact is that I no longer want to leave, escape, cross the border to freedom. I want to be here, with Nick, where I can get at him.
>
> Telling this, I am ashamed of myself. (283)

Of course, telling the story at all is a kind of resistance; it gives her narrative control over her life, if not control over the circumstances in which she finds herself. It empowers Offred while she tells the story, for the communication calls into existence a reader and, therefore, a community.[13]

> By telling you anything at all I'm at least believing in you, I believe you're there, I believe you into being. Because I'm telling you this story I will your existence. I tell, therefore you are. (279)

This now familiar confessional figure of a narrator, who outlines her vulnerability while, at the same time, exercising considerable narrative control, is something that is recently noted by Glenn Deer. Deer argues that the novel is characterized by "paralepsis," defined as:

> the figure of verbal dissimulation and duplicity that asserts its lack of rhetoric while using rhetoric, that on the one hand critiques authority and on the other hand is complicitous with that authority, that feigns powerlessness in order to wield power, that disavows deliberate arrangement while arranging words with great care. (216)

Deer goes on to locate the source of this powerful rhetoric in Atwood's own narrative skill. "It is as if Atwood's skill as story-teller continually intrudes, possessing her narrative creation" (215). What is fascinating about this argument is that it points to the paradoxical power dynamic that I locate as one figure of the confessional mode, without acknowledging or focusing on the specifically confessional nature of Offred's narrative. Consequently, the uneasy combination of Offred's role as "innocent recorder" and "skilled, self-conscious rhetorician and storyteller" (226) can only be explained by recourse to Atwood's own rhetorical skill. What the confessional dynamic I have outlined suggests, however, is that such a combination is deliberate and effective. I would disagree, of course, with Deer's suggestion that Offred's rhetorical expertise is an error on Atwood's part, a moment of authorial disclosure. As Atwood proves in "Siren Song," she is acutely aware of what Deer calls the "power of the powerless, of the seductive prey" (229). Rather, I would argue that Offred is indeed a powerful storyteller, not only because she is recording the events of her victimization, but because through doing so she is confessing to her complicity in her own victimization while defending and justifying her actions. Offred never claims that her account is an objective or "innocent" one; on the contrary, she is making a confession and she has a vested interest in it.

Just as Offred is complicitous in the novel's oppression, so, too, are we implicated in the power politics of the novel. This is made clear when we see how narrative control is finally taken from her by the Historical Notes section which, as Arnold E. Davidson points out, is "the most pessimistic part of the book."[14] Here, we understand that *The Handmaid's Tale* is not *her* tale at all; rather, it may be the product of Professor Piexoto's misguided reordering of Offred's oral narrative. At least one of the novel's internal readers then plays a crucial role in the construction of meaning.[15] Piexoto does not take sole control over the production of meaning, however, because he cannot silence Offred. As the novel's external readers, we soon suspect Piexoto's abuse of power and return to the gaps and fissures of Offred's narrative to discern her story, her message. And such "conspiratorial" readings are rewarded. When Constance Rooke explores

Offred's narrative, for instance, she finds Offred's real name hidden like a treasure within it.[16]

What Piexoto's example tells us is that with the power bestowed upon the reader of the confession comes the responsibility of *witness*.[17] However, I am not as sure as Constance Rooke that our role as witnesses aligns us with Offred. Rather, Offred seems yet another example of someone who is not a responsible witness. She lies — even to herself. Indeed, if one reads closely, the distinction between pre- and post-Gilead on which Offred bases her narrative is flawed. Generally, as Davidson remarks, "*The Handmaid's Tale* portrays the advent of that society as an easy slide into 'final solutions'" (113). More particular to Offred's own experience, Stephanie Barbé Hammer argues that Offred seemed equally passive in her previous life ("she worked, not as an explainer or analyzer but as a transcriber of books to disks in a predominantly female task force — an act which curiously prefigures her own present narrative recording" [43]) and also played the role of mistress to a married man. Concludes Hammer, "[s]een from the point of view of her past, Offred's current existence begins to look less like a nonsensical metaphormosis [sic] and more like a horrible but nightmarishly appropriate extention [sic] of her former life" (43).

Still more troubling than Offred's seemingly subconscious duplicity are the instances when Offred openly acknowledges her tendency to lie. For example, she changes the story of her encounter with Nick at least three times: first promising an honest version, then acknowledging that she provides only a "reconstruction" (275). And, paradoxically, by admitting her temptation to romanticize her encounters with Nick, she appears more honest. I will focus on this second figure of confessed liar and its implications in detail with reference to *Lady Oracle*. For now, though, let me point out that Offred's admitting her escapist tendencies is effective in shaming the reader; for, like Offred, we are tempted to read the narrative in an escapist fashion and accept Gilead as "make-believe."[18] By grounding the story in another time, place, and context, that is, we are able to escape blame. Instead, though, as most readers have been forced to admit, we have to acknowledge that the novel provides a satiric portrait of our world. Put bluntly, Atwood demands that we bear witness not so much to Gilead, but to what we recognize of our society in Gilead.

Figure 2:
The Confessed Liar

READERS OF *The Handmaid's Tale* are disoriented at least three times: when they first encounter the "new" world of Gilead, when Offred admits to altering the details of her story (especially the first encounter with Nick), and when Professor Piexoto reveals his authorial hand. Of the three, however, it is Offred's own duplicity that is most troubling because she disturbs the balance of power by revealing her hand as the producer, rather than the reproducer, of experience — at least within her own text. But Offred is not alone. All of Atwood's fictional narrators disorient their readers. They draw attention either to their own unreliability (Joan Foster), the unreliability of their memory (narrator of "Making Poison" in *Murder in the Dark*), or their mythic or ambiguous status ("Siren Song" and "Corpse Song") within the world of experience.

The most obvious example of the initial disorientation of the fictive confession is enacted in Atwood's "Songs of the Trans-formed" (in *Selected Poems*). In the figure of the disembodied voice, there is the kind of intimacy of detail and communication that signals the confessional dynamic, as well as both a literal and figurative "diminishment" of the self that prompts a recognition of vulnerability. Further, Atwood destabilizes the experience of her narrators such that it is impossible for her readers to ground their confessions in any kind of stable "experience."

Extreme examples, of course, are those narrators who speak from the dead. In "Corpse Song" (in *You Are Happy*) for instance, the narrator cannot fully explain its (his? her?) existence in terms we may understand:

> (My body turned against me
> too soon, it was not a tragedy
>
> (I did not become
> a tree or a constellation
>
> (I became a winter coat the children
> thought they saw on the street corner
>
> (I became this illusion,
> this trick of ventriloquism
> this blind noun, this bandage
> crumpled at your dream's edge (199–200)

And, of course, this "trick of ventriloquism" is Atwood's own; for Atwood's confessional disclosures are "fictive" ones — spoken by fictional characters within a fictional context. The politics of the fictive confession are the politics of ventriloquism.

I began with the figure of the siren, the femme fatale who lures others *to* their death, but I also want to discuss those Atwood heroines who seem to speak *from* the dead: Joan Foster, who narrates *Lady Oracle* after drowning; and Offred, who comes to us as a voice constructed by her future audience. What makes these two novels particularly interesting, in light of the confessional dynamic, is that they highlight not only the dynamics of disclosure but also its ethical implications.[19]

Joan Foster, heroine of *Lacy Oracle*, is a kind of fleshing out of "Corpse Song" since the novel opens with Joan's description of her death. Although an illusion, this introductory strategy alerts us to the problematic nature of the speaker — her identity, her authority. Most obviously, Joan has many names — Joan Delacourt, Joan Foster, Louisa K. Delacourt, Aunt Deirdre — and even more sides to her personality. Unlike the speaker in "Corpse Song," she does have a substantial corporeal body — at first. Within the context of the novel, however, a body is not enough to substantiate a being. In the world of *Lacy Oracle*, bodies shift in size and shape (like Joan's) or they "astro-travel" between the realm of the living and the dead (like her mother's).

It is precisely the instability of Joan's life that provides the basis of her plea for helplessness. Joan's life, and her art, are out of control. The confessional dynamic is signaled in the first chapter as Joan promises not only to outline her life, but also her death. That the latter is badly botched is the humorous cause for her plea for understanding. More importantly, though, she is willing to outline the extent of her perplexity (to us, at least), thereby assuming the vulnerability that signals the confessional exchange:

> I planned my death carefully; unlike my life, which meandered along from one thing to another, despite my feeble attempts to control it. My life had a tendency to spread, to get flabby, to scroll and festoon like the frame of a baroque mirror, which came from following the line of least resistance. (3)

Although Joan seems to tell too many stories for her own good, she is actually extremely careful about information — what she tells and to whom. In one of her younger incarnations, after all, she herself played the role of confidante and is well aware of the kind of power one puts on with knowledge.

> Everyone trusted me, no one was afraid of me, though they should have been. I knew everything about my friends . . . I knew what they thought about each other and what they said

behind each other's backs. But they guessed nothing about me;
I was a sponge, I drank it all in but gave nothing out, despite the
temptation to tell everything, all my hatred and jealousy, to
reveal myself as the duplicitous monster I knew myself to be.
(93)

Joan understands that silence is powerful.[20] After her mysterious
disappearance, Joan exercises considerable power over Sam and
Marlene, precisely by remaining silent. Only when she confesses
will they be found innocent of her murder.

Ironically, then, *Lady Oracle* both signals and resists confession;
for although Joan engages us, as external readers, in what seems
to be a confessional exchange, she confesses that she has no
intention of being powerless and outlines the ways she consciously resists the very act of confession. For instance, her
refusal to reveal her other selves to Arthur is a course of action
that Joan has considered in some detail:

> I should have trusted him more. I should have been honest from
> the beginning, expressed my feelings, told him everything. (But
> if he'd known what I was really like, would he still have loved
> me?) The trouble was that I wanted to maintain his illusions for
> him intact, and it was easy to do, all it needed was a little
> restraint: I simply never told him anything important. (33)[21]

More generally, Joan makes her violation of the so-called confessional credo explicit:

> But it wasn't more honesty that would have saved me, I thought;
> it was more dishonesty. In my experience, honesty and express-
> ing your feelings could lead to only one thing. Disaster. (33)

In other words, Joan's reluctance to tell the truth to Arthur is no
anomaly. It is the rule.

That Joan's reluctance to confess to those around her lies at the heart of her confession to us, her external readers, means that she fabricates a kind of liar's paradox. She appears to be truthful precisely because she acknowledges that she is *not* always truthful. If the first figure of Atwood's fictive confessions is that of the powerful speaker who asserts her own powerlessness, then the second one seems to be that of the confessed liar.

Joan's admission to her propensity for lying, however, does not mean that she changes her ways. At the end of the novel, we see Joan postponing her return to Toronto where she will be compelled to reveal her many identities, and the truth of her faked accident, in order to free Sam. She claims that she has already revealed much of her story to the anonymous journalist, after hitting him over the head with a Cinzano bottle. He, in turn, symbolizes the complicated power dynamics of the confession. Ostensibly all-powerful, he is actually bandaged and hospitalized as a result of Joan's defensive behaviour (not quite as skillful as the siren, Joan is reduced to using physical force). However, Joan warns (paradoxically, driven by the need to confess her duplicity to her external readers) that she has told a few lies to him (344). With this statement, of course, the true story of Joan recedes, as she suggests in the novel's opening: "The trick was to disappear without a trace, leaving behind me the shadow of a corpse, a shadow everyone would mistake for solid reality" (3). For us, as readers, the many Joans we encounter in *Lady Oracle* are merely illusion; as is the illusion of disclosure.

Joan says as much at the end of the novel. "I might as well face it, I thought, I was an artist, an escape artist" (335). Although Joan uses the past tense here, we suspect that she will continue to escape. Certainly, in the last pages of the novel, she escapes any attempt on our part to ground the confession in one single authoritative subject. As readers, we are left with a confession but with no single speaker: the ventriloquist's art."[22]

Consequently, we are left to think about the issues Joan's story raises about our society's expectations of women; and we find ourselves relating those issues to Joan's fictional experience as well as to our own personal experience. Atwood invites us to admit that we, too, are tempted by escape. *Lady Oracle* is an admittedly "good read" precisely because of the romance and humour that provide an alternative to heavy moralizing. But what are the moral and ethical implications of escapism? After all, Joan is not the only escape artist. So are we. And trying to ground the narrative in a single truth, a single Joan, is an unacceptably easy way out.

What I am suggesting is that these fictive confessions are characterized by self-consciousness on the part of the fictional speaker that takes the form of two related figures: the powerful voice that declares its own powerlessness, and the confessed liar. They bestow upon the reader the illusion of power. But it is not power to judge the speaker (as in the priest's right to forgive or pass judgement on the penitent). Rather, by disorienting its readers, the fictive confession forces them to recognize the illusory nature of the speaker and to concentrate on the issues she raises in and through the confession. In an early article Eli Mandel recontextualizes the discussion of gothic elements (particularly duplication) in Atwood's work to that of rhetoric and metafiction. He suggests that an author can be either duplicitous or a magician (172). In this paper, I argue that she can be both. With the paradoxical duplicity of the fictive confession Atwood allows truths to emerge — however constructed they may be.

IN SUMMARY, the fictive confession seems not so much a category as a strategy. Its objectives are twofold: rhetorical and ethical. Rhetorically, the confessional figure serves to (a) lure the reader, (b) initiate the power dynamic of the confessional exchange, and (c) lay bare narrative contrivance. That such exposure does not eliminate contrivance, however, is its central rhetorical confession.

The fictive confession is also a form that enables Atwood to communicate ideological concepts within a fictional framework. In particular, the confessional strategy serves to (a) lure the reader, (b) implicate the reader in the power politics under discussion, and (c) bestow upon him/her both the authority and the responsibility of witness.

As a result of both the rhetorical and moral imperatives of Atwood's fictive confessions, her readers are forced to confront their own expectations. Atwood's fictive confessions are not grounded in the personal experience of the speaker, but rather the thought and self-scrutiny of the reader. Such is the power of the form.

NOTES

1. Reliability, for me, is performative rather than constative (to use J.L. Austin's distinction).

2. I do not, however, offer the suggestion that one might read Atwood's work *as if it were true*. Objecting to such autobiographical readings of her work, Atwood quite rightly points out that her work is "craft" and not "true confessions." "I believe in artistry," Atwood explains, "I believe that there's a difference between true confessions and writing a novel" (Peri 31). Indeed in this paper, by defining confession as a rhetorical strategy, I make a clear distinction between this self-consciously literary form and the unmediated discourse to which Atwood refers when she uses the term "true confessions."

3. Rita Felski 87.

4. Laurence Lerner 64.

5. Judith Whitenack 43.

6. Elizabeth Bruss 5. In this now well-known statement, Bruss is referring specifically to autobiography. However, I feel that her notion that genre can be seen as a strategy rather than a category has far-reaching implications in that it solves the problems of the sheer rigidity of generic classification faced by Northrop Frye (in *The Anatomy of Criticism*) and Alastair Fowler (in *Kinds of Literature*).

7. Laurence Lerner 54. Lerner cites the following as characteristics of pure confession: "factual accuracy of remembering, self-centredness, self-abasement expressed in clichés" (52).

8. From "Songs of the Transformed" in *You Are Happy*.

9. I am thinking here especially of Robert Lowell, Anne Sexton, and Sylvia Plath.

10. Michel Foucault 97.

11. I am by no means suggesting that they are the only power dynamics at work in Atwood's complicated fictive confessions; other important ones would be that between Atwood and her reader, between Atwood's various narrators, between the various selves of her narrators, and between the real reader and the one implied by the text, to mention only a few. However, my aim in this paper is to illustrate the way in which an analysis of confessional power dynamics can provide a useful point of entry in Atwood's fictional oeuvre. That there is no one stable source of power, something Michel Foucault has already taught us, makes this task complicated enough within the limited scope of this paper (93).

12. Stephanie Barbé Hammer 44.

13. Constance Rooke 184, 186.

14. Arnold E. Davidson 120.

15. Ibid 120.

16. Rooke 185.

17. Lorraine York refers to the "explosive poetry of witness" as a traditional way of getting at the ideological projects of Pablo Neruda, Carolyn Forche, Margaret Atwood, Erin Mouré and Mary di Michele (139). Such "literature of witness" is part of the confessional strategy as I outline it here: a way of communicating values within a context of challenge.

18. I am using Gregory Currie's useful term. See *The Nature of Fiction*.

19. I would argue that Atwood's novels, *Surfacing* and *Cat's Eye*, are also fictive confessions. However, the context of the confession's reception is less explicit than in *Lady Oracle* and *The Handmaid's Tale*, since the confessors in these two novels (the Surfacer's parents and Cordelia) are ghostly absences. The seeming absence of the confessor in *Cat's Eye* makes the

novel appear autobiographical (see Cooke, "Reading Reflections in Margaret Atwood's *Cat's Eye*)."

20. The narrator of Atwood's story, "Weight," puts this succinctly: "Knowledge is power only as long as you keep your mouth shut." *Wilderness Tips* 185.

21. "Restraint" is a key term in *Lady Oracle*, for we have a sense that Joan often loses her self-restraint: by over-eating, by over-writing, by being too much and too many. By raising the issue of restraint, Atwood is engaging a different (and seldom theorized) tradition: that of the female confessional novel. In a very convincing article, Virginia Tiger defines the confessional novel as a specifically female form. Tiger defines the tradition as one that is characterized by a self-conscious, perceptive, and thoughtful heroine engaged in scrutinizing the conflict between "female dependence and female autonomy" in which she finds herself. Tiger points to Doris Lessing as a modern example of this essentially "moralist" tradition of novel-writing in which the common theme is the "need for conscious self-restraint" (478). Of course, *Lady Oracle* engages this tradition ironically. Atwood's novel is a send-up of this kind of moral imperative. To read Joan Foster's narrative as a call for restraint is to provide the kind of reading that is satirized and disrupted throughout, to play the role of Joan's mother.

22. Indeed, there is a remote possibility that the story we receive is "ghost-written" by the unnamed journalist.

WORKS CITED

Atwood, Margaret. *Cat's Eye*. Toronto: McClelland & Stewart, 1988.

———. *Lady Oracle*. Toronto: Seal, 1976.

———. *Murder in the Dark*. Toronto: Coach House Press, 1983.

———. *Selected Poems*. Toronto: Oxford UP, 1976.

———. *The Handmaid's Tale*. Toronto: McClelland & Stewart, 1985.

———. *True Stories*. Toronto: Oxford UP, 1981.

———. *Wilderness Tips*. Toronto: McClelland & Stewart, 1991.

Bruss, Elizabeth. *Autobiographical Acts: The Changing Situation of a Literary Genre*. Baltimore: Johns Hopkins UP, 1976.

Cooke, Nathalie. "Reading Reflections in Margaret Atwood's *Cat's Eye*." *Essays on Life Writing*. Ed. Marlene Kadar. Toronto: U of Toronto P, 1992. 162–69.

Currie, Gregory. *The Nature of Fiction*. Cambridge, MA: Cambridge UP, 1990.

Davidson, Arnold E. "Future Tense: Making History in *The Handmaid's Tale*." *Margaret Atwood: Vision and Forms*. Eds. Kathryn Van Spanckeren and Jan Garden Castro. Carbondale: Southern Illinois UP, 1988. 113–21.

Deer, Glenn. "Rhetorical Strategies in *The Handmaid's Tale*: Dystopia and the Paradoxes of Power." *English Studies in Canada* 17 (1992): 215–33.

Felski, Rita. *Beyond Feminist Aesthetics: Feminist Literature and Social Change*. Cambridge, MA: Harvard UP, 1989.

Foucault, Michel. *The History of Sexuality: An Introduction*. Vol. 1. Trans. Robert Hurley, 1978. New York: Vintage, 1990.

Frye, Northrop. *The Anatomy of Criticism*. Princeton: Princeton UP, 1957. New York: Atheneum, 1969.

Hammer, Stephanie Barbé, "The World as It Will Be? Female Satire and the Technology of Power in *The Handmaid's Tale*." *Modern Language Studies* 22 (1990): 39–49.

Lerner, Laurence. "What Is Confessional Poetry?" *Critical Quarterly* 29 (1987): 46–66.

Mandel, Eli. "Atwood Gothic," *Malahat Review* 41 (1977): 165–74.

Peri, Camille. "Witchcraft." *Mother Jones* 14 (1989): 28–45.

Rooke, Constance. *Fear of the Open Heart*. Toronto: Coach House Press, 1989.

Tiger, Virginia. "The Female Novel of Education and the Confessional Heroine." *Dalhousie Review* 60 (1980): 472–86.

Walker, Nancy. "Ironic Autobiography: From *The Waterfall* to *The Handmaid's Tale*." *Women's Studies: An Interdisciplinary Journal* 15(1988): 203–20.

Whitenack, Judith. "A New Look at Autobiography and Confession." *Forum* 23 (1982): 40–48.

York, Lorraine. "Poetic Emergenc(i)es." *Essays on Canadian Writing* 44 (1991): 133–41.

Lorraine M. York

"Over All I Place
a Glass Bell":
The Meta-Iconography
of Margaret Atwood

ASK ANY REASONABLY WELL-READ Canadian
which literary figure s/he can conjure up in the mind's eye, and
more likely than not, a curly-haired, blue-eyed, strikingly Pre-
Raphaelite woman will appear. This familiar figure gazes at us not
only from her book jackets and the pages of literary journals, but
at regular intervals from the glossy leaves of popular magazines
like *Maclean's* and *Chatelaine*. Her books appear in numerous
languages, and her sales worldwide are enormous. (The first
printing of *Survival*, for example, was an impressive 20,000 cop-
ies.[1]) Surveying the first decade of her publishing career, Robert
Fulford announced that "by now it's difficult to separate Atwood
the 'real' poet, novelist, publicist, from the various Atwoods of our
imagination, the Atwoods we may have created to satisfy our
cultural needs . . . Feminist, nationalist, literary witch, mytho-
logical poet, satirist, formulator of critical theories."[2] "For the
media," Fulford mused, "Atwood is endlessly reusable because
she is endlessly Protean" (98). This image of Atwood as the
recycling blue box of Canada's literary lineup has been so pervasive that Frank Davey was forced to conclude that "An in-depth
biographical study of Atwood will eventually be needed, not to

explain her work but to demythologize it, to free it of its 'Margaret the Mother' or 'Margaret the Monster' associations by making clear the specific and actual of her private life."[3] None of this, of course, is news; as early in her career as 1973, Atwood complained to the rather unlikely audience of the Empire Club in Toronto that she had become, much to her bemusement, a Thing. As William French reported in the *Globe and Mail*, "The difference between being a Thing and being Distinguished, [Atwood] explained, is that when someone who is Distinguished is asked a question, no one pays any attention to the answer. But a Thing is both icon and target, both worshipped and shot at. People make up what they think a Thing said or should say, then attack them or praise them for it."[4]

Indeed, Atwood, the recyclable, Protean icon of Canadian Literature, has attracted as much buckshot as veneration. Three years after his celebration of Margaret the Metamorphosician, Robert Fulford examined the darker side of literary iconization. "Do Canadians fear excellence?" asks the title of his short note in *Saturday Night*, "Consider the case of Atwood." Atwood is now a "case," a literary psychosis in search of medication. Trying to account for the negative reviews that *Life Before Man* received in Canada, Fulford resorted to the following parable: How would you like it if your sister won the Nobel Prize? The American professor who provoked Fulford's question by wondering aloud why so many Canadian readers seem to despise Atwood replied in one word: "shitty."

Shit, to be frank, is precisely the compound that routinely gets lobbed at iconized literary targets. A perfect example of this phenomenon is a nasty piece by Scott Symons in a 1990 issue of *The Idler*, "Atwood-as-Icon." In my search for references to the literary iconization of Atwood, I naturally came across this item, though nothing prepared me for the vitriolic attack, not even some years of teaching Atwood and getting sharply polarized student responses to her work — or, rather, to her iconic status.

"If we can locate the meanings of Atwood-as-Icon," Symons promises, "we'll surely know more about our nationhood."[5] These "meanings" are, for Symons, connected with Atwood's putative power-lust: the fact that her work examines women in bondage to patriarchy becomes, by an odd turn of logic, proof that Atwood herself is obsessed with sadomasochistic control. In a dead giveaway, Symons quotes Norman Mailer to the effect that women who wish to be equal are already dominant. By a similar philosophical reasoning, one supposes, jailed student protesters in China are dictators.

I have spent this much time outlining Atwood's literary iconization, in both manifestations as canonization and witch-hunt, because the question of Atwood as icon needs to be addressed more seriously than it has been to date, as a genuine intellectual issue rather than as a publicity stunt or journalistic sound bite. Some of Atwood's academic critics have examined the basic paradox of iconography in her work, although they mostly use other terms for it: Sherrill Grace, for example, in *Violent Duality*, argues that "the central dialectic and tension in Atwood's work" is "the pull towards art on one hand and towards life on the other. How," Grace asks, "does one capture living forms in imaginative and verbal structures?"[6] Frank Davey, in his article, "Atwood's Gorgon Touch," rephrases the same dialectic as a choice between the "aesthetics of space" and the "aesthetics of time": product versus process.[7] But there remains one more layer of inquiry to be unearthed in a study of Atwood and iconization: How does Atwood turn her concern with iconization and its implications back on herself — as an iconized writer? She does this by creating, in her fiction and prose, what I will call a meta-iconography.

THE SEEMS LITTLE doubt that, in all of her work to date, Atwood has undertaken a critique of iconization, that powerful

aesthetic and emotional desire to reify. Indeed, icons, by definition, consist of constructed cultural power. Heinz Skrobucha, an
authority on visual icons — early Eastern religious paintings —
tells the story of a Russian man asking his priest, "'Is it permitted
to sleep with a woman in a room in which there are icons?'" The
answer was: "'Don't you take the cross from your neck when
you go to a woman? In just the same manner you may sleep with
your wife in your apartment only when the icons have been put
away or are veiled.'"[8] The advice recalls a comic moment in
Timothy Findley's *Famous Last Words*, when the abdicated King
Edward and Wallis Simpson enjoy making love in front of a
picture of the Queen Mother, thumbing their noses at their
bedroom icon of regal power.

In early works such as *The Circle Game* and *The Edible Woman*,
Atwood thumbs *her* nose at the iconic. Indeed, *The Circle Game* is
the most resolutely iconoclastic of her poetry collections. "I
want to break . . . all the glass cases," the speaker of the title
poem announces, and this desire undoubtedly extends to the
icons that would be encased by those glass shells (55.1,5). The
title of another poem from that collection, "Against Still Life,"
effectively sums up Atwood's response to icons at this early
stage of her career. In *The Edible Woman*, Marian enters her living
room, bearing the cake-woman to Peter, "with reverence, as
though she was carrying something sacred in a procession, an
icon or the crown on a cushion in a play" (284). This description
echoes the earlier scene of Marian walking home after being duly
lacquered and polished — iconized — at the local temple of
beauty, "carrying it [her red sequined dress] now in its pink and
silver cardboard box as she walked towards the house across the
slippery road, balancing her head on her neck as though she was
a juggler with a fragile golden bubble" (217). This fragile golden
icon of a head is metaphorically smashed when the cake-woman
is devoured by Duncan. "It's mostly the head," Marian announces
as she unwraps the cake remnant, and Duncan, working from the

mouth, to the nose, to the eye, to the hair, is obviously severing the head from what remains of the torso (293).

This association between heads and icons is a marked feature of Eastern icon painting. Though there are many icons that depict full-length figures and detailed scenes involving numerous characters (for example, Last Suppers, Days of Judgement), the bust-sized portrait is instantly recognizable to many people as iconic. This may be because early icons were intended for personal rather than institutional use,[9] and many of these paintings featured particular — private or patron — saints. The predominance of the bust figure may also owe something to the influence of Egyptian mummy portraits: their full, frontal presentation of the face, their soulful gazes.[10] At any rate, the last scene of Atwood's first novel is one of explicit iconoclasm; this act of de-iconizing an icon will become a virtual trademark of Atwood's later works. Clearly, Atwood is conversant with the iconic — not only in the general, aesthetic, and philosophical sense, but in the original art historical sense as well.

To a certain extent, the works that follow do continue to issue warnings about the dangers of iconolotry. The narrator of *Surfacing*, a former art student, is also conversant with early religious iconography; in her eyes, the "snout"-like arm of the handless "Madame" who ran the general store in the village is "miraculous in an unspecified way like the toes of saints or the cut-off pieces of early martyrs, the eyes on the plate, the severed breasts, the heart with letters on it shining like a light bulb through the trim hole painted in the chest, art history" (27). She prays for a similar miracle for herself: an iconic, fragmentary stasis. And so she feels "betrayed" by Paul's wife's new stove, just as she wonders earlier, when her father said he didn't build the cedar house to last forever, "Why not? Why didn't you?" (20, 34). The narrator's father has refused the narrator's psychological icons a fittingly time-insulated cathedral in which to hang, just as his mortal body refutes her iconic dream-vision of stasis by dying.

Consequently, in a number of Atwood's poems and fictions, fecundity and iconography are directly opposed. The speaker of "One More Garden" from *True Stories* describes this opposition in terms of a choice:

> I should throw my gold watch
> into the ocean and become
> timeless. I'd stand more chance
> here as a gourd, making
> more gourds, as a belly
> making more. Kiss your
> thin icon goodbye, sink memory
> & hope. Join the round
> round dance. Fuck the future. (17.9–17)

So, too, in *Life Before Man*, Lesje Green is in danger of becoming Nate's "thin icon." When a nervous Nate prepares to call Lesje for the first time, he imagines that "At the other end of the line a thin woman waits, her pale face framed by dark hair, her hand lifted, fingers upraised in blessing" (27). Even when he decides to become seriously involved with her, she remains "that cool thin body, the face turned in upon itself in statue-like contemplation" (119). But Lesje, as her fecund-sounding surname suggests, fights iconization with fertility; at the end of the novel, she tosses her birth-control pills away and decides to "join the round / round dance" — to "Fuck the future" into being.

For every fecund iconoclast in Atwood, there is at least one lover-icon who is unwilling to surrender his stasis — or his sterility. The lover of *Power Politics*, for example, manages the lonely feat of being self-iconizing — a truly narcissistic, masturbatory form of iconography, since icons are, by definition, empowered by the faithful beholder. "[Y]ou become slowly more public," the speaker of the poems tells him (30.4); "turning yourself to an / impervious glass tower" (32.24–25). George

Bowering observes that many of the arresting images to be found in this collection are, in fact, those of "people turned into their iconic representations."[11] This lover-turned-icon makes a return appearance in Atwood's next collection of poetry, *You Are Happy*; there, the sinister Odysseus of the "Circe-Mud Poems" stands at Circe's door, "bright as an icon" (53.2).

The way out of this circle game of romantic iconography is, for Atwood, to substitute the conventionally ugly or disgusting for the socially desirable. Writing about the heart, itself a potent icon of romance, in *Two-Headed Poems*, Atwood rejects the candy-shaped variety in favour of

> . . . this lump of muscle
> that contracts like a flayed biceps,
> purple-blue, with its skin of suet,
> its skin of gristle . . . (14.6–9)

At the end of the last story in *Bluebeard's Egg*, "Unearthing Suite," the narrator's parents wax enthusiastic over animal feces: "For my mother . . . this deposit of animal shit — is a miraculous token, a sign of divine grace; as if their mundane, familiar, much-patched but at times still leaking roof has been visited and made momentarily radiant by an unknown but by no means minor god" (285). But if one is rating repugnant Atwoodian anti-icons, the "Hairball" of the story of the same name in *Wilderness Tips* must surely take the prize. Kat, the fired fashion magazine genius, wrapping up her pet tumour in a truffles box, complete with a sprinkling of powdered cocoa, and sending it to her fickle lover, echoes Atwood's anti-iconic strategy: she reveals the "gristle," "shit," and "hairballs" that lie at the heart of iconized candy-heart romance. "[I]t was all iconography," muses Kat of her former profession of making the ugly beautiful; now she has learned iconography's potent reverse art.

The Handmaid's Tale and *Cat's Eye* seemingly continue this iconoclastic trend. After all, in the land of Gilead, for example, visual icons virtually replace verbal forms of communication: "Now places are known by their signs alone," observes Offred of the store "Milk and Honey," which is identified by a picture of "three eggs, a bee, a cow" (35). Visual language figures what Gileadan authority wishes to promote as desirable (as opposed to the subterranean language of desire: the written word). As Offred observes of another store window, "Loaves and Fishes," "They put the picture [of delicious fillets] in the window when they have something, take it away when they don't. Sign language" (173). This "sign language" is a microcosmic version of Gilead's state-sanctioned iconolotry; the handmaids, too, function as signs in a window, representing the sexual goods that are available only to the powerful and taken away from the undeserving. As Moira sums up the Commander's smuggling of Offred into Jezebel's, "Some of them do that, they get a kick out of it. It's like screwing on the altar or something: your gang are supposed to be such chaste vessels. They like to see you all painted up" (255). This is true iconic megalomania: the desire to control not only icons but even iconoclasm.

In *Cat's Eye*, a novel that explores the private and public iconography of one painter's oeuvre, Atwood has written the most explicitly iconographic novel of her career. Even the setting, Toronto, has settled into a calcified, iconic form: "Some of the street signs are subtitled in Chinese, multiculturalism on the march, others have *Fashion District* underneath the names. Everything is a district now. There never used to be districts" (43). In this observation as in so many others, Elaine Risley places herself as a visiting iconoclast in the land of solidified "districts." As a teenager, she smashes the current adolescent icons and replaces them with versions of Kat's "hairball": "Frank Sinatra is The Singing Marshmallow, Betty Hutton is The Human Grindstone" (235). As a mature artist whose own career is being carved into "districts" (i.e., given a "retrospective" showing), Elaine ignores the obligatory black costume of the *artiste* in favour of a wimpish powder-blue jogging suit: "It could be iconoclasm, how do they know?" (87). In a similar way, by embracing figural representation in the face of the abstract expressionist onslaught of her time, Elaine has redefined iconoclasm: it now means, for Atwood, resisting the pressures of the avant-garde, of the iconoclasts. The confident iconoclasm of her earlier fictions and poems is cracking at the seams; how can one define iconoclasm anymore, if the most iconic act one can perform is to follow the iconoclasts?

THIS QUESTION should tip us off that Atwood's iconoclasm is not itself a stable concept. Most critics, however, tend to see Atwood's position as consistent over time: Atwood, they would argue, hates icons, wants them "broken." And, in having it thus, they themselves ironically iconize Atwood, chart her philosophical "district." Frank Davey, in "Atwood's Gorgon Touch," however, is one of the first to allow such dualistic formulations to crack and crumble. After proposing his own scheme of Atwood playing off the "aesthetics of space" and the "aesthetics of time," Davey watches as his own terms of analysis overlap; though "circle games" tend to be destructive in Atwood's work, he recognizes that there is "a doubleness" there, too: "Games are sterile but fascinating; statues are cold but beautiful; illusory order is false but addictive."[12]

Such a paradoxical formulation is itself in danger of sounding stable, like a balancing of opposites. But there is a historical process, an evolution at work in Atwood's iconoclastic thought, from fairly straightforward iconoclasm, based on dualities, to the complex realization of the inherent instability of icons. The Royal Porcupine of *Lady Oracle*, who prides himself on being a master iconoclast in the art world, is himself a romantic icon — but he soon shrivels into plain, Edgar Linton-like Chuck Brewer, sporting a Honda T-shirt. The Commander, Offred notes with some surprise, is "no longer a thing" (176) once he starts to invite her to his room for some surreptitious Scrabble. And Cordelia, that Jamesian child-demon, collapses, like the Wicked Witch of the West, into a bundle of insecurities by the end of *Cat's Eye*. Partly, these de-iconizing processes are products of Atwood's increasingly politicized viewpoint; by the time she writes works such as *Bodily Harm* and *True Stories*, all forms of power, she perceives, are based on their opposites: insecurity, a perceived lack of power.

As a result of this increasingly political aesthetic, Atwood slowly recognizes that iconoclasm pure and simple is not enough. An early hint of this new position appears in the poem "An Icon," from *The Animals in That Country*:

> You are
> the lines I draw around you;
> with this cleaver of a pencil
> I hack off your aureole.
>
> I can make you armless, legless;
> I deny
> your goldrimmed visions
> by scratching through your eyes.
>
> I prune the ferns from your hair;
> I cut you down to size,
> crayon clever
> footnotes on your forehead
> so I can seize you.
>
> But you are
> slipperier than clumsy colour
> But you evade me,

break the cages
of black circumferences
by which I would surround you

and whistling and destructive, and
carefree as a hurricane

you take my fourcornered
measure, scroll me
up like a map. (60)

The breezy destructiveness of the icon that Atwood characteristically targets in her early work is here, but so, too, is a profound skepticism about the efficacy of iconoclasm. This icon is a paradoxically iconoclastic force, for it resists all attempts to circumscribe its power. Ironically, it is the iconoclastic artist who ends up drawing lines around the icon, reinscribing its halo, and scratching out its eyes, an act reminiscent of the tendency of Renaissance audiences to scratch out the figures of the demons in religious paintings. Conversely, the icon in her poem takes up strangely iconoclastic activities: breaking "cages." Which, then, is the icon, and which the iconoclast? The distinctions begin to blur at the edges because iconoclastic destruction has become, for Atwood, increasingly disturbing in its power associations.

As "An Icon" wittily points out, every iconoclast must acknowledge how blurry these edges are, by recognizing her/his complicity in acts of iconization. When the narrator of *Power Politics* decides that all the iconic manifestations of her lover are "inaccurate" ("the hinged man, the fragile man / built of glass pebbles, / the fanged man with his opulent capes and boots"), she also admits that "It was my fault but you helped, / you enjoyed it" (55.1, 2–4, 6–7). In the works that follow, Atwood reverses the emphasis: it may have been the fault of the icon for embodying power, but the consumer/victim of the icon has had a part to play, too. Joan Foster is the most obvious example of a willing iconizer; meditating on *her* cast of male icons — Paul, the Royal Porcupine (another "man with . . . opulent capes and boots"), Arthur — she realizes that "I'd polished them with my love and expected them to shine, brightly enough to return my own reflection, enhanced and sparkling" (284–85). Rennie Wilford, from *Bodily Harm*, like Marian McAlpin before her, is implicated as an iconizer by the work she engages in, though Atwood's critique has sharpened in the intervening decade. Rennie goes so far as to forge new icons, something the unsuspecting Marian never does, caught up as she is in charting the marketability of icons others have established: "But sometimes Rennie liked to write pieces about trends that didn't really exist, to see if she could make them exist by writing about them" (25). By the time Atwood writes *The Handmaid's Tale*, her study of complicity in acts of iconization has deepened to the extent that even women who are as oppressed as the handmaids will participate in rituals which legitimize the icons of their oppressors: the jealousy directed towards pregnant handmaids by the others, for example, and the horrific salvagings. As Offred uncomfortably recalls about the salvaging of a handmaid, ". . . I've leaned forward to touch the rope in front of me, in time with the others, both hands on it, the rope hairy, sticky with tar in the hot sun, then placed my hand on my heart to show my unity with the Salvagers, and my consent, and my complicity in the death of this woman" (288).

For Atwood, the hands of the writer are always on this rope. In an early poem, "Woman Skating," from *Procedures for Underground*, Atwood constructs an apparent duality — an iconic representation of "a woman skating" and a parenthetical portrait of this woman, "actually" her mother, complete with the anti-iconic details of the scene: the sooty snowbank, the "faded maroon earmuffs" (64.4, 9, 18). But at the end of the poem, Atwood muddies this easy-seeming opposition of iconic and "actual":

"Over all I place / a glass bell" (65.16–17). Even the writer's formulation of an iconoclastic stance is tinged by the poem's — memory's, language's — inevitable complicity in the formation of icons. To recall the earlier poem "An Icon," Atwood once again confesses to the icon, "You are / the lines I draw around you"; the "glass bell" of the iconic descends "over all."

This awareness is particularly pressing for an explicitly political poet — as Atwood is by 1981 in *True Stories*. As its very title suggests, "Notes Towards a Poem That Can Never Be Written" grapples with this dilemma of writerly complicity. The victims of state atrocity become, in effect, icons in the bloodied hands of the political poet: "we count them like beads, / we turn them into statistics & litanies / and into poems like this one" (66.11–13). In the more recent *Wilderness Tips*, though, the explicit political content of *Bodily Harm* and *True Stories* is now muted; a couple of the stories close with reminders of the power of narrative to deaden, to iconize stories of pain. "[T]he story itself seems to her outmoded," thinks Joanne in "True Trash" about the story of the pregnant camp waitress. "It's an archaic story, a folk-tale, a mosaic artefact. It's a story that would never happen now" (37). The reference to mosaic art reveals that Atwood's discomforting thought of the iconic power of a narrative lyric has not lost its force — or its visual associations.

This argument about writing as an iconizing force may appear to contradict my earlier contention that the iconic may increasingly attract positive as well as threatening overtones in Atwood. But both the thought of complicity and the reevaluation of the icon partake in the deconstruction of a simple, oppositional iconoclasm. At first, in works such as *The Edible Woman* and *The Circle Game*, there is not a breath of a suspicion that an icon can be anything but destructive, imprisoning. By the time of *Surfacing*, however, there appear to be, for Atwood, both nurturing and destructive icons: witness, for instance, the true icons left to the narrator by her parents. In the "Atwood Vocabulary" section of his *Margaret Atwood: A Feminist Poetics*, Frank Davey remarks under the heading "Signposts/Totems" that "The narrator now is obviously aware of the iconic significance of objects, and actively seeks to interpret them" — clearly, to her benefit.[13]

Even the poem "Woman Skating," which I cited above as implicating the writer in forming stifling icons, offers a potentially revisionist reading of icons. The "glass bell" that descends on the poem at the end, like a heavy stage curtain, is not only a token of inevitable authorial power and complicity; it is also memory itself, which allows both versions of the skating mother to survive. Glass bells may cut off air, but they also allow for perception, for re-vision.

This same complexity appears some years later in *The Handmaid's Tale*, a novel that celebrates memory as one of the most potent, subversive forces. As I've already suggested, much of Gilead's authoritarianism is associated with the enforcement of state icons. Not surprisingly, the victims of that system desire, for their part, to appropriate icons, to have the power of defining them; as Offred confesses,

> I would like to steal something from this room. I would like to take some small thing, the scrolled ashtray, the little silver pillbox from the mantel perhaps, or a dried flower: hide it in the folds of my dress or in my zippered sleeve, keep it there until this evening is over, secrete it in my room, under the bed, or in a shoe, or in a slit in the hard petit-point FAITH cushion. Every once in a while I would take it out and look at it. It would make me feel that I have power. (90)

Though Scott Symons would see this passage as a prime example of Atwood's counter power-lust, there is a deeper reason for Offred's desire for the iconic: it is a response to her loss of positive icons. The next time Offred confesses that she wants "to steal something," she has just been meditating on the icons she has lost: "I want Luke here so badly. I want to be held and told my name. I want to be valued, in ways that I am not; I want to be valuable. I repeat my former name, reminding myself of what I once could do, how others saw me" (108). People's names are analogous to painted icons — they stand for a prototype (the person or deity so designated) at the same time that they are a thing in themselves: an assemblage of letters. Like other icons, they solidify and, in the case of Western surnames, they are patriarchal, complicit in gender oppression. Still, flawed vessels though they are, names can carry the commodity Offred prizes: value — being valued by oneself and by others. No one can attach value to "Ofglen" or "Ofwarren"; such names merely point to a succession of women who have had one role in common. For these reasons, Offred's extended musings on the subject of her former name explicitly invoke iconic metaphors:

> I tell myself it doesn't matter, your name is like your telephone number, useful only to others; but what I tell myself is wrong, it does matter. I keep the knowledge of this name like something hidden, some treasure I'll come back to dig up, one day. I think of this name as buried. This name has an aura around it, like an amulet, some charm that's survived from an unimaginably distant past. I lie in my single bed at night, with my eyes closed, and the name floats there behind my eyes, not quite within reach, shining in the dark. (94)

This reevaluation of the icon reaches a climax in that consciously iconographical novel, *Cat's Eye*. Elaine, like Atwood, moves from iconoclasm to a renewed, reformulated desire for the iconic. As a child, playing with Eaton's catalogues, she feels weighed down by "the accumulation of all these objects, these possessions that would have to be taken care of, packed, stuffed into cars, unpacked" (53). Here Elaine is roughly at the stage of Marian McAlpin in *The Edible Woman*: groaning under the weight of consumer icons. But, as she explores art history and painting,

Elaine makes a truce with objects, and she does so by returning to painted icons:

> I don't like these shadowy, viscous pictures. I prefer the earlier ones, with their daytime clarity, their calm arrested gestures. . . . What I want instead is pictures that seem to exist of their own accord. I want objects that breathe out light; a luminous flatness. (326)

In a sly reference to her childhood disgust for "things," Elaine admits that, in her apprenticeship paintings of domestic objects, she has created "nothing that doesn't look like a random sampling from the Housewares Department of the Eaton's Catalogue" (327). Elaine has, in effect, turned iconic oppression into liberation through the iconic, and she continues to do the same in her painting career. Describing one canvas, which juxtaposes a modernist landscape, the figures of her parents, painted in super-realist style, with a "row of iconic-looking symbols painted in the flat style of Egyptian tomb frescoes," Elaine reveals that the latter are, in fact, logos from gas stations of her childhood. "They call into question the reality of landscape and figures alike," she concludes (406). So do the positive icons of memory in Atwood's more recent works: they have the power to "call into question" contemporary styles and usages that are often taken for granted or unthinkingly accepted as "real," revealing them, too, to be formed, artful, iconic. So, though her lover Jon fatuously excuses his own return to figural art by saying that he is using "common cultural sign systems to reflect the iconic banality of our times" (335), Elaine has discovered that icons — both contemporary and ancient — are anything but banal.

FROM ABOUT 1976 on, Margaret Atwood, too, has discovered that icons are not banal, and not necessarily constricting. That said, are we still left with an irresolvable paradox, with another "violent duality"? Has Atwood, as Eli Mandel wrote in 1977, embroiled herself in "an impossible dilemma about writing and experience" (174)? No; for Atwood, "paradox," "duality," and "dilemma" are not terms that signal the terminus of artistic exploration. Instead, Atwood takes her radical study of iconography beyond these conventional stop signs, by turning it into self-conscious art. She uses the unstable concept of iconography to survey the processes by which she herself has become an icon. Like John Barth's postmodern author par excellence, Atwood reaches the end of the artistic road, only to turn that terminus into the starting point for new fictions.

Visual icons have always had a similarly ambiguous referentiality. As Heinz Skrobucha points out, the church fathers tended to equate picture and prototype; to worship the iconic portrait of an Emperor or the Christ was to worship that ruler or deity as well.[14] In an analogous way, Atwood's portraits of iconized authors exist as shadowy palimpsests, revealing both their own figurations and those of Atwood-as-icon. In this portion of my argument I am indebted to George Bowering's exploration of various layers of self-referentiality in Atwood; in "Atwood's Hands" he argues that, in *Power Politics,* the narrator "sometimes lifts the mask to take a breath; she too breaks the rules, fracturing the artificial construct, turning the 'I' of the poem into Margaret Atwood . . ." (44). He also sees Atwood self-consciously playing on this persona overlap, by parodying the trademarks of her earlier work (47). Such a critique does raise some philosophical problems, such as the definition of "Margaret Atwood" as against a persona, and the potential reduction of all artifice to autobiography. Still, the element I propose to add to Bowering's study — that of self-conscious iconography — involves investigating the slippage, the murky areas between the Atwood persona and the Atwood icon (the latter to be distinguished from a living person named Margaret Atwood). The Atwood icon — or

Thing, as Atwood herself would have it — is a fairly easily isolated, defined constellation of trademarks and traits.

The earliest, explicit example of this iconic double-referentiality is Joan Foster from *Lady Oracle*, who parodically plays on a number of Atwoodian iconic trademarks. In fact, Joan herself uses the word "trademark" to refer to her hair, in the opening pages of the novel (9). When she proceeds to hack off her trademark with nail scissors, Joan, in effect, replays the final scene in *The Edible Woman*, where Marian's iconic cake woman has her head full of tresses sheared off by Duncan — except that in the later novel the act has acquired a whole new self-reflexivity. There are, of course, many other jesting self-references in the novel, which have already been traced by its critics, such as the reincarnation of Atwood's publishers, McClelland and Stewart, as the elephantine literary duo, Morton and Sturgess. But more important to my own study of Atwood's iconography of the public self is Joan's ironic status as a living dead poet. Surveying the newspaper clippings sent to her in Terremoto after her faked suicide, Joan realizes that "I'd been shoved into the ranks of those other unhappy ladies, scores of them apparently, who'd been killed by a surfeit of words." Not only that, Joan notes that "Sales of *Lady Oracle* were booming, every necrophiliac in the country was rushing to buy a copy" (315). Joan has become a dead poet who lives to survey her death by iconization; the situation self-consciously mirrors Atwood's meta-iconographical positioning in her own *Lady Oracle*.

Two stories from *Wilderness Tips* confirm Atwood's continuing fascination with the self-reflexive, iconized woman writer. The poet Selena from "Isis in Darkness" is engaged, like the early Atwood, in a deiconizing project; her tales of the underworld take place "not in the ancient Middle Kingdom of the Egyptians, but in flat, dingy Toronto, on Spadina Avenue, at night, among the darkened garment factories and delicatessens and bars and pawnshops" (66). (Consider Atwood's final poem from *The Jour-*

nals of Susanna Moodie, wherein Moodie returns from the under-world, riding a bus on St. Clair Avenue.) Selena, like Joan, becomes an iconized dead woman writer, though Richard, and not Selena herself, lives to document the process: "the academics are swarming like bot-flies," he reports (82). More important, the dead Selena is described in terms of a mosaic, though it is an icon of the critic-lover's making: Richard places a filecard "neatly in the mosaic of paper he is making across his desk . . . fitting her broken pieces back together" (83).

In "Uncles," the iconized figure is not a writer, nor does she die. But Susanna, a radio-then-television "national institution" (148) eerily reminiscent of the late Barbara Frum, undergoes some of Joan's and Selena's iconic transformations. Prime among these is what I would call the "embitchification" of the female icon. Susanna's former mentor Percy's tabloid-style exposé paints her much as Scott Symons renders Atwood: "DRAGON LADY REVEALED" (153). Atwood has spoken frankly about her own embitchification at the hands of the Percys of the literary world: "I'm quite happy to line up for a group spit on sexist reviewers, since over the years I've been on the receiving end of every bias in the book. . . . Witch, man-hater, man-freezing Medusa, man-devouring monster. The Ice Goddess, the Snow Queen."[15] She even adduces evidence from one critic's icono-graphical studies of her jacket photos: "not enough smiles, in her opinion. Girls, like the peasants in eighteenth-century genre paintings, are supposed to smile a lot" (20). A fictional version of this celebrity iconography appears in *Lady Oracle*; Joan tries to explain away a photograph of her fat former self with Aunt Lou by calling the plump figure her Aunt Deirdre, "a bitch" (89). Joan has succumbed to the myth of the "thin icon"; to be anything else, for her, is to court the danger of being labeled a "bitch."

Atwood's most sustained self-conscious study of the iconized author is, not surprisingly, Elaine Risley from *Cat's Eye*. Elaine picks up the story of the female literary icon where Atwood has left off at the end of *Lady Oracle*, and resumes with the figure of an older — and consciously aging — female artist. In this novel, though, the self-referentiality is not limited to a few trademarks; *Cat's Eye* narrates not only Elaine Risley's retrospective, but Margaret Atwood's as well. For example, Elaine is not the newborn celebrity that Joan Foster is; she is, in fact, so well worn an icon that her face invites transgression. One of the photographs that accompanies the newspaper notice of her retrospective is, Elaine comments, "shot a little from beneath so it looks as if I have a double chin" (225). Walking to the gallery where her retrospective is to be held, Elaine spots a flyer with another photograph of her on it, this time festooned with a moustache. The Maurice Duchamp echo reinforces Atwood's play on literary iconization: only the truly iconic invites such desecration.

This portrait of the aging female artist as disfigured icon engages a whole web of self-conscious Atwoodian references: from Atwood's apparently surprising physical petiteness (88), to her "embitchification" by the media (what Elaine christens "those witch-and-succubus pieces" [90]), and even her November birthday (108). Not only that, there is a corresponding web of inter-textual references to Atwood's other works; "I become fascinated with the effects of glass, and of other light-reflecting surfaces," says Elaine of her early paintings. And so might say early Atwood of works such as "Tricks with Mirrors" or "This Is a Photograph of Me." Another self-reflexive trick with a mirror found in this novel is Atwood's fictional return to her icon-obsessed poem, "Woman Skating." "Worse, she's taken up ice-dancing," a young Elaine says of her mother.

> She goes to classes at the local indoor rink, and tangoes and waltzes in time to tinny music, holding hands with other women. This is mortifying but at least she does it indoors, where no one

can see her. I can only hope she won't take to practising, later
when it's really winter, on the outdoor rink, where somebody I
might know could see her. (214)

"Over all this" — "this" referring here to her own career —
Atwood "place[s] a glass bell."

There are many more iconic self-portraits buried in Atwood's
poems and narratives, but the one that speaks most tellingly, to
my mind, of her (dis)figuration as a literary icon is that of the
weeping Madonna. Atwood is obviously struck by the Mexican
version of the Madonna icon; as she told Karla Hammond, when
she was in Mexico she saw a group of about six Virgin Marys,
which "all had little tin arms, legs, pigs, and cows pinned on
them, which were offerings that people had made when the
Virgin had saved something of theirs" (28). This memory becomes part of the fictional landscape of *Bodily Harm*: Rennie,
entering a church of St. Antoine,

> thinks of the Virgins in Mexico, several of them in each church,
> dressed in red or white or blue or black; you chose one and
> prayed to it according to your needs. Black was for loss. The
> skirts of the Virgins had been studded with little tin images, tin
> arms, tin legs, tin children, tin sheep and cows, even tin pigs, in
> thanks for what had been restored, or perhaps only in hope that
> it might be. (70)

In *Cat's Eye*, this pierced Madonna makes a return appearance;
this time she appears to Elaine on a stray religious picture,
"smiling sadly in a disappointed way; her hands are outstretched
as if in welcome, and her heart is on the outside of her chest, with
seven swords stuck into it" (182). In one form or another, this
sad or weeping Madonna makes appearances throughout
Atwood's career: mascara-besmudged, in the case of Mrs. Foster's

astral body in *Lady Oracle*, Anna in *Surfacing* (after her humiliation in front of the camera), and Serena Joy (in her former reincarnation as a Tammy Faye Bakerish gospel singer) in *The Handmaid's Tale*. There is also the shocking spectacle of the once stone-like Auntie Muriel of *Life Before Man* suddenly weeping at the thought of her own mortality. Frequently in Atwood, this image suggests the cracking of masks, of elaborate defences (themselves typically symbolized by the running make-up).

This slippage between mask and emotion, between icon and flesh, has always fascinated Margaret Atwood. If Atwood herself is an icon, she is not only the public one of which Robert Fulford wrote, and which Atwood herself christened the "Thing"; she is a textually self-conscious one as well. In truly meta-iconographical style, she is one more in her series of weeping Madonnas, a flesh-bound icon who breaks out of her iconhood only to cry out her vision of the icons that circumscribe her.

NOTES

1. Frank Davey 1984, 153.

2. Robert Fulford 1977, 95.

3. Davey 1984, 14.

4. William French 28.

5. Scott Symons 36.

6. Sherrill Grace 130.

7. Davey 1978, 173.

8. Heinz Skrobucha 62.

9. Kurt Weitzmann 11.

10. Ibid 8.

11. George Bowering 43.

12. Davey 1978, 181.

13. Ibid 1984, 123.

14. Skrobucha 16–17.

15. Margaret Atwood, "If You Can't Say Something Nice, Don't Say Anything at All," 20.

WORKS CITED

Atwood, Margaret. *The Animals in That Country*. Toronto: Oxford UP, 1968.

———. *Bluebeard's Egg*. Toronto: McClelland & Stewart, 1983.

———. *Bodily Harm*. 1982. Toronto: McClelland & Stewart-Seal, 1983.

———. *Cat's Eye*. Toronto: McClelland & Stewart, 1988.

———. *The Circle Game*. 1966. Intro. Sherrill E. Grace. Toronto: Anansi, 1978.

———. *The Edible Woman*. 1969. Toronto: McClelland & Stewart-Seal, 1981.

———. "If You Can't Say Something Nice, Don't Say Anything at All." *Language in Her Eye: Writing and Gender: Views by Canadian Women Writing in English*. Eds. Libby Scheier, Sarah Sheard, and Eleanor Wachtel. Toronto: Coach House Press, 1990. 15–25.

———. *The Handmaid's Tale*. Toronto: McClelland & Stewart, 1985.

———. *Lady Oracle*. 1976. Toronto: McClelland & Stewart-Seal, 1981.

———. *Life Before Man*. 1979. Toronto: McClelland & Stewart-Seal, 1980.

———. *Power Politics*. Toronto: Anansi, 1971.

———. *Procedures for Underground*. Boston: Little, Brown, 1970.

———. *Surfacing*. 1972. Toronto: PaperJacks, 1979.

———. *True Stories*. Toronto: Oxford UP, 1981.

———. *Two-Headed Poems*. Toronto: Oxford UP, 1978.

———. *Wilderness Tips*. Toronto: McClelland & Stewart, 1991.

———. *You Are Happy*. Toronto: Oxford UP, 1974.

Barth, John. "The Literature of Exhaustion." *Atlantic* (August 1967): 29–34.

Bowering, George, "Margaret Atwood's Hands." *Studies in Canadian Literature* 6:1 (1981): 39–52.

Davey, Frank. "Atwood's Gorgon Touch." *Brave New Wave*. Ed. Jack David. Windsor: Black Moss, 1978. 171–95.

——— *Margaret Atwood: A Feminist Poetics*. Vancouver: Talonbooks, 1984.

French, William. "Icon and Target: Atwood as Thing." *Globe and Mail* April 7, 1973: 28.

Fulford, Robert. "Do Canadians Fear Excellence? Consider the Case of Atwood." *Saturday Night* May 1980: 12.

———. "The Images of Atwood." *Malahat Review* 41 (1977): 95–98.

Grace, Sherrill E. *Violent Duality: A Study of Margaret Atwood*. Ed. Ken Norris. Montréal: Véhicule, 1980.

Hammond, Karla. "An Interview with Margaret Atwood." *American Poetry Review* 8:5 (1979): 27–29.

Mandel, Eli. "Atwood Gothic." *Malahat Review* 41 (1977): 165–74.

Skrobucha, Heinz. *Introduction to Icons.* Trans. Giovanni Rossetti and Marguerite Buchloh. Recklinghausen: Aurel Bongers, 1961.

Symons, Scott. "Atwood-as-Icon." *The Idler* May 1990: 36–39.

Weitzmann, Kurt. *The Icon: Holy Images — Sixth to Fourteenth Century.* New York: George Braziller, 1978.

Patricia Merivale

From "Bad News" to "Good Bones": Margaret Atwood's Gendering of Art and Elegy

MARGARET ATWOOD'S SECOND COLLECTION of short prose pieces or poems, *Good Bones* (1992), follows by a decade her first, *Murder in the Dark*. As John Bemrose points out (and Neil Besner implies), such texts, however we wish to designate their ambiguous and variegated genres, seem to have taken the place of the lyric poem in Atwood's earlier work. In a 1990 interview with Eleanor Wachtel, Atwood spoke of an organizing principle in her lyric collections, making them "cognate with sonnet cycles . . . a number of short poems connected together in a narrative way. And the book [*Power Politics*, 1971] is arranged so that the first section is personal, the middle one is political and the third one is mythic" (Wachtel 197–98). It seems plausible to suppose that the two collections taking (at least for the moment) the place of the lyric in her oeuvre may follow similar principles, although it seems unlikely that the "sonnet cycle" is still the generic model. These books are as closely related, perhaps, to Baudelaire's prose-poem sequence, *Spleen de Paris*, as *Power Politics* is to the sonnet cycles of Shakespeare or Elizabeth Barrett Browning. I have asserted elsewhere that *Murder in the Dark,"* consists largely, if not entirely, of prose poems, in a sense that Baudelaire would have understood (if not appreciated). If, as the anonymous jacket blurb writer puts it, *Good Bones* is "continuing in the tradition of . . . *Murder in the Dark*, the texts in the more recent collection may also gain a purpose, indeed a synergy, from their juxtaposition as a prose-poem sequence, however fortuitously driven it may in fact have been by Atwood's rhythms of publication.

While a good deal of *Murder in the Dark* was "coming from" Atwood's poetry, it could be argued that *Good Bones* was, to about the same degree, coming from Atwood's prose, given its increased emphasis on revisionist prose genres and metanarrative. From either direction, one arrives at the often anecdotal, tightly organized, refrain-shaped, even internally rhymed short prose pieces, turning on a point at the end, all of which, in either collection, deserve consideration as prose poems.

The book is organized in much the same way as *Murder in the Dark*. There are the same number of poems, twenty-seven, many of them segmented into five or six parts. (These subdivided poems seem more "cognate with sonnet cycles" than do the collections as a whole.) Atwood herself divided *Murder in the Dark* into four groups of poems, the first group containing eight poems, the next consisting of one in five sections, the next six, and the last twelve. Within each group internal relationships of type, form, image, and theme are evident. *Good Bones* seems similarly divisible into groups of six, fifteen, and six, although, as I will indicate, the demarcations are somewhat more fluid, especially in the middle group. Other readers might align them differently.

The blurb writer (like the reviewers) emphasizes the generic mélange, or "stimulating miscellany" of the collection: "parable, monologue, mini-romance and mini-biography, speculative fiction, prose lyric, outrageous recipe and reconfigured fairy tale." A "cornucopia," to be sure, but a cornucopia of highly revisionist generic clichés. One text, indeed, is not even set out as prose: the thematically key text, "Let Us Now Praise Stupid Women," is in a comic, but unrhymed, Ogden Nash meter, with strongly rhythmical lines of radically uneven lengths.

Many of the *Good Bones* poems could be added to the *Murder in the Dark* groupings without obvious dislocation and have similar relationships to Atwood's other works. The substantial grouping of five sci-fi satires of the sex war ("Epaulettes," "Cold-Blooded," "Alien Territory," "Adventure Story," and "Homeland-ing"), plus a pair of futurist polemics, "Hardball" and "We Want It All" (all except the last are in the middle group), constitutes the major shift of emphasis from the mixture found in *Murder in the Dark* (though "Simmering" offers a precedent), while anecdotally shaped epiphanic units of "autobiography" are distinctly less frequent (and not as successful: "Poppies," "Theology") in *Good Bones* than they were in *Murder in the Dark*. The elegantly comic self-reflexive meditations on art, gendered female, are given pride of place here; in *Murder in the Dark* the "autobiographical" group was placed first. There are numerous echoes, ties, and links between the two books — doubtless articulating matters of enduring and repeated interest to Atwood — that may be considered "intertextualities."

The few reviews of *Good Bones* are on the whole appreciative. But it is somehow "in the air" that this book is not only more miscellaneous, but also consists of a running down of techniques and inspirations, providing weaker examples of Atwoodian strategies for the compact prose text (to beg the question of genre for the moment) than *Murder in the Dark*. Not perhaps a major Atwood, the Conventional Wisdom seems to run, but simply a Fact of Publishing. She has, we all know, at intervals of several years, selected, tidied up, and then published in collections, her poems and short stories, most or all of which had appeared singly or in small groups in an astonishing variety of magazines, from mass-circulation to the "littlest" and most esoteric, during the intervening years. There are also a few pieces that may have languished without previous appearances (some of the *Good Bones* texts have appeared previously as many as half a dozen times). Be that as it may, the resulting collection gains a textual life of its own. I will allude to the intra-textualities in *Good Bones* as well as to its numerous echoes of other texts in the Great World of texts, both key elements in these highly, deliberately, and (if I am right about seeing them largely as prose poems) inevitably "inter-textual" works.

As my title suggests, I see the chiasmic framing of the book between its brilliant opening poem, "Bad News," and its equally brilliant closing poem, "Good Bones," to be the major clue to its structure. Further, the fifteen middle poems, which are not, in my view, the "central" ones, are framed between the six opening poems (devoted in Atwood's characteristically subversive way to the question of Woman and Story) and the six closing poems, each of a strikingly elegiac nature. These twelve make up the meat of this inside-out sandwich.

In the corresponding thematic structure, "good bones" (note the irony in that subtle oxymoron) can be seen as both a riposte and a partial solution to the problem of living with "Bad News," of which this book, like the world, is full. There is a lot of bad news here — indeed the Atwood world is largely bad news — but it is dealt with self-reflexively in the first poem, a metagossip poem. "Bad News," personified as the artist of the microart of gossip (as well as an intertextual artifact), makes "good stories" out of "bad news." Atwood's particular art here is to demonstrate the making of art out of gossip, using the colloquial and oral to speak about the social and psychological.

Good bones, conversely, are both literally and figuratively the supporting structure of our survival in this world of bad news, as well as our *memento mori*, the raw material of elegy, where textual and fleshly bones occupy the same verbal premises. The book seems divided between these two antinomies. I am claiming that the book has indeed some unifying "structural principles" (149) — has, as it were, its own "Good Bones" — in at least one of the several senses that Atwood teases out of that cliché in her concluding poem.

The Woman and Story section, the first group of six, is so tightly organized as to constitute a kind of rhyme scheme: A BB CC A. "Bad News" and "Let Us Now Praise Stupid Women" frame the other four poems, which form two pairs: "The Little Red Hen Tells All" and "Gertrude Talks Back," and "There Was Once" and "Unpopular Gals." The group is further unified thematically (like *Murder in the Dark*'s "Women's Novels" and "Happy Endings"), by the patterns of metatextually gendered art, here exemplified in images of vocalization: "news," "tells all," "talks back," "Skip the description," "My turn [to talk]," "let us praise."

Good Bones offers a different kind of metatextuality from *Murder in the Dark*: its emphasis is on narrative instead of on verb-image-text. I have already suggested that it moves towards "prose poem" from the direction of Atwood's prose, whereas parts of *Murder in the Dark*, at least, move towards prose poem from the direction of Atwood's poetry. There is not much, in *Good Bones*, equivalent to *Murder in the Dark*'s reifying and gendering of words, with their "octopoid arms of labial polysyllables" and "arachnoid grace" ("Women's Novels" #3). "Metaphor leads me by the nose, into the maze" ("Women's Novels" #7), but it is plot that leads into the narrative mazes of *Good Bones*. We are never invited to "fall back into these rhythms as if into safe hands" ("Iconography," *Murder in the Dark* 52). For instance, we, the implied readers of "Let Us Now Praise Stupid Women," are urging a ditzy gothic heroine, a positive hyperbole of dumbness, too dumb even for a role in the inner narratives of *Lady Oracle*, to save herself: "But trapped inside the white pages, she can't hear us . . . this girl couldn't tear her way out of a paper bag" (35). "Paper" swivels from the potentially metatextual to the dead-metaphorical without a tremor, whereas in "The Page," to be trapped in the page is an altogether more metaphysical danger; for the explicitly poetic consciousness, "the page closes over their heads without a sound . . . " (*Murder in the Dark* 45).

"Bad News," the eponymous central character of the first poem, is the personification of an ironic emblem in which Virgil's allegorical character, "Rumour" (Aeneid IV: 173–98; VII: 329–56 [Allecto]), is renamed "Bad News," while keeping her classical "brass wings" and "literate serpents." She is bored these days, and, like all of us, eager for a disaster, any disaster, both to break the monotony and to comfort us in our own lesser afflictions. The reader becomes embroiled with the persona of the implied reader: "No news is good news, everyone knows that. You know it too, and you like it that way." "No news" flips over, by a syntactic pun, into meaning "There is no such thing as good news," trapping us into agreeing that we long to hear Bad News, trapping us into the identification that Atwood makes more explicit in "Let Us Now Praise Stupid Women": "Hypocrite lecteuse! Ma semblable! Ma soeur!" (37).

"The Little Red Hen Tells All" is a revision of the familiar animal fable, turned into a female artist parable (and a seemingly autobiographical one at that). It is also a reworking of the favourite Atwood topos of "bread" (used in *Murder in the Dark*), and a fountain of good advice: "Keep your eyes to the grindstone and you could find a grain of wheat, too." "Gertrude Talks Back," its companion piece, is a dramatic monologue (the only one in the book, in the strict Robert Browning sense), where a specific listener (Hamlet) is implied in the monologue of the specific speaker (Gertrude) in her revisionist *Hamlet*. A feminist Gertrude, with proleptically "ageing bones," reenacts that most magisterial of English patriarchal master narratives, in much the same tone of voice as the Little Red Hen.

The title "There Was Once" translates the German version — *Es war einmal* — of the standard fairy-tale opening, better known in English as "once upon a time." Using "there was once" as a synecdoche for storytelling, it is a metafictional fairy tale on narrative method, which demonstrates the difficulties of carrying on with a story that is being interrupted and corrected one word at a time. It is a skit on the all-too-easy and local targets of Political Correctness, whose personified proponent is shown as deconstructing this particular narrative out of existence. In "Let Us Now Praise Stupid Women," Atwood asks us to "Imagine a world without stories!" (32); in "There Was Once," by a different set of rhetorical strategies,[1] Atwood shows one way of bringing about this disaster.

"There Was Once" is perhaps the least successful of these gendered metafictions; "Unpopular Gals" is a more impressive example of the pseudogenre of fake fairy tale. It revises the ferocious witch (as many other feminist revisions have done) by suggesting the justness of her cause and the magnitude of her own wrongs, using such familiar Atwood topoi as "red-hot shoes" and the cutting off of feet; but, more interestingly, by means of a self-reflexive self-defence, this witch identifies herself as that strong character of (meta)fiction: "I'm the plot, babe, and don't ever forget it" (30). In its version of the plot of Fall and Redemption, "Unpopular Gals" anticipates the theme of "Let Us Now Praise Stupid Women": that patriarchal narrative is dependent for its key plots on the stereotypical follies of women. As in "Good Bones," "Good daughters," those who, like Wise Virgins, "miss out" on what Plot has to offer, get "'a dutiful wife' . . . engraved on their tombstones." As in "Bad News," Plot says, "I stir things up, I get things moving."

"Let Us Now Praise Stupid Women" is, like "Bad News," worth examining in intertextual detail. Its title is at least doubly parodic, of "Let us now praise famous men," from Ecclesiasticus (Apocrypha) 44.1, and of James Agee's well-known book of the same name (1939). In it the Wise and Foolish Virgins exemplify, hilariously, the biblical revisionism so crucial in *The Handmaid's Tale*. There are two key intertextual allusions, both intriguingly mediated by T. S. Eliot[2]: Goldsmith's "lovely woman stoops [or bungles her way into] folly" with the assistance of Eliot's *The Waste Land* (line 250); and, again by way of *The Waste Land* (line 76), Baudelaire's "Hypocrite lecteur! Mon semblable! Mon frère!" supplies the poem's punch line (with "lecteur" inaccurately re-gendered into "lecteuse" rather than "lectrice"). "Let Us Now Praise Stupid Women" deploys the Bad News binaries of monotonous calm and exhilarating storm, for the tediously virtuous Wise Virgins supply no narrative interest at all, while the Foolish Ones yield "much satisfactory uproar" (34). We are reminded of Eve, who, with the help of the snake, makes all of Judeo-Christian theology happen.

"The Female Body," a transitional poem, looks back over its shoulder at the matter of gendered art in its self-reflexive topic-body, to which we are introduced in the epic catalogue of its first section, through the personified verbalization, "my limping topic." The harassed author, being (in real life) solicited for a text (this one), goes off in search of "an avocado, an alderman, an adjective," that is to say, a Word, with which to accomplish her commission. This first section is very much a prose poem of the *Murder in the Dark* variety. Its variegated subsequent sections, although not without bony prolepsis ("The skeleton, as you might expect, is white" 41), on the whole look forward to the second group, heavy (perhaps too heavy) with satirical poems of the Sex War.

"The Female Body" begins, like "The Little Red Hen," as fake autobiography, and like "Let Us Now Praise Stupid Women," as a metafictional satire. It is paired, both thematically and in terms of publishing "occasion," with "Alien Territory," which could equally well be titled "The Male Body."[3] Most of "Alien Territory" deals with the specifically male psychic landscape of birth trauma, castration complex, and anxiety over the size, unreliability, and vulnerability of the penis. Men's bodies are dangerous to each other (see section 3, on war), as well as to women (see section 6, on Bluebeard). There are strong internal parallels between "The Female Body" and "Alien Territory"; both spin seven variations (sections) on their "capacious topic," and both end lyrically. "The Female Body" ends negatively, as the male imprisons the female. As if in reply, the poem on the male body, "Alien Territory," ends affirmatively, for a male is found (or imagined) in a prose-poem repetition of "poverty" and "beggar," to bless the woman's body, saying it is "made of light." Then reciprocal compassion can begin, for when the male "says" his own body, i.e., his feelings, he can then articulate that key, equally shared word/fact, Death, "making the word sound like the backwash of a wave." Compare the sardonically observed social world of "Men at Sea," in which men are so pointedly unable to reciprocate compassion by sharing their feelings.

"The Female Body" and "Alien Territory" are not printed consecutively; in fact, they frame the six poems that constitute the most miscellaneous (and, with the conspicuous exception of "Men at Sea," the least successful) grouping of all: "In Love with Raymond Chandler," "Stump Hunting," "Making a Man," "Epaulettes," "Cold-Blooded," and "Men at Sea." "Epaulettes" and "Cold-Blooded," plus another five poems printed after "Alien Territory," are largely stuck in the sci-fi mode of what Marleen Barr calls "feminist fabulation," or, for a more Canadian comparison, in the mode of Louky Bersianik's *L'eugélionne*, the world "made strange" by means of satiric gender inversions.

"Men at Sea," however, is formally an almost perfect prose poem. As in several of the prose poems of *Murder in the Dark*, its title is "turned" at the end into a framing refrain; here, by punning punctuation, it becomes "Men, at sea." Yet, although this conclusion comments sardonically on the masculine glory suggested by the title, the poem expresses some compassion for the male of the species. Like the tentative map of the reconciliation of male and female at the end of "Alien Territory," it offers an unusually affirmative variation of the sex war pattern that dominates the central grouping. "Men at Sea" is a short bridge-poem from "The Female Body" to "Alien Territory"; it sets out the gendered dilemma to which "Alien Territory" provides a possible answer.

"My Life as a Bat" is, of course, another parody title: Philip Roth's *My Life as a Man* (1974), or Reinar Jönsson's *My Life as a Dog* (novel, 1983; film, 1989), are among the most chronologically apposite among dozens of similar formulations being spoofed here. The poem is, like several of the others, a sort of sonnet cycle made up of five variations on a theme. Its first segment makes the case for reincarnation, the narrative premise for the speaker's memories of bat life; its second tells the Bat-narrator's nightmares, in which light rather than dark is the negative element: thus, more properly perhaps, daymares? "For some of us, the mythologies are different" (100): evil, for bats, consists of humans seen as violent and hostile, and thus "made strange" by the bat perspective. Apart from the charm of Atwood's bat world, which stands on its own, there is clearly an allegory of Otherness and its perceptions, whether those of women or artists, or animals. The third section critiques vampire films as clues to bat life, finding them laughably unrealistic in terms of the speaker's tangential memories: "O Dracula, unlikely hero! O flying leukemia, in your cloak like a living umbrella . . ." The fourth is an anecdote of World War II on "The Bat as Deadly Weapon," i.e., as another innocent victim of the war establishment. The concluding section, "Beauty," links back to the opening propositions about reincarnation: perhaps the speaker's human life is the interlude, and her bat life real. She yearns to return to bathood, to reencounter the otherness for which she has made so eloquent a lyric case, while, at the same time, using it to critique humanhood.

There are strikingly elegiac elements in "My Life as a Bat," "shrivelled to a few small bones" (100), as there are in "An Angel." This angel, the Angel of Suicide, is a messenger, of sorts, with the unnervingly surrealistic "face of a grey egg." "Poppies:

Three Variations" is, as its title suggests, a triple meta-elegiac turn on the greatest and most familiar of Canadian historical elegies. It starts as pseudoautobiography: the child meditates on the veterans' experience of "rusty shells, broken skulls" (113–14), transmuting them into the lost or abandoned toy soldiers "lying down there . . . waiting to be dug up" (115). It concludes as meta-elegy: "The sharp blades of the reapers . . . Disaster sells beer . . . below thought, below memory, below everything, the guns" (119–20). The entire triad is an exercise in variant vocabulary (although, arguably, one too reliant on the gimmick of deploying McCrae's stanza three times), as each clichéd word is turned to new purposes in each of its three new contexts, forming an elegiac meditation on the past, the present, and the future.

The last six poems of this middle section (from "Hardball" through "Homelanding"), modulate from the sci-fi sex-war satire into the explicitly elegiac concluding poems. Even the futurist polemics, "Hardball" and "We Want It All," turn science fiction towards elegy, in terms of apocalyptic visions supplying communal elegies for the Earth and all its living creatures. "Hardball" is by far the stronger of the two, starting with its title, which turns out to be a subtle pun, both colloquial and literary. The Marvell echoes at the opening (in the "hard [stone] ball") glide smoothly into an antique advertising cliché from my youth and Atwood's: "so round, so firm, so fully packed" — we cannot help but add, *sotto voce*, "so free and easy on the draw." There is flexible as well as superabundant intertextuality in this poem, including the Bible, "Kubla Khan," and the philosophical analogies of the world, first to "an eighteenth-century ship, with stowaways but no destination," and then to "a nineteenth-century lifeboat . . . with castaways but no rescuers" (95), whose inhabitants' fate is computerized cannibalism. "We Want It All" is, in comparison, a merely readable tract, and its title a relatively cheap shot (for Atwood) at un-gendering a gender slogan.

But particularly elegiac is "Homelanding," sections 5–6, where the science fiction explorer first describes "death in our world," and then transposes the clichéd request "take me to your leaders" into "take me to your deaths," suggesting the ultimately nongendered focus of the Atwood elegy: "It's this knowledge of death, which we share, where we overlap. Death is our common ground. Together, on it, we can walk forward . . . take me to your deaths" (127–28).

The six concluding poems are elegiac, but although they link back to the gendered art of the first section, they are not gendered in the same sense, for perhaps, as "Homelanding" seems to suggest, Death is an Equal Opportunity Employer, and elegy can only be human. On the whole Atwood's elegies, combining elements of her elegiac short stories with reminiscences of her more gothic lyric poems, are neither polemically gendered nor comic-satiric.

"Third Handed" invites comparison with the *Murder in the Dark* poem, "Instructions for the Third Eye" — the eye (as in Jay Macpherson's poem "The Third Eye") of artistic or visionary epiphany. But artist parable is subordinate to elegy here. The poem gives us the "Third Hand" in a dozen iconic, pictorial, and semiotic variants, culminating in the theme from W. W. Jacobs's ghoulish ghost story "The Monkey's Paw": "No one notices the third hand creeping away painfully on its fingers . . . trailing raw blood from its severed wrist" (130). The iconic hand then turns into an extended metaphor, for "It writes, and having written, moves" ("nor all your Piety nor Wit, / Nor all your Tears wash out a Word of it," Omar Khayyám informs us); the hand "writes" us, as language "writes" destiny. "Vacant spaces belong to it, the vowel O, all blank pages . . . the hour before birth and the minute after death . . . " (131). Its last metamorphosis is into what it was all along, the hand of the uncanny, of the child-guide to the land of death.

"Death Scenes" is plainly a *poème à clé*, memorializing the death of a specific woman. Whose death? I wonder, very much as I did when first reading Atwood's *conte à clé* on the death of a female artist, "Isis in Darkness" (*Wilderness Tips*, 1990) usually understood to be about Gwendolyn MacEwen. "Death Scenes" opens with seven speech-paragraphs in the dying woman's voice, continues with four interpolated in the voice of an attendant, and concludes with seven in the voice of the Atwood-speaker (the implied listener of the first section). It is structured on pastoral elegy motifs, anticipating the subtler strengths of "Good Bones": "I want to get the rose bushes in first . . . I want to see what comes up, in the spring" (133–34), says the first voice; "I went over there, did a little weeding" (136), says the third, or Atwood-voice. The word "scenes," from the title, is picked up in the punning "Glorious scenes" (135), where the "scenes" she made when alive segue into the "scenes" of her death.

"Death Scenes" forms a gender-pair with the more easily decoded riddle poem that follows it, "Four Small Paragraphs," an elegy for the male artist, Albert Camus. Its epigraph, "For Mr. Flat," reveals his identity by way of the word "camus," a French adjective meaning "flat-[nosed]." Both the spare North African setting of this graveyard poem and its much sparer style match the spirit of its subject, making the poem an impressive variation on Atwood's usual voices.[4] The "tough and pungent [mountain] shrubs, the *maquis* they're called" (138), stark and stoical "with [their] dark cryptic foliage . . . No hope, no armfuls of petals," correspond to what the elegist has found in Camus's dark and cryptic books: "*Don't expect mercy.*" This is also a poem about the right way to memorialize the dead: it concludes with the speaker's view of the contrast between "other graves" decorated with bright porcelain flowers and Camus's grave with its "greyness, the elegance of plainsong . . . Later, when I went back, someone had left six withering real roses in a kitchen jar" (139).

Camus is one of Atwood's rare nonsatirized male protagonists, and this almost pastoral elegy for him is remarkable in Atwood's work for gendering both art and elegy masculine.

"Dance of the Lepers" is "a dance of going on despite everything," an inner performance, a story as/of inner artifact, like so many of the artist parables of *Murder in the Dark*, which it also resembles in the parallel refrains of its epiphanic catalogue: "They [the Lepers] looked like animated mummies from an old horror film . . . They looked like war casualties . . . They looked like your own face in the steam-covered mirror after a bath, your own face temporarily nameless" (146). They warn us with their bells that (as we have known at least since *Lady Oracle*), "Dancing can be dangerous." But the moral of this parable of the artist's struggle for form turns out to be, "If you can dance, even you, why not the rest of us?" (147). And the elegiac affirmations of "Good Bones," the masterly concluding poem, come within reach.

"Good Bones" is in five sections, like "My Life as a Bat" and several other poems in *Good Bones*. These sections are subdivided, with patterned symmetry, into two, three, four, three, and two paragraphs respectively, making "Good Bones" as formally complex a poem as any in the volume. Furthermore, the poem picks up many echoes from the rest of the collection. The extended metaphor adumbrated in the title and played out in its subsequent variations is like, but far cleverer than, the different recipes for "Making a Man"; it forms a scaffolding, or even a skeleton, for the poem. The compacted multiple word plays of "Good Bones" make it very much a prose poem; its title in particular is varied into a refrain, which forms, in conclusion, its frame in a way we have found typical of prose poems like "Men at Sea" and many in *Murder in the Dark*.

From the end of the first section, where "the bones come out like flowers," and throughout this poem, we are invited to think of the pastoral, of pastoral elegy, and perhaps also of "les fleurs du mal."

The second section, a sequential episode of childhood autobiography in the *Murder in the Dark* manner, merges the minstrelsy of the (Darktown) Strutters with the Prophet Ezekiel by the synecdoche of "them bones" becoming "them dry bones." The "Hallowe'en skeleton, white and one-dimensional" leads into the autobiographical summary: "So much for death, at that time, there." At this time, here (the present time of the poem), death has clearly come much closer.

In the third section, set in the cemetery, the Donne reference, "circlets of bright hair" around the bone, suggests metaphysical elegy, while the dichotomy of "good" and "bad" bones looks back to the "good" and "bad" women of the gendered metafictions at the beginning of the collection. In the fourth section, the images of osteoporosis hold together another more compact and poetically stronger "Death Scene," or elegy, for a woman whose ashes are to be buried "under the tulips." The epitaph, "We are both fond of gardens," points back to "bones . . . like flowers" of the first section.

All the cold pastoralism here (and to a lesser degree in the other elegies) reminds us once more of the so far distinctly underestimated influence of Jay Macpherson's poetry upon Atwood's. There are echoes of her gothic poems in the "bad bones" of the third section and in the horror movies of "Dance of the Lepers" and "My Life as a Bat." And, again, the equivalence of bones and flowers in the first section, like the ashes under the tulips, reminds us of Macpherson's poems, "Girl with Buck Teeth" and especially "The Gardeners," with its own ironic anticipation of "We are both fond of gardens" and its deployment of cliché:

My next neighbour
Worked herself to bone
Raising prize bokays
In a yard mostly stone. . . .

But I lie pushing daisies
Fat and white as me
(*Poems Twice Told* 57)

In the fifth section of "Good Bones," beginning "Today I speak to my bones as I would speak to a dog," the "aching bones" and the "limping topic" from earlier poems find their final resting place: "Good bones, good bones, I coax . . . do one more trick, once more" (153). Here it is the vocative intonation that produces the pun.

Such subversion of prose genres through compact parody and canny intertextuality, in which an anecdotal structure is soaked in the acrid sauces of black humour, has been a recipe for one branch of the oxymoronic genre of the prose poem since the time of Baudelaire (see Evans et al.). It is this kind of prose poem that interests Atwood, rather than the lyrically surreal and melodious prose poems of the 1890s (see Phyllis Webb's recent collection, *Hanging Fire*, for examples of that mode), or the more abstractly meditative and philosophical kind represented by, say, John Ashbery (see Murphy), or those found in the works of many Canadian poets influenced more by the "redskins" (Pound-Williams-Olson-Black Mountain) than by the "palefaces" (Baudelaire and Eliot, for our immediate purposes). Atwood has, for the moment, the Baudelairean mode almost to herself in Canadian poetry, as she quite brilliantly demonstrated in *Murder in the Dark*. *Good Bones* consolidates her generic monopoly in such prose poems, while extending her range, first in the gendered metatextualities of the opening section, and then, especially, in the elegiac intertextualities of the closing section.

"Bad News," the opening poem, flips over at its conclusion onto the Baudelairean (or Eliotic) hypocrisy of "you," the "lectrice," or implied reader, settling back in (her) chair to rustle the paper — the daily paper, containing all that bad news, but perhaps also the "paper" of this book of poems. The book concludes, or very nearly, with "That's what it says here: the last word" (151) of an epitaph for another set of "good bones," and does in fact conclude with the words "*Good* bones! Good *bones!* Keep on going," giving two more senses of the polyvalent cliché that Atwood has permutated so skillfully throughout the poem. What is Atwood gaining by so exact (and obviously deliberate) a framework for a collection whose middle is indeed so miscellaneous? Are any of these poems fulfilling the function for *Good Bones* that Sherrill Grace attributes to "Instructions for the Third Eye," *Murder in the Dark*'s concluding poem, which is "teaching the reader how to read" the collection? Surely "Good Bones" itself, very nearly the "last words" of the book, must be (very nearly) the last words about it, for the image of the "good bones" turns out to be a satisfyingly inevitable self-reflexive metaphor for the structure of the book as a whole.

NOTES

1. See Salman Rushdie's *Haroun and the Sea of Stories* for similar strategies aimed at censorship from the Right.
2. Atwood's early poetry gathered momentum "once I hit T. S. Eliot," she says. In Wachtel 192.
3. These poems first appeared in "The Female Body" and "The Male Body" issues, respectively, of the *Michigan Quarterly Review*, 1990.
4. Compare Atwood's short story, "The Grave of the Famous Poet" (*Dancing Girls*, 1977), on a somewhat similar topic.

WORKS CITED

Atwood, Margaret. *Good Bones*. Toronto: Coach House Press, 1992.

———. *Murder in the Dark*. Toronto: Coach House Press, 1983.

Barr, Marleen. *Feminist Fabulation: Space/Postmodern Fiction*. Iowa City: U of Iowa P, 1992.

Bemrose, John. "*Good Bones*" (Review). *Maclean's* 105.40 (October 5, 1992): S10-S11.

Besner, Neil. "A Poet's Bones" (Review). *Canadian Literature* 138/9 (Fall-Winter 1993): 105–6.

Draper, Gary. "*Good Bones*" (Review). *Books in Canada* 21.7 (October 1992): 40–41.

Drobot, Eve. "*Good Bones*" (Review). *Globe and Mail*, September 19, 1992, sec. 6: 10.

Evans, Margery A. *Baudelaire and Intertextuality: Poetry at the Crossroads*. Cambridge: Cambridge UP, 1993.

Grace, Sherrill E. "Stories 'beneath the page': Atwood's New Fiction." *CRNLE Reviews Journal* 1 (1984): 68–71.

Kemp, Peter. "The Atwood Variations" (Review of *Good Bones*). *Times Literary Supplement*, November 6, 1992: 20.

Macpherson, Jay. *Poems Twice Told: The Boatman & Welcoming Disaster*. Toronto: Oxford UP, 1981.

Merivale, Patricia. "'*Hypocrite lecteuse! Ma semblable! Ma soeur!*': On Teaching Atwood's *Murder in the Dark*." Forthcoming in *Approaches to Teaching Atwood's* The Handmaid's Tale *and Other Works*. Eds. Thomas Friedman, Shannon Hengen, Sharon Wilson. New York: Modern Languages Association, 1995.

Murphy, Margueritte. *A Tradition of Subversion: The Prose Poem in England from Wilde to Ashbery*. Amherst: U of Massachusetts P, 1992.

Perrick, Penny. "*Good Bones*" (Review). *Sunday Times*, November 8, 1992, sec. 6: 10.

Wachtel, Eleanor. "Margaret Atwood." *Writers & Company: In Conversation with CBC Radio's Eleanor Wachtel*. Toronto: Knopf, 1993. 190–203.

Webb, Phyllis. *Hanging Fire*. Toronto: Coach House Press, 1990.

Shannon Hengen

Zenia's Foreignness

SEVERAL YEARS AGO I presented a paper at the Association for Canadian Studies in the United States conference, in which I argued that Linda Hutcheon's theories of postmodernism fail to account for agency, either in literary criticism or in the objects of its study. I now realize that, in fact, *I* lack a theory of agency, and will therefore use Hutcheon's ideas as a starting point in suggesting a place for Margaret Atwood's most recent novel in a canon of postmodern, postcolonial, Canadian literature, with a view to generating further discussion about agency in Canadian criticism and art. My canon could be described further as postfeminist, postimperial, postnational, and postgeneric, and it emerges from ideas proposed by such commentators on Canadian culture as Frank Davey, Robert Lecker, Donna Bennett, Diana Brydon, and Jonathan Hart. Their work has the potential to reinvigorate Canadian culture by showing its unique place in the larger world.

Despite the negative evaluations of Linda Hutcheon's oeuvre, including my own observation that the Canadianness of the Canadian postmodern is never adequately described (see also Brydon, "The White Inuit Speaks"; McGregor; and Weir), the contributions she has made to defining and indicating the Canadian postmodern are invaluable. Particularly in *The Canadian Postmodern, Remembering Postmodernism, Splitting Images,* and *Other Solitudes*, Hutcheon discusses or anthologizes provocative and evocative Canadian art, art that has the power to redefine nadianness. Although she does not show in sufficient detail precisely how these works have the power to change, or indeed why she chooses these works to study, she provides sophisticated theoretical bases and interpretations, and contributes immensely to the discussion of Canadian literary history by so thoroughly addressing Canadian art after modernism. While she has not fully achieved what Robert Lecker calls "the rehistoricization of Canadian literature" ("Canonization" 671), she has done much to broaden the scope of what we study as art. And her recent essay, "Eruptions of Postmodernity: The Postcolonial and the Ecological," does recontextualize Northrop Frye's views of Canadian nature within the discourse of postcolonial critique. As well, she devotes the last chapter of her most recent book, *Irony's Edge: the theory and politics of irony* — a book whose subjects range from Richard Wagner's opera to Kenneth Branagh's films and the photographs of contemporary German artist Anselm Kiefer — to a controversial show at Toronto's Royal Ontario Museum, entitled "Into the Heart of Africa." Thereby Canada and things Canadian are read in a postnational, postmodern context.

If other critics do not share Hutcheon's view of the pervasiveness of irony and parody in Canadian postmodern art, we are then called to discover what we do see as recurring techniques. My own discussion of Atwood's novel will argue, for example, that postimperial characterization might be seen as a recurring strategy in contemporary Canadian art. This kind of characterization recalls the old oppressions of a Eurocentric view (or the oppressions of racist and sexist views) by undercutting those oppressions through other, New World characterizations. Thus a third subject position emerges from the conflict. My description of Atwood's novel as postmodern thus arises directly from Hutcheon's convincing arguments that a peculiar kind of dialogic discourse appears in Canadian postmodern novels, particularly Atwood's. While Hutcheon calls that discourse ironic, I call it postimperial — a term of my own coinage — to specify what ideology is being addressed. Whereas Hutcheon writes that "Atwood's ironies are multi-edged, . . . cutting against both cultural stereo-typing and women's own complicity with that process" (*Splitting Images* 101), I would conclude that her postimperial characterizations are "multi-edged," challenging both Old and New World ideologies to form something other. Similar characterizations in works of art that show Canadian oppressions of other Canadians, beyond foreign imperialisms, might be brought together with future discussions of *The Robber Bride*.

Reading Atwood's novel as postcolonial (the international form of postimperial) is enabled by the commentary of Jonathan Hart, Diana Brydon, and Donna Bennett. In an article that I would call an example of postimperial criticism, Hart addresses the threat of a neo-imperialist criticism arising from the fact that literary critics take their methodologies from the Anglo-American and Continental traditions rather than from those of any of the other postcolonial cultures under study. "In the beginning was not English," Hart writes. "Unfortunately, there is such a rush to publish in English that this sometimes centralizes the debate into some of the world's richest and most powerful countries" ("Perspectives" 84). In Brydon's "Response to Hart" she clarifies that "[a]s Canadians, we occupy an ambivalent position within the postcolonial dynamic" (101) because we are both subject to and complicit with imperial powers, but that we might also be able to fashion a more appropriate and effective methodology if we reconsider the value of a Commonwealth — rather than a more broadly postcolonial — perspective (105–11). Fundamentally, both Hart and Brydon defend a politically engaged methodology, thereby strengthening the agreement among theorists that the objects of postcolonial critique, and as a result the critique itself, have more potential for efficacy than those concerning postmodernism alone. To this discussion, Donna Bennett adds a cautionary note in her study entitled "English Canada's Postcolonial Complexities," a historical review of, among other things, what Bennett calls "an internal postcolonialism" (177), resembling closely what I call postimperialism. If postcolonial critics "take contestation as the only valid methodology and practice," Bennett writes, and "if we make marginality and resistance our only measures of authenticity," then we limit the questions we can ask and predetermine the answers we will receive" (196). But the critical stance I envision would attempt to be between margin and centre, offering a changed, not a predetermined, view of both.

The next step would be to suggest what a Canadian postimperial methodology might entail. Apparently, it would run completely counter to the tradition of Canadian literary criticism and the literature canonized by it. "[T]he canonized criticism," writes Lecker, "like the enshrined poetry and fiction, remains conservative, moral, documentary, sociological, and realistic in approach" (670–71). Frank Davey, in his "Critical Response" to Lecker's essay, states that Lecker "offers no sense of competing canons" (675), and Tracy Ware argues that "Lecker's historical perspective is too narrow" (481), but Lecker's assertion that we should reflect upon the values shaping our sense of canon seems undeniably valid. And indeed Lecker himself does so thoroughly in his "Privacy, Publicity, and the Discourse of Canadian Criticism," an article calling for a new integration of private (theoretical) literary critical debate and public intervention. Our assuming that "Canada is worth talking about" (71) would "allow Canadian critics to extend their intellectual agency" (75). Presumably critics might then reach the same audiences as our most popular novelists.

Several other critics have noted that the Canadian literary canon has historically been an "unstable" (Bennett, "Conflicted," 132), "fluid" (Ware 487), and "malleable" (Gerson 47) thing, despite attempts by many English professors — from the beginning of English studies in Canadian universities (see Murray) through the cultural awakening of the 1960s and beyond — to "show how the literary development mimes the social, political, and cultural progress of the nation, and further, how that progress is both material and spiritual, as well as coherent and cohesive" (McCarthy 38). Consensus has never been fully achieved, it seems, although preference has apparently been given to a national canon, comprised of realistic novels from Ontario whose themes can be said to define Canadianness (see Bennett, "Conflicted").

Curiously, while Atwood's writing is studied by thematic-nationalist critics, it is also stressed by those (Davey, Hutcheon, and Mathews, for example) whose criticism would not fit the description of thematic-national and, therefore, canonical. Hence my conclusion that Atwood's writing, including the most recent novel, is both canonical and postcanonical, nationalistic and postnationalistic, realistic and postmodern. The most appropriate methodology for interpreting her work would therefore bring combinations of those perspectives to bear. To Frank Davey's thinking, poststructuralist and "thematic" methodologies can be combined in the service of a "re-situation of a culture's literary texts within its socio-political text" (*Post-National* 22); I would add to this an explicitly political agenda — postfeminist and postimperial.

The Robber Bride

IN THIS TALE of female bonding caused by female betrayal, both the bonding and the betrayal speak directly and loudly to those Canadians who contributed to *The Robber Bride*'s topping the national bestseller list in Canada for many weeks. I use the term postfeminist to describe a wider ideological purview that would include not only feminism, but also postmodernism, and especially postcolonialism and its local variant, postimperialism. Admittedly, the theorist who most influenced my adoption of this dangerous term is Atwood herself, in her address to the

American Booksellers' Association convention in June 1993, when she comments on — among other things — what her newest novel is about:

> I was sitting around one day thinking to myself, Where have all the Lady Macbeths gone? Gone to Ophelias, every one, leaving the devilish tour-de-force parts to be played by bass-baritones. Or, to put it another way: If all women are well behaved by nature — or if we aren't allowed to say otherwise for fear of being accused of antifemaleism — then they are deprived of moral choice, and there isn't much left for them to do in books except run away a lot. Or, to put it another way: *Equality* means equally bad as well as equally good. (11)

In a postfeminist milieu, women face difficult moral choices amid the lingering hindrances posed by an imperfect world to distract and undermine them, with or without the support of other women to guide them. Zenia, who fully embraces that imperfect world, remains isolated throughout the novel, finally suffering from an ovarian cancer that would have killed her within six months if the heroin overdose had not done so first. An obvious contrast to the image of Zenia dead in the Arnold Garden Hotel fountain is the three other women laughing and telling stories together in Charis's kitchen at the novel's end, each one having mourned Zenia in her own way. But the three carrying Zenia's ashes together to Lake Ontario en route to Charis's island provides a third, transitional image of the women, an image of unity.

By acknowledging and turning against the oppression women inflict upon one another, women can find a support that partly frees them from what Roz refers to as "male fantasies" (456). The term postfeminist thus fits this novel, though its further applicability seems unclear. I use it to describe the new view of morality achieved by the novel's three protagonists, a morality that moves beyond both "Canadian" prudery and the "European" decadence lived out by Zenia, and that acknowledges popularized (or postmodern) forms of feminism in the 1990s.

But reviews of this capacious novel in Canadian print media do not adequately explain the very postimperial and postfeminist aspects that partly account for its wide appeal to Canadians. Zenia, for example, is variously condemned or praised in the reviews, but is never discussed as treacherous precisely because of her disaffection with Canada. And the mothers or grandmothers of the three protagonists — Tony, Charis, and Roz — are similarly ignored in reviews while, in fact, they provide important information about their daughters' peculiar vulnerability to or, conversely, power over the orphaned and nationless Zenia. While not claiming an authoritative reading of *The Robber Bride*, I hope instead to encourage comparisons of this very popular novel with other examples of contemporary Canadian cultural production in order to consider the extent of the appeal of postimperialism in Canadian art.

In the *Quill & Quire* Sandra Martin notes but does not elaborate upon the idea that the novel's challenge is in "confronting politically correct feminism" (59). In *Books in Canada* Joan Thomas writes that the "chivalry of women is high-lighted, the way they over-function in relationships" (31). According to Sherrill Grace in *Canadian Forum*, Zenia is "an image of what ordinary men imagine they want in a woman and what ordinary women wish they could be to attract (and destroy?) men" (45). In *The Globe and Mail* Marina Warner muses that this novel "grants deeper, stranger powers to women's friendships" than Atwood's previous work (C24). Judith Timson dismisses the novel in her *Maclean's* review in part because of Atwood's "curious lack of compassion for her characters," as "less than a serious work and more like an upmarket melodrama" (55). Atwood herself claims that "[m]y book is about war, death, treachery and lies," as well as "sustaining relationships" ("Playing" C2).

This reading will stress the ways in which Zenia forces each woman to confront her buried past, particularly her sense of difference from other women, and therefore her immoderate dependence on the good opinion of men. This introspection eventually enables the three to find strength in a female friendship that is tested and found to be real. Although Zenia may appear to come from nowhere, her various fabricated origins are, significantly, all European. In one version her mother is a White Russian, perhaps a countess (189), and her father — in the three accounts Zenia's own lying mother gives of him — is Greek or Polish or English; in another version her mother is a Roumanian gypsy (312) and her father a Finnish communist; finally she is German with two Jewish grandparents (418). Readers might be tempted to discount Zenia as a kind of postmodern simulacrum (to borrow the theory of Jean Baudrillard), a "renovated" and inhuman (118) creature, to use the words of Roz from Atwood's novel — in other words, as a character with no conceivable referent in the real world — but I will not be so tempted. Rather, I will argue that Zenia's foreignness, her difference, is precisely what each of the other three main characters must come to understand, and that difference is as powerful as any other force in their lives.

Zenia's assessment of Canada is that it is "a *gentle* place" (426), by which Roz assumes Zenia really means "*boring*" (427). But Roz herself defends Canada, suggesting that "*boring* has something to offer, these days. Maybe they should export a little *boring*. It's better than getting your head shot off" (427). A distinction is thus put in place between other parts of the world, which are "*interesting*" (426), and gentle Canada. Since Tony and Roz have both felt like foreigners in their own country, their task is to attempt to reconcile the two traditions of Old World and New, in order to produce a third choice. Charis, the other main character, finds Toronto beautiful and has "belief" in it (60). Most obviously the healer in this novel, with her grandmother's powerful hands,

Charis has the most to learn from Zenia's foreignness, since she is the one explicitly described as "soft" (47) and vulnerable.

All three find some relief from thraldom to the men in their lives, and perhaps also from the concomitant negative views of other women most clearly voiced in this novel by Roz, paradoxically by first embracing Zenia. Roz congratulates her friends on finding new men to date, because "a good man is hard to find":

> maybe . . . because so many of the good men have been eaten, by man-eaters like Zenia. Most women disapprove of man-eaters; not so much because of the activity itself, or the promiscuity involved, but because of the greed. Women don't want all the men eaten up by man-eaters; they want a few left over so they can eat some themselves. (455)

But none of the surviving three manifests such "greed" and is indeed seen to rely more and more upon sustenance from the others, having found a position between man-eater and such an obvious victim of male fantasies, as the young Karen.

Each of the three protagonists befriends Zenia, and for a time Zenia exclusively, when other women shun her. Tony, first of all, admires and indeed subsidizes Zenia precisely because she defies a "social order" (194) upheld by the other women with whom Tony lives in residence and attends university. Toronto is "so puritanical!" according to Zenia (194), an observation borne out by the other young women's judgement of Zenia. Although "Zenia is the incarnation of how plainer, more oblong women wish to look, and therefore to be," and is "thought also to be brilliant," she is "fearsome. Wolfish, feral, beyond the pale" (154). After Zenia asks Tony what her obsession is, Tony meditates on this question and realizes that the other young women in her dormitory Common Room would think Zenia "was full of it, and also a slut. . . . They would disapprove of her slutty hair" (150).

But Tony is drawn to Zenia's disregard for the oppression of socially rigid behaviour, or moral prudery, especially that imposed by other women. Zenia's momentary confusion with Tony's mother, Anthea (198), and indeed with Tony's own dark and powerful twin, "Ynot" (220), partly explains Tony's need for her, since Tony has never identified with her own mother's imperfect fit with conventional Toronto society. The English war bride Anthea's contempt for Toronto and Canada as "this narrow-minded provincial city, in this too-large, too-small, too-cold, too-hot country" (169) leads her to run away to the U.S. with one of her husband's colleagues, the husband of one of her bridge club partners, abandoning her very young daughter Antonia. Zenia thus finishes the lesson Anthea begins — a lesson concerning passion and moral choice beyond the conventional world in which moral choice is predetermined and passion is outlawed. Only by exploring her own "obsessions" for West and for the history of war can Tony claim her desire, and perhaps her mother's legacy.

The unpredictable outlaw Zenia similarly forces Roz to reclaim her own status as "outsider" (425). When a teenager at Forest Hill Collegiate Institute, Roz feels she is in a "foreign country" (399), where she "can see that she will never be prettier, daintier, thinner, sexier, or harder to impress than these girls [at the collegiate] are. She decides instead to be smarter, funnier, and richer" (401). But Roz does not transcend the local sexist ideology in her slavish attitude towards male approval. She submits to Mitch's highly conventional rituals of courtship (i.e., no sex) and tolerates his many extramarital affairs. Idealizing her husband even more than the other two protagonists idealize their men, Roz is made to confront Zenia's degraded image of Mitch, thereby giving her back some emotional balance. Mitch as Roz describes him is a kind of handsome child, but as Zenia states, "he was a control freak" (509), a "sick lech" whom Roz "never gave . . . any credit." Rather, she "always saw him as a victim of women, just putty in their hands. You babied him. Did it ever occur to you that Mitch was responsible for his actions?" (510). Roz's belief that men are somehow powerless against competitive, antifeminist women prevents her both from seeing Mitch clearly and from learning to protect herself and other women from a sexist ideology that harms women and men. Zenia — a competitive, antifeminist woman to be sure — paradoxically forces Roz to acknowledge that strength comes from alliances with other women who share her contempt for those, like Mitch and like the girls she attended high school with, who encourage a "[s]ex-role stereotyping" that keeps men in charge (362) and women in charge of babying them.

Charis's lessons from Zenia are more complex. The least conflicted in terms of her place in Canadian society, Charis is drawn to Zenia because of Zenia's illness. Charis's natural healing powers, inherited from her Canadian grandmother, have not been effective in healing Charis's own damaged and discarded self, the person called Karen. Only when Charis recognizes that "she has part of Zenia inside herself" (309), and openly admires — as have the other two protagonists on many occasions — Zenia's courage, can she begin to enjoy sex with Billy and, in fact, become pregnant with his child, overcoming her childhood sexual abuse. "When she makes love with Billy she doesn't think about being Karen, or Charis either. She thinks about being Zenia" (307), and Zenia thus becomes one of three possible mothers of August(a). Zenia teaches Charis about the betrayal men are capable of, after which Charis "has more confidence" (310). Near the novel's end Charis is able to throw off her belief that she caused Billy's abandonment and think instead that "maybe it's just as well Billy didn't stick around" (523).

Curiously, it seems that Zenia needs Charis as much as Charis needs Zenia. The innocence and sweetness, or gentleness, of the most thoroughly New World character becomes necessary for

Zenia to reclaim her soul and be forgiven by another woman before death (498). Charis assures the reader finally that *"Zenia has returned to the Light"* (524) — a fate most would not have expected for her. Therefore the intermingling of Old and New World ideologies, innocence and sophistication, integrity and cunning, conventionality and passion, occurs in each of the four main characters in Atwood's novel, as though to indicate other possible subject positions for postcolonial, postmodern, postfeminist Canadian women. Perhaps the novel is an example of what Brydon calls the "new globalism," which "simultaneously asserts local independence and global interdependencies" ("The White Inuit Speaks" 196).

But a kind of close reading of this book cannot in itself be construed as a postcanonical interpretation. The very con-textualizing that I argue would expand and democratize our work as Canadianist critics must at least be attempted here, in closing. The fact that all of Atwood's main characters are white and bourgeois can exclude many Canadian readers, just as her nonwhite character, Shanita, in *The Robber Bride* feels excluded from mainstream Canadian culture. The naive Charis suggests that when people inquire about Shanita's origins they are really asking where her parents are from, to which Shanita responds that that's not what they mean: "What they mean is, when am I leaving?" (65). That this novel examines the European-Canadian connection can be argued, but that it looks at Canada's connec-tions with countries and peoples non-European cannot. As Zenia shouts — and Roz to her horror gives some assent — *"Fuck the Third World! I'm tired of it!"* (113). While readers of European descent can explore and review their complicity with the poten-tial imperialism of a Eurocentric view by joining the three protagonists in uncritical praise of Zenia, readers cannot discover anything of substance about Canadian racism by studying *The Robber Bride.* Thus the context of Atwood's novel may seem limited to other fiction by white Canadians.

Yet what might break down such distinctions between fiction by whites and nonwhites is discussion of them under the rubric of the postimperial. Perhaps characterizations occur in novels by nonwhite Canadians in which a white Canadian holds attitudes as intolerant as Zenia's, attitudes in need of revision. Indeed the boundary between fiction and other genres, or between fiction and other arts, can be removed in order to study this book in its broadest contexts. Surely oppressive characters appear in other pieces by Canadian artists, characters who are oppressive particularly because of their elitist beliefs, which are based in false assumptions about racial or ethnic superiority.

A comparison of the interplay between European, or European-style, and Canadian females in Atom Egoyan's films, for example, might bring Zenia's relationship with the three more stodgily Canadian females in *The Robber Bride* into clearer focus.

The two sisters in Egoyan's 1991 film *The Adjuster*, for example, one Canadian and one European, taken together might describe a kind of sexually sophisticated and powerful postcolonial Canadian woman, who is both voyeur (or consumer) *and* producer of erotica, rather than victim of others' sexual fantasies. And the ironically maternal figure in Egoyan's 1994 film *Exotica* also might signify a female who can survive in both the "natural" and "healthy" atmosphere of the New World, and the other imported, cosmopolitan atmosphere of the night club she owns. As Canada interacts in the postnational world, or global village, of the future, women who successfully combine old and new seem more likely to thrive, a supposition that might partly explain not only the popularity of *The Robber Bride* but also the critical and popular acclaim given Egoyan's films, especially his latest one.

I suggest that the postimperial, postmodern, postfeminist interpretation I believe Atwood's most recent novel demands might be portable to other products of Canadian culture. Such a methodology would lead eventually to a theory of the agency of some of our most compelling contemporary Canadian art to forge renewed identities. This postimperial Canadian canon would have as its focus the study of art that mingles oppressive with liberating ideologies, with special emphasis on such timely issues as gender, nationalism, and ethnicity. My proposed theory of the agency of Canadian culture and its critics derives, in a sense, from the relationship between Zenia and each of the three protagonists in *The Robber Bride*. In coming to understand and specify the similarities and — more importantly — the differences between what might be termed mainstream Canadian culture and other Canadian cultures, as well as those foreign, both the mainstream and the other are seen anew. Using that agency specifically to forge the postimperial Canadian canon I have hinted at would result not in a threat to but rather an expansion of our art.

WORKS CITED

The Adjuster. Dir. Atom Egoyan. Alliance, 1991.

Atwood, Margaret. "Margaret Atwood's Address to the American Booksellers Association Convention, Miami, Florida; June 1, 1993." *The Book Group Companion to Margaret Atwood's* The Robber Bride. New York: Nan A. Talese/Doubleday, n.d. 7–13.

———. "Playing the Atwood Guessing Game." Interview with Val Ross. *The Globe and Mail* October 7, 1993: C1–2.

———. *The Robber Bride*. Toronto: McClelland & Stewart, 1993.

Baudrillard, Jean. *Simulations*. Trans. Paul Foss, Paul Patton, and Philip Beitchman. New York: Semiotext(e), 1983.

Bennett, Donna. "Conflicted Vision: A Consideration of Canon and Genre in English-Canadian Literature." *Canadian Canons: Essays in Literary Value*. Ed. Robert Lecker. Toronto: U of Toronto P, 1991. 131–49.

———. "English Canada's Postcolonial Complexities." *Essays on Canadian Writing* 51–52 (Winter 1993–Spring 1994): 164–210.

Brydon, Diana. "Response to Hart." Arachnē 1.1 (1994): 100–12.

———. "The White Inuit Speaks: Contamination as Literary Strategy." *Past the*

Last Post: Theorizing Post-Colonialism and Post-Modernism. Eds. Ian Adam and Helen Tiffin. Calgary: U of Calgary P, 1990. 191–203.

Davey, Frank. "Critical Response: Canadian Canons." *Critical Inquiry* 16 (Spring 1990): 672–81.

———. *Post-National Arguments: The Politics of the Anglophone-Canadian Novel Since 1967.* Toronto: U of Toronto P, 1993.

Exotica. Dir. Atom Egoyan. Alliance, 1994.

Gerson, Carole. "The Canon between the Wars: Field-notes of a Feminist Literary Archeologist." *Canadian Canons.* 46–56.

Grace, Sherrill E. "Atwood's Postmodern Fairytale." Review of *The Robber Bride*, by Margaret Atwood. *Canadian Forum.* March 1994: 44–45.

Hart, Jonathan. "Response to Shaffer and Brydon." *Arachnē.* 1.1 (1994): 113–19.

———. "Traces, Resistances, and Contradictions: Canadian and International Perspectives on Postcolonial Theories." *Arachnē* 1.1 (1994): 68–93.

Hutcheon, Linda. "Afterword: Postmodernism's Ironic Paradoxes: Politics and Art." *Remembering Postmodernism: Trends in Recent Canadian Art.* Mark A. Cheetham with Linda Hutcheon. Toronto: Oxford UP, 1991. 109–33.

———. *The Canadian Postmodern: A Study of Contemporary English-Canadian Fiction.* Toronto: Oxford UP, 1988.

———. "Eruptions of Postmodernity: The Postcolonial and the Ecological." *Essays on Canadian Writing* 51–52 (Winter 1993–Spring 1994): 146–63.

———. *Irony's Edge: the theory and politics of irony.* New York: Routledge, 1995.

———. *Splitting Images: Contemporary Canadian Ironies.* Toronto: Oxford UP, 1991.

———. and Marion Richmond, eds. *Other Solitudes: Canadian Multicultural Fictions.* Toronto: Oxford UP, 1990.

Lecker, Robert. "The Canonization of Canadian Literature: An Inquiry into Value." *Critical Inquiry* 16 (Spring 1990): 656–71.

———. "Privacy, Publicity, and the Discourse of Canadian Criticism." *Essays on Canadian Writing* 51–52 (Winter 1993–Spring 1994): 32–82.

Martin, Sandra. "Playful with razor blades." Review of *The Robber Bride*, by Margaret Atwood. *Quill & Quire* 59.9 (September 1993): 59.

Mathews, Lawrence. "Calgary, Canonization, and Class: Deciphering List B." *Canadian Canons.* 150–66.

McCarthy, Dermot. "Early Canadian Literary Histories and the Function of a Canon." *Canadian Canons*. 30–45.

McGregor, Gaile. "Postmodernism and its discontents." Review of *A Poetics of Postmodernism: History, Theory & Fiction*, and *The Canadian Postmodern: A Study of Contemporary English-Canadian Fiction*, both by Linda Hutcheon. *Border/Lines* 18 (Spring 1990): 43–45.

Murray, Heather. "English Studies in Canada to 1945: A Bibliographic Essay." *English Studies in Canada* XVII.4 (December 1991): 437–67.

Thomas, Joan. "Taking No Prisoners." Review of *The Robber Bride*, by Margaret Atwood. *Books in Canada* October 1993: 30–31.

Timson, Judith. "Return of the she-devil." Review of *The Robber Bride*, by Margaret Atwood. *Maclean's* 4 October 1993: 55.

Ware, Tracy. "A Little Self-Consciousness Is a Dangerous Thing: A Response to Robert Lecker." *English Studies in Canada* XVII.4 (December 1991): 481–93.

Warner, Marina. "Atwood dips into Plath depths." Review of *The Robber Bride*, by Margaret Atwood. *The Globe and Mail* October 2, 1993: C24.

Weir, Lorraine. "Normalizing the Subject: Linda Hutcheon and the English-Canadian Postmodern." *Canadian Canons*. 180–95.

Contributors

DIANA BRYDON teaches English literature at the University of Guelph. She has published widely on Canadian and postcolonial topics. Her most recent book is *Decolonising Fictions*, coauthored with Helen Tiffin.

NATHALIE COOKE teaches in the English department at McGill University. She is coeditor of the revised and abridged *Oxford Anthology of Canadian Literature in English*, and has published articles on contemporary Canadian prose and poetry. She is currently working on a book manuscript, *Lying Is a Writerly Craft: The Politics of Duplicity in Margaret Atwood's Novels*.

SANDRA DJWA teaches English literature at Simon Fraser University. Her books include *The Politics of the Imagination: A Life of F. R. Scott* and *E. J. Pratt: The Evolutionary Vision*. She is coeditor of *The Complete Poems of E. J. Pratt*, and editor of *Giving Canada a Literary History: A Memoir by Carl F. Klinck*.

SHERRILL E. GRACE is professor of English at the University of British Columbia. She has published books on Malcolm Lowry, Margaret Atwood, and on literary expressionism, as well as more than one hundred articles on Canadian, American, and British literature. She has recently completed editing two volumes of *The Collected Letters of Malcolm Lowry*, and has begun research for a book on the representation of "North" in Canadian culture.

SHANNON HENGEN has been a member of the English department at Laurentian University since 1988. She is the author of *Margaret Atwood's Power: Mirrors, Reflections and Images in Select Fiction and Poetry*, and coeditor with Sharon Wilson and Tom Friedman of *Approaches to Teaching Atwood's* The Handmaid's Tale *and Other Works*. Her article on Canadian women's drama, "Towards a Feminist Comedy," will appear in *Canadian Literature* in 1995.

MOLLY HITE is associate professor of English at Cornell University. She is the author of two book-length studies, *Ideas of Order in the Novels of Thomas Pynchon* and *The Other Side of the Story: Structures and Strategies of Contemporary Feminist Narrative*, as well as two novels, *Class Porn* and *Breach of Immunity*.

HILDA HOLLIS is a doctoral student at McMaster University, primarily working on Victorian women writers, and is interested in the response of female authors to dominant philosophy. She has an article on Phyllis Bentley forthcoming in the *Dictionary of Literary Biography*.

CORAL ANN HOWELLS is Reader in Canadian Literature at the University of Reading, and former president of the British Association for Canadian Studies. She has written and lectured extensively on Canadian women's writing in Britain, Europe, North America, India, and Australia. Her published works include *Private and Fictional Words: Canadian Women Novelists of the 1970s and 80s, Jean Rhys, Narrative Strategies in Recent Canadian Literature* (coedited with L. Hunter), *York Notes on* The Handmaid's Tale, and *Margaret Atwood*. She is currently researching a book on Alice Munro.

PATRICIA MERIVALE is professor of English and Comparative Literature at the University of British Columbia, and author of *Pan the Boat-God: His Myth in Modern Times* and of numerous comparative articles. She is currently working on the theory and practice of the metaphysical detective story, on apocalyptic artist parables, and on the prose poem. A companion paper on *Murder in the Dark* will appear in the MLA volume, *Approaches to Teaching Atwood's* The Handmaid's Tale *and Other Works*.

LINDA WAGNER-MARTIN is Hanes Professor of English and Comparative Literature at the University of North Carolina, Chapel Hill. She has written widely on American and women writers, with recent books being *Telling Women's Lives: The New Biography* and both *The Oxford Companion to Women's Writing in the United States* and *The Oxford Book of Women's Writing* (coedited with Cathy N. Davidson). Editor of the contemporary section of the *Heath Anthology of American Literature*, Wagner-Martin serves as president of the Ernest Hemingway Foundation and Society. A revisionist biography of Gertrude Stein and her family is forthcoming.

GLENN WILLMOTT is assistant professor of English at Dalhousie University. He received his doctorate from Duke University in 1992 after completing a dissertation on Marshall McLuhan. He has published articles and reviews on Canadian literature and on modernism.

LORRAINE M.YORK is associate professor of English at McMaster University. She has written books on Timothy Findley and on photography and contemporary Canadian fiction. Her work-in-progress is entitled *Collaboractions: Theorizing Contemporary Women's Collaborative Art*.